D0723461

Politics in the Developing World

Politics in the Developing World

A Concise Introduction

Jeff Haynes

Blackwell
Publishing

350 Main Street, Malden, MA 02148-5018, USA
108 Cowley Road, Oxford OX4 1JF, UK
550 Swanston Street, Carlton, Victoria 3053, Australia
Kurfürstendamm 57, 10707 Berlin, Germany

First published 2002 by Blackwell Publishers Ltd, a Blackwell Publishing company

Library of Congress Cataloging-in-Publication Data

Haynes, Jeffrey.
    Politics in the developing world: a concise introduction / Jeff Haynes.
        p. cm.
Includes bibliographical references and index.
    ISBN 0-631-22555-2 (hbk.) – ISBN 0-631-22556-0 (pbk.)
    1. Developing countries – Politics and government.   2. Globalization.
I. Title.
    JF60.H385 2002
    909′.097240825 – dc21

                                                            2001007500

A catalogue record for this title is available from the British Library.

Set in 10.5 on 12.5 pt. Palatino
by Ace Filmsetting Ltd, Frome, Somerset
Printed and bound in United Kingdom
by TJ International, Padstow, Cornwall

For further information on
Blackwell Publishing, visit our website:
www.blackwellpublishing.com

Contents

Tables

1

Politics, Economics, and Societies in the Developing World at the New Millennium

What do you think of when you think of the politics, economics, and societies of African, Asian, Latin American, and Middle Eastern countries? While views no doubt differ widely, it is probably a safe bet that many people think primarily or at least to a considerable degree of negative images. Why? It may be because it often seems from newspapers, television, and radio reports that politics, economics, and social interactions are played out in arenas characterized by political violence and instability, greed and corruption, avarice and malice. In other words, our perceptions of what goes on in many developing countries may be strongly informed by widely reported political and economic conflict and societal disharmony.

To explain this we need to bear in mind that, as Manor (1991) notes, "the scope of politics in Third World settings is usually broader than in the West." As a consequence, "modes of analysis must accommodate themselves to that reality more effectively than the familiar paradigms have done" (ibid: 5). The "familiar paradigms" that Manor refers to are modernization theory, with its focus on domestic factors, and dependency or underdevelopment theory, primarily concerned with the impact of external determinants. However, a third view, one that I adopt in this book, believes that the best analysis is made by focusing on both domestic and external factors. In the chapters that follow, I shall also refer to the importance of *structural* and *contingent* factors to explain variations in outcomes between countries. While I shall discuss them in detail later in the current chapter, it may be useful briefly to explain these concepts now. "Structural factors" pertain to a country's "immovable traditions [and] power structures" (Pinkney 1993: 139–40) and are important in helping determine political and economic outcomes. This is because they impose limits on the range of choices available to political and economic actors, who consequently opt for certain courses of action and not others. "Contingent factors," on the other hand, refer to the role of human agency and of one-off events in helping determine outcomes. In other words, what occurs in a country is not necessarily set in stone because of its structural characteristics. What individual actors do at certain times can also be important.

For analytical convenience, I group the countries of the developing word into regions. In this book, "Africa" refers to all African countries south of the Sahara desert. "South Asia" is the Indian subcontinent plus Pakistan, while "East and Southeast Asia" embraces the countries of Asia – apart from Japan – between the Indian subcontinent and the Pacific. The "Middle East" includes the predominantly Muslim countries of West Asia and Africa north of the Sahara. "Latin America and the Caribbean" includes the countries of South America plus the islands of the West Indies.

The Book's Structure

Primarily written for university undergraduates, this book features up-to-date analysis and data throughout. My overall purpose is to present an analysis of recent political, economic, and social developments in the countries of Africa, South Asia, East and Southeast Asia, the Middle East, and Latin America and the Caribbean since the end of the Cold War in the late 1980s. I examine both domestic and international factors and, where appropriate, highlight their interaction. Using this approach, I seek to present a different perspective from that in many comparable standard texts. Often, the tendency is to focus primarily upon *either* domestic *or* external factors to explain political and economic events and developments.

I start from the premise that both domestic and external factors can be important in shaping outcomes in the countries of the developing world. My aim is to examine the breadth, nature, range, and complementarity of some of the most pressing and topical issues that affect these countries. Consequently, in the following chapters we focus on globalization, especially its economic and political dimensions;

economic growth and development; democratization and democracy; religious and ethnic conflict; human and women's rights; and the sociopolitical impact of environmental damage.

The book builds upon and supplements a previous publication of mine: *Third World Politics: A Concise Introduction* (TWP), published in 1996. Why not a second edition of TWP? Why the need for a new book? I felt that it was not sufficient merely to produce a second edition of TWP, for two main reasons. First, events over the last few years – especially globalization, economic liberalization, and democratization – have affected all developing countries. Consequently, it seemed to me that a completely fresh analysis was required. Second, TWP's analysis was arranged in terms of the primary importance of domestic factors, interpreted via contending analytical paradigms: (1) modernization theory and (2) dependency theory. However, such a bifurcated focus no longer seems appropriate: at the new millennium the analytical insights of these approaches now seem to many passé (Randall and Theobald 1998).

No analysis of the developing world can now ignore the phenomenon of globalization, a key analytical and conceptual term. However, there is often a lack of precision in specifying precisely what globalization is. Having spawned innumerable conference papers, articles, book chapters, and whole books, much interest in the concept stems from two key events that took place over a decade ago. First, the collapse of the USSR in 1991, along with the contemporaneous disintegration of the Eastern European communist bloc, was an epochal event whose full significance is still unfolding. Second, the demise of Europe's communist countries did not start, yet encouraged, both the "third wave of democracy" and a global trend towards economic liberalization, developments we shall examine in depth in later chapters.

In this book we focus on the post-Cold War era (that is, the period since 1989) for several reasons. First, these years are a convenient period of time, notable for dramatic political and economic changes that have affected many developing countries, such as democratization, economic reforms, and demands for human rights. Second, the 1990s saw a focus upon an array of international trends and developments that began or were stimulated by the end of the Cold War. Recent interest in globalization helped stimulate a fundamental re-examination of how to explain political and economic outcomes in developing countries. Informed by the ensuing debate, chapter 2 focuses upon globalization and its impact on the developing world. The key question we examine in this chapter is to what extent do developing countries have freedom of action in an increasingly globalized environment? To answer the question we examine (1) the Non-Aligned Movement which, between the 1960s and the 1990s, was the main organization of developing countries to project and promote a collective voice in international relations; and (2) the rise of regionalism as a perceived antidote to the malign effects of globalization.

Chapter 3 turns to the issue of economic growth and development in the developing world. It clearly notes the recent changes in the global economy, including the East Asian economic crisis of 1997–8 and its aftermath. It also examines the nature of post-Cold War economic determinants which have helped develop a complex new global economy, superseding the old simplicities of First, Second and Third Worlds, "rich" and "poor," "haves" and "have-nots," "industrialized" and "non-industrialized." I illustrate what is happening in this regard by focusing on the interconnectedness of national economies, and examine both the economic marginality of some developing countries, as well as two economic "success stories": South Korea and Taiwan. Both seem clearly to have benefited from economic globalization, despite the hiccups of 1997–8. Others, including impoverished African, Latin American, and South Asian countries, have benefited much less, if at all.

In chapter 4 we shift attention to democracy and examine its progress in the developing world since the 1980s. We examine several key concepts, including democratization and democracy, and the related terms "civil society" and "social capital," the strength of which is widely seen as essential to democratic progress. We also assess the importance of both domestic and external factors to democratization and democracy in the developing world and see how and why after the Cold War Western governments and agencies encouraged many developing countries to democratize.

Chapter 5 examines ethnic and religious conflicts. In numerous developing countries political and economic developments have been linked to the existence of both ethnic and religious tensions. While there are various reasons put forward as to why this is the case, we analyze the issue primarily in relation to a quest for power by ethnic and/or religious groups which, in the past, feel that they have been denied it. We also examine the importance of external factors in encouraging such groups to express their disaffection.

In chapter 6 we turn to human rights. Human rights issues are highly controversial, not only in individual countries and international relations, but also more generally in the academic world. Various disciplines, including area studies, international law, and political theory, have all produced debate and conflicting interpretations over human rights theory and practice. This is because there are fundamental – as well as definitional – disagreements over the content of human rights, notably the comparative status of individual and collective rights. Sometimes, for example, governments seek to defend their apparently arbitrary or harsh treatment of individuals or groups in the name of the collective or national good.

Chapter 7 focuses on gender and highlights the patchy, but generally poor, position of females in most developing countries. The first section of the chapter explores the general socioeconomic and political position of females in the regions of the developing world. In recent years, economic malaise in many developing countries has served to reduce still further the already inferior position of many poor women. In this context we examine the impact of globalization and structural adjustment programs on women and girls. The chapter also describes and assesses a representative range of women's groups in developing countries in terms of (1) what they do and (2) how they do it. I suggest that the main sociopolitical significance of women's groups is not that they threaten the stability of the state. Rather, it is that in the male-dominated societies of the developing world, albeit imperfectly and partially, such organizations can help women improve their collective position.

We focus on the political, economic, and social dimensions of environmental issues in chapter 8. The overall aim is to explain how and why environmental issues are often linked to wider demands for sociopolitical change and/or economic reform, especially from groups lacking power. We examine (1) environmental groups within developing countries; (2) their interaction with transnational environmental organizations such as Greenpeace International; and (3) case studies from a number of developing countries. The overall conclusion is that while environment groups do not always gain their objectives, they should not be written off as insignificant. Collectively, they comprise an important new element in emerging civil societies in many developing countries, helping challenge state power and thus increasing the power of ordinary people.

Chapter 9 is the concluding chapter. There, I summarize the important points made in the book.

What's In a Name? "Developing World," "Third World," or "the South"?

Before going further we should deal with a controversial issue: what to call the collectivity of African, Asian, Latin American, and Caribbean and Middle Eastern countries. Rather than constantly – and clumsily – referring to "the countries of Africa, South Asia, East and Southeast Asia, Latin America and the Caribbean, and the Middle East," we need an acceptable shorthand term. But there is no consensus on this issue; you will see several terms in the literature. Three are particularly common: the "Third World," "the South," and the "developing countries." Let us look at the pros and cons of each.

The "Third World"

Because dozens of African, Asian, and Middle Eastern countries decolonized in the 1950s and 1960s, "Western political scientists found themselves increasingly challenged to develop frameworks for understanding and predicting the[ir] politics" (Randall and Theobald 1998: vii). Alfred Sauvy, a French economist and demographer, is usually credited as the first person to use the term "Third World," in an article published in 1952. Its use caught on, and by the late 1950s it was in widespread use. For Sauvy and others, the "Third World" referred not only to the then-decolonizing countries, but also to the economically weak countries of Latin America, many of which had been independent since the early nineteenth century.

The term "Third World" also had a meaning in international relations. It reflected the fact that by the 1960s the world was divided into three ideologically defined blocs:

- The "First World," that is, the industrialized democracies of Europe and North America (plus Australia, New Zealand, and Japan).
- The "Second World," that is, the communist countries of Eastern Europe. Some analysts also included their ideological allies in Asia (North Korea, China) and Latin America (Cuba).
- The "Third World," comprising a large number of countries organized in the Non-Aligned Movement, and claiming to be neutral in the Cold War.

Thus the label "Third World" had two separate, yet linked, senses during the Cold War. It was used to refer to certain countries' poor development position and also to their relatively unimportant place in international politics. Developmentally, the term sought to capture the notion of a certain type of country: postcolonial, and compared to the rich countries of the First World, economically weak and underdeveloped. Regarding international relations, a bloc of postcolonial countries emerged and formed an alliance: the Non-Aligned Movement (NAM), whose member countries claimed, sometimes with good reason, to be followers of neither the USA nor the USSR. While, individually, most developing countries played relatively minor roles in international relations during the Cold War, their collective voice focused in the NAM was relatively loud, and at irregular intervals, influential. In sum, the term "Third World" had a dual meaning. On the one hand, it referred to a large group of economically underdeveloped, developmentally weak African, Asian, Middle Eastern, and Latin American countries. On the other hand, it connoted the proclaimed neutrality of a large bloc of mostly postcolonial developing countries, organized in the NAM.

The Cold War, because of its ideological division between the superpowers, was crucial in defining the concept of the Third World. Consequently, it is hardly surprising that the end of the Cold War in 1989 produced significant changes; not least, a key justification for use of the term "Third World" disappeared. The demise of the Second World, and the growing economic and political diversity of developing countries, led Bayart (1991) to argue that the term "Third World" could logically no longer be analytically useful. Two events were of particular importance. The first was the political collapse and eventual dissolution of the communist Second World, as the dramatic collapse of the Eastern European communist bloc removed at a stroke the chief ideological challenge to the West. The second was the contemporaneous wave of democratization and economic liberalization that swept across Africa, Asia, and Latin America (but not the Middle East) in the 1980s and 1990s. Dozens of new democracies emerged in Latin America, Asia, and Africa, yet overall there was much political diversity among developing countries. The result was a variety of political systems: large numbers of democracies and numerous non-democracies, including communist one-party rule (Cuba, Laos, Vietnam, North Korea), military dictatorship (Pakistan), and various kinds of theocracies (Afghanistan, Iran, Saudi Arabia, Sudan). Economic diversity and developmental diversity were reflected in strikingly different per capita gross national products (GNPs): in 1999, the GNP of Singapore was US$29,610, South Korea's was US$8,490, and Ethiopia's a mere US$100, one third of 1 percent of Singapore's! (World Bank 2001: 274–5).

For Bayart (1991), the consequence of these developments was that the very notion of a single Third World was now a "fantasy" without analytical or conceptual utility. It was a convenient but now inappropriate label, unwarrantably conjoining diverse nations with very different cultures, societies, political systems, and economies. Other critics, such as Berger (1994), also suggested that the very concept of a Third World was meaningless, but for a different reason. Berger argued that even the richest Western countries had often substantial impoverished "underclasses" – that is, groups of people who lived in what were essentially "Third World" conditions. In addition, groups of political and economic elites (often the same people) in developing countries were integrated into a global class structure and enjoyed very good living standards, even by Western standards. The overall point was that there was no longer a clear division between the rich countries of the First World and the poor countries of the Third World. In part, this was because there were large numbers of impoverished people living in the West and much smaller, although still significant, numbers of elites in the developing countries.

In sum, by the early 1990s, critiques suggested that old, familiar simplicities – reflected in the term "Third World" – no longer had analytical utility. Three developments were important: (1) the collapse of the communist Second World; (2) the "third wave of democracy" and widespread economic liberalization; and (3) a blurring of the division between rich First World and poor Third World countries.

"The South"

If the term "Third World" was no longer analytically useful, what of a possible alternative: "the South"? For many people, the term "Third World" has an unacceptable, pejorative connotation, implying poverty, lack of development, low status – in short, "third rate." Reflecting such concerns, a report compiled in 1980 by a team led by the former West German chancellor Willy Brandt, suggested what it saw as a suitable alternative: the "South." This term lacked the pejorative connotations of the Third World. Justification for its use was that it highlighted the unjust global economic order by dichotomizing developmental distinctions between the rich "North" – the developed countries of North America and Western Europe (also, confusingly, known as "the West") – and the economically poor countries of Latin America, Asia, Africa, and the Middle East ("the South"). However, just as the blanket term "Third World" obscured considerable cultural, economic, and political differences among individual countries, so too "the South" can be seen as an unsatisfactory analytical term. This is for two main reasons. First, "the South" is essentially a geographic expression that ignores the fact that two "Northern" countries, Australia and New Zealand, are actually located in the geographical South. Second, it fails to differentiate between individual countries in political, developmental, and economic terms.

"Developing countries"

"Developing countries" is another alternative for a shorthand term for the aggregation of African, South Asian, East and Southeast Asian, Latin American and Caribbean, and Middle Eastern countries. I shall use it in this book. Acknowledging that these countries' economic, developmental, and political positions vary widely, I justify its use not least by the fact that it is the term favored by most governments of the countries themselves, as well as by global institutions, such as the United Nations.

This is not to imply that the term is uncontroversial. As Thomas points out, while "modernization, industrialization and development often appear effectively to be synonyms, the concept of 'development' actually embodies considerable ambiguity" (Thomas 1999: 46). For critics, the use of the adjective "developing" has a big drawback: it seems to imply that there is a spectrum with "underdeveloped" at one end and "developed" at the other. In this way of thinking, "developing" countries logically move over time from underdeveloped to developed status. But the problem is not only that there is great economic and developmental diversity among developing countries. It is also that it is very unlikely that all "developing" countries are in fact moving from underdeveloped to developed status. In fact, in some countries – including Afghanistan, Somalia, and the Democratic Republic of the Congo – development seems most conspicuous by its absence. On the other hand, as a perusal of United Nations Development Program reports over time would indicate, the great majority of developing countries, measured in overall terms, have seen – sometimes substantial – economic development since the 1970s (UNDP 1996; World Bank 2001).

Another problem is that it is not immediately clear what connotes a "developed" country. Does it simply imply a nation with a certain (relatively high) degree of economic growth? Does it suggest an element of redistribution of the fruits of growth? What of widely divergent socio-economic conditions, of the kind referred to earlier by Berger (1994), in both "developed" and "developing" countries? It is not easy to answer such questions. However, despite problems and ambiguities, I use the term "developing countries" in this book, not least because to my mind there is currently no better alternative. But remember that it is at best a shorthand term, one used for convenience. It does not imply that all "developing countries" share all or even a majority of political, social, and economic characteristics.

Domestic and External Factors in Explaining Outcomes in Developing Countries

To understand contemporary political, economic, and social outcomes in developing countries we need to focus upon the impact of both domestic and external factors, including globalization. This is not to imply that globalization began only recently. It is often suggested that it began in the seventeenth century, characterized by the spread of capitalism from Europe and the subsequent growth of colonial empires. More than 90 percent of developing countries were, at one time or another, colonial possessions of a handful of Western powers, including Belgium, Britain, France, Germany, Italy, Japan, the Netherlands, Portugal, Spain, and the USA. Decolonization came in two main waves, separated by more than a century. The first occurred in the early nineteenth century, resulting in the independence of 18 Latin American and Caribbean countries. The second occurred between 1945 and 1975, set in train by World War II. During this period around 90 colonies achieved freedom from foreign rule. Decolonization was virtually complete by 1990, marked by the independence of Namibia (see Hadjor 1993: 73–8, for a complete list of former colonies in Africa, Asia, Latin America and the Caribbean, and the Middle East).

   Independence was not necessarily a panacea for solving the former colonies' economic, political, and social problems. Despite the huge achievement of throwing off colonial rule, the great majority of former colonies in the developing world found themselves with two basic problems:

1   Relative economic impoverishment and weakness. Harnessed to the international economy on a detrimental basis, many countries, especially in Africa, became dependent on Western aid after decolonization.
2   Political instability and failure to develop democracy. In many developing countries, democratically elected governments were deposed, many soon after independence. Typically, they were replaced – often for decades – by unelected civilian or military rule.

The overall point is that independence from colonial rule brought two major problems for most of the new governments. First, to achieve political and social stability, it was necessary to construct nation-states from often disparate peoples, typically separated by ethnic, linguistic, and/or religious divisions. In many cases, this was very difficult to achieve. Second, how could the postcolonial governments develop their countries' productive capacities so as to deliver sufficient and sustained economic growth to ensure that all their people's living standards improved?

Modernization and Dependency Theories

Until recently, examinations of these issues were usually investigated via the insights of one of two analytical paradigms: modernization theory and dependency theory. The modernization paradigm focused squarely on domestic factors, paying little explicit attention to external factors and issues. Dependency theory, on the other hand, sought to explain political and economic outcomes in developing countries by reference primarily to external factors. Each paradigm enjoyed a prolonged period of analytical predominance: modernization theory in the 1950s and early 1960s, dependency theory in the late 1960s and early 1970s. Smith (1985: 559) notes that the main problem with modernization theory "was that it was too fragmented," while dependency theory was "too holistic." Taken separately, the central concerns of the paradigms could not adequately explain the recent array of political and economic developments in the developing world.

We turn to a brief summary of the key concerns of each paradigm, and note their analytical drawbacks. This will help us appreciate the importance of the new issues which have emerged in recent years and support the contention that the most analytically productive way to understand what has happened is through an assessment of the interaction of domestic and external factors.

Modernization theory and modernization revisionism

Modernization theory was preoccupied with domestic conditions for political and economic development, such as the impact on development of "institutional transformation" and "agents of modernization." The first wave of criticism broke in the late 1960s. It focused on what critics saw as the approach's over-simple conceptualization of "tradition" and "modernity" and their interrelationship. This was part of a broader reaction against some underlying assumptions, especially the assumption that there are recognizably traditional institutions which constitute a barrier to modernization; and the assumption that the extent to which modernization takes place means that traditional institutions must decline (Randall and Theobald 1998: 45). In general, early modernization theory seemed to fail to understand (1) the diversity and perseverance of various forms of tradition; (2) the complexity of tradition's relationship with modernity; and (3) the political significance of so-called traditional phenomena, such as clientelism, religion, ethnicity, and caste.

The critiques of modernization theory soon led to a refinement of the approach, known as modernization revisionism. In making analytical room for "the specific character and consequences of indigenous social structures and culture[s]," modernization revisionism not only exposed early modernization theorists' simplistic and ethnocentric assumptions about tradition and modernity, but also underlined that "traditional" phenomena – such as caste, ethnicity, religion, and clientelism – were often of contemporary political salience (ibid: 84–5). But this led to additional questions. What causes such factors to become politically salient in some countries but not in others? How does tradition impinge on "modern" political structures and processes, such as states, political parties, and elections?

Building on the insights of modernization theory, modernization revisionism privileged a variety of often newly observed "traditional" domestic structures and processes as the key to understanding political outcomes within developing countries. But, critics pointed out, on their own such factors could not provide coherent, holistic accounts to explain why things turned out one way rather than another. The main problem was that they could only make sense within a framework that they could not themselves supply. That is, they failed to factor into the analysis wider structural factors, including, domestically, social class structures and, at the global level, the influence of Western economic and political interests and the international economic system.

Dependency and neo-dependency theory

Dependency theory emerged in the 1960s as a critique of the modernization approach. It focused on the allegedly baleful legacy for developing countries, not only of imperialism, but also of the Western-dominated international economic system, while showing little or no concern for domestic factors. However, following a period of intellectual primacy its star waned in the 1970s, primarily because some developing countries, such as South Korea and Taiwan, were enjoying strong economic growth and development – only to reappear in the early 1980s in the form of neo-dependency theory. The apparent decline of the salience of dependency theory coincided with the emergence of a new phase of North–South relations, which saw the emergence of neo-dependency theory.

Neo-dependency theory pointed to a new – or at least dramatically extended – component of actual relations between rich Western countries and poorer developing ones: the international debt crisis that occurred in the early 1980s. Its trajectory seemed to neo-dependency analysts to be a striking illustration, under certain circumstances, of the power of international structures to mold outcomes in the developing world. International indebtedness soared while international lending agencies imposed stringent conditions for debt rescheduling, including the ubiquitous structural adjustment programs (SAPs). The imposition of SAPs reflected the new ascendancy of neoliberal economics and an associated desire to roll back the economic influence of the state. However, critics pointed out that the actual implications of SAPs were actually contradictory: a strong state would be needed to implement and carry out SAP-linked reforms, but one of the aims of the latter was to reduce the state's economic significance! Let's look next at the ins and outs of the developing countries' debt crisis and the West's response.

The West's response to the developing countries' debt crisis

By the early 1990s, developing countries were collectively burdened by a level of international debt which had risen 15-fold in 20 years – from US$100 billion to around US$1,500 billion (George 1993: 59). Many observers, including Sweezy and Magdoff (1984), Pool and Stamos (1985), and Magdoff (1986), judged that the growth of international indebtedness among developing countries was an indication that dependency theory had been right all along. They argued that the growing debt burden seemed to reflect a renewal of Western neocolonialism to ensnare numerous developing countries. To such critics the foreign debt problem represented an intensification of financial dependency, "a process that has played a crucial role in the shaping of the development of [many developing] countries" (So 1990: 116). Foreign indebtedness was seen as a clear example of developing countries' economic policy being dictated by the West, in two ways. First, the West failed to come up with a comprehensive global solution to deal with developing countries' spiraling foreign indebtedness. This meant that many heavily indebted countries were compelled annually to send large proportions of their export proceeds – 60 percent or more was not unknown – to Western creditors so as to service their debts. Second, in numerous indebted developing countries the International Monetary Fund (IMF), assisted by the World Bank, imposed its own economic policy: SAPs.

Attempting to deal with the implications of the debt crisis, deeply indebted developing countries came under the economically onerous regime imposed by the IMF and the World Bank, the two leading Western-dominated international financial institutions (IFIs). This regime, critics argued, clearly showed how Western interests could dictate outcomes in developing countries. The point was illustrated by detailing how the West responded to the developing countries' debt crisis. Seeking to account for swiftly expanding international indebtedness in the 1980s, George (1993) distinguished between two sets of factors. On the one hand, she noted the salience of elements that were in some sense "avoidable" for indebted developing countries, such as poor governmental decisions. But, on the other hand, she suggested that "avoidable" factors were actually outweighed by the "unavoidable" ones: notably two external "shocks": (1) major oil price rises in the 1970s and (2) consequential significant rises in international interest rates that followed in the early 1980s. These external shocks, George suggested, were highly important in accounting for what happened in relation to debt in developing countries.

Anxious to recycle swiftly accumulating "petrodollars," commercial banks lent billions of dollars to the governments of Latin American and other developing countries. However, the banks became nervous about further lending when international indebtedness burgeoned and the risk of default grew. Under these circumstances, the banks looked to the IMF as a "neutral" agency able to impose economic discipline on debtor countries. The IMF argued that most governments of developing countries had for too long pursued "misguided" strategies of economic growth, relying too much on the state as the key motor of growth. Neo-dependency critics argued that the main point of the IMF's desired economic "reforms" was not to stimulate development per se but to encourage seriously indebted developing economies into a suitable position to repay their foreign debts.

Mexico provides a good example of what happened. By the early 1980s Mexico's foreign debt mushroomed to US$55 billion. With nowhere else to turn, the IMF was brought in by the government to oversee essential economic reforms. The initial objective was relatively limited: monetary stabilization. But the IMF's strategy and subsequent arrangements for debt recycling extended Mexico's conditional requirements to include far-reaching economic structural changes. Later, the IMF's generic formula for debt assistance was applied to more than a dozen additional Latin American and numerous other developing countries.

Western governments were determined that the debt crisis should not seriously undermine their leading banks. The latter had lent billions of dollars to developing countries, especially in Latin America, and the ramifications of countries' debt defaults could have led to global monetary collapse. Consequently, Western policies were primarily geared to protecting the banks and were not, as a result, particularly concerned with ameliorating developing countries' indebtedness. Over time, the banks managed gradually to adjust their balance sheets – that is, they gradually wrote off unpayable debts. As a result, they became much less vulnerable to developing countries' threats to default on their international debts. But increasing numbers of developing countries were unable easily to service their debts and the result was a number of essentially stop-gap solutions, including debt renegotiations and partial rescheduling of debts; unilateral moratoriums on repayments; fixed – relatively low – proportions of export earnings to service debt; and SAPs. None in isolation or collectively was sufficient to end the debt crisis.

This is not to imply that there was absolutely no action to deal with the debt crisis, only that it was piecemeal and too limited in its application. For example, Western countries (grouped in the Organization of Economic Cooperation and Development) converted about US$5 billion from debt to grants in the mid-1980s, and SAPs amounted to roughly the same amount. A summit meeting held in Toronto in 1988 came up with another US$5 billion, and some concessions were made to "low-income" developing countries, that is, those with per capita GNPs of less than US$635 in 1991 (Dolan 1993: 266). In addition, a few "middle-income" developing countries – that is, with per capita GNPs between US$636 and US$2,555 – managed to get some of their commercial debts to Western banks restructured in the 1990s. Welcome though these concessions no doubt were, it is important to put this aid into perspective. On the developing countries' total debt of US$1,500 billion, Western assistance – of around US$15 billion – amounted to just 1 percent of the total debt. What critics saw as a very disappointing Western response to the debt crisis was seen as evidence of the West's clear and continuing economic dominance over the developing countries. As we shall see in chapter 3, in the early 2000s, two decades after the debt crisis broke, foreign debt continues to be an enormous economic burden with serious social and political consequences in numerous developing countries in Africa, Asia, and Latin America.

Overall, critics argued, Western governments' and IFIs' handling of the debt crisis provided evidence of a "divide and rule" strategy: debt-restructuring negotiations were conducted on a country-by-country basis, and certain – but limited – incentives were offered to those who accepted bilateral deals, but there was nothing for those that refused them. One impact was to reduce the capacity of the developing countries to act as a bloc. "As the Cold War drew to a close, Southern institutions seemed incapable of advancing their quest for economic justice for the world's poorer nations" (Acharya 1999: 92). Add to this the fact that the end of the Cold War not only generally reconfirmed the West's global clout, but more specifically presented two new important economic challenges to developing countries: (1) they had to deal with the possibility that a proportion of Western aid would be diverted to help in the rebuilding of Eastern European post-communist economies; and (2) the collapse of the Eastern European communist bloc increased pressure on developing countries to integrate their economies more closely into the world capitalist order.

The imposition of fundamental economic liberalization and reform programs in the 1980s and 1990s was an important manifestation of the continued incorporation of developing countries' economies into the global capitalist order. The content of SAPs was strongly influenced by the rise of neoliberal thinking that ideologically characterized both the Reagan government in the USA (1980–8) and Britain's Thatcher administration (1979–90). What began as a piecemeal policy to deal with the short-term impact of foreign indebtedness in Latin America, developed into the ubiquitous SAPs applied to numerous developing countries from the 1980s. While varying in their details from country to country, SAPs were always rooted in the same general formula: it stressed, on the one hand, the importance of markets, competition, and strong linkages to the world economy and, on the other, a reduced economic role for the state.

But the prescription was not to be limited to changing the economic role of the state and creating a new, liberal economic environment. The

IMF claimed that necessary domestic changes, augmented by appropriate changes at the global level, such as new globalized capital markets and a reborn world trading order, would result in the gap closing between the world's rich and poor. However, contrary to the IMF's expectations, SAPs did not lead to increased prosperity across the board, but rather to widespread exacerbation of preexisting social inequalities, increased poverty and political conflict, and declining health and educational programs (Randall and Theobald 1998: 160–2). Disappointing economic outcomes encouraged demands for political reforms. As we shall see in chapter 4, many commentators believe that the disappointing outcomes of SAPs were a key factor in the recent wave of democratization in the developing world. In sum, SAPs were prescribed by Western governments and supported by Western commercial banks, acting through the IMF and the World Bank. Critics saw SAPs as an ideologically orientated response to developing countries' international indebtedness, which, however, did little to tackle development questions.

The Analytical Importance of Structure and Contingency

Our brief survey of modernization and dependency theories has showed the following: (1) the analytical significance of both domestic and international factors to political, economic, and social outcomes in the developing world; (2) the importance of structural factors to outcomes. What structural factors in particular are important to help understand and explain outcomes in the countries of the developing world?

To answer this question we need to take into account the analytical importance to political and economic outcomes of both structure and contingency. To illustrate their importance it will be useful to examine them briefly in relation to democratic consolidation. Democratic consolidation is the phase of democracy that, following a transition to democracy from authoritarian rule, not only involves significant challenges to leading political actors, but also implies that democracy is widely accepted among political actors (Haynes 2001a).

After democratic transition, the main challenge is to institutionalize democratic competition between groups and organizations with conflicting interests and aspirations, previously united in opposition to authoritarian rule. To facilitate democratic consolidation, political actors must now agree to subordinate their strategies and divisions so that, at the very least, a return to authoritarian rule is not facilitated.

This places considerable demands on political actors' skills and commitment to democracy. Now they must demonstrate "ability to differentiate political forces rather than draw them into a grand coalition, the capacity to define and channel competing political projects rather than seek to keep potentially divisive reforms off the agenda, and the willingness to tackle incremental reforms ... rather than defer them to some later date" (Karl 1990: 17). But this outcome is often difficult to achieve as, post-transition, political actors typically settle back into largely predictable positions, competing with each other for power. Here, the underlying distribution of power in society is an important factor in determining post-transition outcomes; that is, when politics becomes routinized again, and follows largely predictable patterns. At this stage, typically, "the same configuration of institutional forces" conditioning "the process of transition will regain saliency at increased levels" (Bratton and Van de Walle 1997: 274). All political actors work within a framework of political restraints and opportunities that not only limit the range of plausible alternatives open to them, but also make it highly likely that certain courses of action will be selected over others. The point is that certain structures of power reappear after democratic transition and help determine which actors will predominate in the new political environment. Let's look in more detail at the relevant structures.

Structures

The kinds of structures I have in mind include a country's "immovable traditions [and] power structures" (Pinkney 1993: 139–40). They are important because they impose limits on the range of choices available, predisposing political and economic actors to opt for certain courses of action over others. O'Donnell (1994: 65) suggests that decisive factors generating medium-term outcomes are strongly linked to "various long-term factors" that many governments inherit, such as serious socioeconomic problems. This suggests that countries' political and economic characteristics will differ from region to region and from country to country.

Domestic and international factors

What structures are analytically relevant? First, there are formal political institutions found in practically all states: permanent edifices of public life, such as laws, organizations, public offices, and elections. Second, informal institutions can also be important, such as the "dynamics of interests and identities, domination and resistance, compromise and accommodation" that may run parallel or counter to formal democratic ones (Bratton and Van de Walle 1997: 276). It is the interaction of such aspects, coupled with contingent factors (described below), that determine political and economic outcomes in a country. Overall, while the relative weight of these factors, as well as the factors themselves, will differ from country to country, four structural characteristics are important: (1) the character of a polity's social and economic system; (2) constellations of power at the state and lower levels; (3) the political effectiveness of civil and political societies; and (4) a range of external factors and actors. Let us look at each.

First, relationships between class divisions and state power are often analytically significant. In developing countries, relations between various classes – wealthy capitalists, large-scale landowners, urban middle classes, industrial-sector workers, small-scale farmers, landless agricultural workers, and so on – can profoundly affect political and economic outcomes. This is a way of saying that what happens in a country is strongly linked to and by various domestic structures, including class, state, and transnational power, driven by particularistic histories of capitalist development (Cammack 1997).

Second, the overall economic position of a country – is it rich or poor? – and its degree of social polarization are important structural factors. For example, it is often suggested that democracy requires a rough balance of power between, on the one hand, the state, and, on the other, societal interests organized in political and civil society (Haynes 2001a).

Third, democracy is unlikely to be sustained when the state is either excessively powerful in relation to traditionally subservient social classes, as in many Middle Eastern countries, or is overdependent on powerful landed classes that benefit from control of labor-repressive agriculture, as in many Latin American nations.

Fourth, various external factors and actors – including background conditions, influential actors, and individual, decisive events – can also be important in helping determine what happens within developing countries. In this regard, important international structures can include international law, transnational civil society, and IFIs such as the World Bank, the IMF, and the World Trade Organization.

In sum, while the precise mix differs from country to country, important domestic *structures* related to political and developmental outcomes in developing countries include the following:

- personalistic rule, with a corresponding lack of relevant political institutions;
- unhelpful national political cultures that do not value democracy higher than other forms of political engagement;
- weak or declining economies, heavily dependent on international financial assistance;
- serious societal conflicts, rooted in religious, ethnic, and/or ideological schisms;
- weak, fragmented civil societies;
- highly politicized militaries anxious to maintain the existing structures of power;
- unrepresentative and unaccountable governments;
- unrepresentative, undemocratic political parties, dominated by self-serving leaders;
- numerically small yet politically powerful landowning elites that deny landless people enough access to agricultural land;
- politically and economically powerful individuals at the local level;
- religious and cultural traditions that are not only hostile to liberal democracy but also to more and better human rights.

Overall, the explanatory value of domestic structures is that outcomes are often strongly influenced by a country's weight of inherited political, economic, and social institutions. This is a way of saying that "institutional edifices have inertia – and social trends have momentum – that generally exceed human intent and control" (Bratton and Van de Walle 1997: 22). In addition, there is an important international structure to which we have already referred: the Western-dominated global economic system.

In sum, varying from country to country in their precise mix, domestic and international structures help mold political, economic, and social outcomes in developing countries. In other words, there is no *tabula rasa*: no government, whatever its stated ideological proclivities or goals, democratically orientated or not, can erase historically produced societal behavior and the structures that accompany it. On the other hand, a myopic focus on structures alone would lead us to overlook the important role of human agency and one-off events in helping determining outcomes. That is, structures are only part of the story. We must not ignore what individual political actors do and the circumstances leading them to act in a certain way. This raises the issue of contingency, to which we turn next.

Contingency

International factors

In recent years several one-off international events have been analytically important in helping explain political, economic, and social outcomes in developing countries. At the end of the 1980s, both the end of the Cold War and the "third wave of democracy" challenged authoritarian rulers across the developing world. Reflecting the demise of the Soviet Union, this period was notable for a situation where numerous developing countries were subject to demands from Western countries not only to democratize but also to bring into effect the structures and processes of "good governance." These "political conditionalities" were stipulated by Western governments – including those of the United States, Japan, France, and Britain, collectively the largest aid donors to developing countries in quantitative terms. The Western governments wielded much influence because of their ability to grant or deny aid. This involved significant policy conditions, sometimes backed by the threat of material sanctions if economic and political reforms were not forthcoming (Carothers 1997; Ottaway and Carothers 2000).

A second international contingent factor of relevance to the developing countries is what might be referred to as "background conditions" or the *Zeitgeist*: that is, recent and significant changes in thinking at the global level, for example in relation to human rights, the social, political, and economic position of women, and protection of the natural environment.

Note, however, that there was a variegated impact of such international factors on developing countries. For example, many observers would agree that the end of the Cold War was a major – and general – fillip to democratization around the world. On the other hand, many economically weak developing countries were highly dependent on injections of foreign aid to help balance budgets. Such countries were subject not only to Western pressures to democratize but also to embark upon often fundamental economic change. The success of Western demands in these matters would often be linked to certain factors, including the geographical size and economic weakness of targeted countries. For example, the impact of external factors on the large countries of the southern cone of Latin America (Brazil, Argentina, and Chile) was less than on the small, economically weak countries of Central America, geographically contiguous to the USA. Another example comes from Africa: small, economically weak regional countries, such as Ghana and Benin, were highly dependent on foreign aid injections to balance their budgets and, as a result, were more willing to listen to foreign demands than a large, economically powerful, oil-exporting country, such as Nigeria.

Domestic factors

A consolidated democracy requires that democratic institutions are not only built but also valued. Democracy can be installed without democrats, but it cannot be consolidated without them. Political actors may initially see a founding election as the "least worst" alternative to solve an intractable political standoff or to induce political movement in an ossified regime. Democracy may even survive in the short run under the force of these kinds of strategic calculations, but democracy will truly last only when political actors learn to love it. Until elites and citizens alike come to cherish rule by the people and exhibit a willingness to stand up for it, there will be no permanent defense against tyranny. (Bratton and Van de Walle 1997: 279)

This is the closing paragraph of Bratton and Van de Walle's book on democratic transitions in Africa. It highlights the importance to democratic consolidation of contingent factors; that is, the role of human agency and one-off events in helping determine political outcomes. Implicitly, however, Bratton and Van de Walle are suggesting that it is actually impossible to construct a handy checklist of contingency factors to which we can turn when wishing to assess chances of democratic consolidation in Africa and, by extension, elsewhere. This is because the events that can send things in a democratic direction, or reduce that possibility, are simply too varied to list. Much the same could be said for economic outcomes.

Africa provides several recent examples illustrating the importance of contingency to recent political outcomes. The first is the pivotal role of Nelson Mandela, former president of South Africa (1994–9). Imprisoned for over 30 years by the white-dominated apartheid regime, Mandela's personal decision to enter into political negotiations with the government, following his release from prison in 1990, was central to South Africa's democratization.

A second, less well known, example of the importance of contingency to political outcomes occurred in the East African country of Uganda. From the mid-1980s, Uganda's government, under the leadership of Yoweri Museveni, has presided over an unconventional "no-party" form of democracy, known as the "movement system" (Hansen and Twaddle 1995). In the early 1990s, when many other African countries were turning to conventional forms of multi-party democracy, Uganda's government refused to follow suit. Why? It was not necessarily because the government feared it would be ousted at the polls; indications were that the government was popular enough to win elections. In other words, there was little doubt that the regime would have won elections had it chosen to allow a multi-party system. One answer to the question is that the country's powerful leader, Yoweri Museveni, sincerely believed that multi-partyism was the cause of the evils of tribalism and religious prejudice at the root of two decades of conflict in Uganda prior to his rule. The overall point is that Museveni's personal decision to pursue an unconventional form of democracy highlights the importance of contingency to Uganda's current political arrangements.

A third example highlighting the analytical importance of contingency also comes from Africa, this time from Nigeria. The election to power of a former military leader, Olusegun Obasanjo, in early 1999 led to optimism that the country would finally put behind it a long history of military governments and a lack of democracy caused, it was argued, by the country's unhelpful structural characteristics. President Obasanjo was seen as fervently pro-democracy and, as a result, the government of the United States focused much development assistance on the country. However, it soon became clear that Obasanjo could not easily or quickly overcome Nigeria's unhelpful structural legacies, including serious ethnic, religious, and regional friction, a long-significant political role for the military, and much oil wealth in the hands of a numerically tiny elite (McGreal 2000). The overall point is that President Obasanjo's personal desire for democracy, bolstered by US financial assistance, was not enough, in the face of unhelpful structural characteristics, to set the country on a clearly democratic path.

It might be argued that Africa's political heritages and circumstances are different from those of other developing countries and regions. For example, not only in most Latin American, but also in some Asian countries, notably South Korea and Taiwan, political legacies of authoritarian government took on a particular form, known as "bureaucratic authoritarianism." Consequently, attempts at democratization commenced from a different starting point than in Africa. However, in all three regions, democratization outcomes were also linked to human agency. For example, despite democratic rule in the Latin American country of Venezuela since 1958, the nature of the political system – which in fact privileged the elites – became increasingly unpopular among ordinary people. Two political parties that carved up power between them dominated the political scene for decades. Eventually, in the late 1990s, Hugo Chavez, a charismatic politician and former coup leader, was elected national president. Chavez could have simply continued with the form of the old political regime and retained the existing power equation. Instead, he proclaimed that he wanted to bring in a new form of popular democracy; to change the system by removing from power the old, discredited parties and "pass it to the people." While critics claimed that he was presiding over a new form of charismatic authoritarianism, the point is that Venezuela is an example of a political environment where the importance of both contingency and structures has been significant in explaining political events.

Conclusion

Uganda's Museveni, South Africa's Mandela, and Hugo Chavez in Venezuela are three important political figures whose personal decisions, in the context of structural characteristics, were of great importance to political outcomes in their respective countries. The examples highlight the essence of what I call *structured contingency*, and suggest the following hypothesis:

> *While inherited structures form the context within which political leaders act, individuals are not slavishly bound by structure. Human agency and one-off events can also be of great importance to explain political and economic outcomes in developing countries.*

The concept of structured contingency highlights that (1) all polities have structures – that is, inherited rules and institutions and recurrent patterns of behavior – to which those engaged in political competition are attuned; and that (2) political outcomes are also linked to what individual political actors do, sometimes in the context of one-off events. In summary, structured contingency is informed by the following:

- All polities have historically established, informal and formal, structures of power. They are reflected in established rules and institutions that limit the available – that is, realistic – alternatives open to political actors; consequently, they will tend to select certain courses of action over others.

- Because political outcomes are not entirely random but reflect to a large degree institutionalized patterns, structured contingency is concerned with "the interaction of the uncertainties of politics with persistent institutional structures" (Bratton and Van de Walle 1997: 278).

2

Globalization and International Relations

Global interdependence will dominate the twenty-first century. What happens in sub-Saharan Africa or the Indonesian jungle is already being felt in the UK. (Bunting 2001)

The global village. The new world order. The peace dividend. These are all buzzwords of the 1990s that reflected an optimistic outlook for the dawning of the next century. Each idea brought a sense that finally we could progress from the dysfunction caused by failing to understand that we are one family. . . . Unfortunately, it has become obvious that the corner turned did not lead to a smooth road on which racism, nationalism and a plethora of insular, myopic attitudes were put behind us. In fact it seems that we have entered a period where many of the demons of the Cold War era – whether economic, environmental or social – still loom like an ominous cloud on the horizon. (Elizabeth Dowdeswell, Executive Director of the United Nations Environmental Program, quoted in Bretherton 1996: 10)

The issue of globalization has increased in importance since the end of the Cold War in 1989. Initially, as Bretherton's quotation implies, it brought widespread hopes for enhanced international cooperation between peoples and countries, and fresh commitment to strengthen the role of international organizations, especially the United Nations. These developments, many people hoped, would facilitate attempts to address a range of perennial global problems, including economic, social, and political injustices; war; human rights abuses; and environmental degradation and destruction. To see how things turned out in relation to the developing world, chapter 2 has the following structure. First, it looks at "positive" and "negative" characterizations of globalization.

Second, it focuses on globalization in relation to its technological, economic, political, and cultural aspects. Third, it investigates how globalization has affected the ability of developing countries to organize at the international level by highlighting the decline of the Non-Aligned Movement. Fourth, it examines the trend towards regionalization in the developing world as an antidote to the perceived malign effects of globalization.

"Positive" and "Negative" Globalization

While "globalization" names a process that is still unfolding, there has been no shortage of attempts to define it. The quotation from Bunting (2001) above emphasizes that globalization is about enhanced interdependence between peoples and countries. But is it possible to understand the impact of globalization as an "objective" process that simply involves mapping the relevant "facts" in order to assess key global trends in relation to social, political, and economic organization? Because analysis of globalization is almost always cast in wider normative and ideological contexts, with value judgments to the fore, many would answer "no." Reflecting such concerns, two schools of thought differ in their interpretation of the impact of globalization upon the developing world. I shall refer to the first as the "positive globalization" (PG) view, and the second as the "negative globalization" (NG) approach.

"Positive globalization"

Hurrell and Woods (1995: 449) identify a powerful cluster of liberal assumptions attached to the PG view. The first is that globalization is not only irresistible but also to be welcomed. Second, globalization is bringing overwhelmingly beneficial consequences, including greater economic efficiency, via the spread of markets; more effective international institutions; better mechanisms for problem-solving; and more political choice and openness as a result of the third wave of democracy. Much of the PG literature has resonances with the functionalist writings of the 1960s and 1970s that appeared in relation to the problems and prospects for the European Union. Then, functionalist theorists such as Ernst Haas argued that technical cooperation to manage specific problems would ultimately yield a superstructure of political behavior in which the sovereignty of the nation-state would be steadily eroded and circumvented. This would be a welcome development. The liberal proponents of globalization similarly believe in its progressive impact in relation to economic, political, and social behavior.

In the PG view, the end of the Cold War clearly demonstrated the superiority of the West's values and belief systems over those of its communist rival. Now, it was believed, we would see not only the final achievement of capitalism's global expansion, but also the universal extension of liberal democracy. The outcome would be a peaceful and prosperous new world order, a modern golden age. Globalization would advance the well-being of millions of people around the world, through the liberating impact of the spread of markets, democracy, and enhanced human rights. To further these developments, international organizations and global institutions would be strengthened and better focused to address pressing global problems. In addition, informal cross-border structures would develop further, involving the interaction of "local groups and grassroots organizations from all parts of the world," known as transnational civil society (Bretherton 1996: 8).

Western governments and Western-controlled IFIs see economic globalization/liberalization as overwhelmingly positive for developing countries. It is argued that benefits are especially clear when seen in the context of the dismal failures of various types of economic planning. These include both communist central state planning and the *dirigiste* – that is, state-led, non-communist – variety practiced for long periods in many developing countries. Two problems of such planning are highlighted: politicians' and bureaucrats' economic mismanagement and the problems of "rent seeking" (that is, "the attempt to gain profit from becoming the sole producer and/or distributor of a good or service": Bealey 1999: 284). Both are seen as habitual, unwelcome aspects of state economic involvement that seriously limit the desirability of state economic involvement. Instead, proponents of economic liberalization argue that the "discipline of the marketplace," on balance, results in fewer errors of judgment than when the state is heavily involved. Those errors that do occur will be on a reduced and hence less damaging scale.

Critics of the economic liberalization/"marketization" approach point to two problems. First, in practice, as opposed to theory, the "benefits" of marketization misrepresent the past by exaggerating state economic failures in the developing world. Second, removing or even drastically scaling down the state's economic role is problematic, as it removes or restricts the possibility of social measures "to protect the weak from market failures and the exercise of political power" (Sen 1999: 61). A counter-argument is that the evolving yet partial regionalization of the world economy – that is, economic activity that clusters around a number of geographic poles, such as the European Union, the North American Free Trade Association (USA, Canada, Mexico), and the Pacific Basin and Japan – will provide a degree of scope for some state regulation of market trends.

"Negative globalization"

A monstrous plot is afoot. Public schools and hospitals are under threat. So is the right of governments to set standards that protect our health and environment. The World Trade Organization is trying to resurrect the ill-fated Multilateral Agreement on Investment, or MAI. It must be stopped before it is too late. (Moore 2001)

Economic liberalization refers to measures which extend and enhance the operation of market forces, including both microeconomic and macroeconomic aspects of the economy, and including both denationalization of industry and freeing labor markets from state control. The NG view is that economic liberalization, as an integral aspect of globalization, has been hijacked by a market liberalism which puts the mechanisms of the market before both the natural environment and the well-being of many communities. As Sen puts it, economic globalization is "the economic outcome of liberalization for which there are socioeconomic and human consequences." Macroeconomically, "the most significant retreat has been from the policy of demand management to reduce unemployment. The adoption of floating exchange rates and the abandonment of capital controls are also an aspect of macroeconomic liberalization" (Sen 1999: 61).

In the quotation above, Mike Moore, Director General of the World Trade Organization (WTO), refers sarcastically to widespread popular fears in relation to the aims and objectives of the WTO, the global organization founded in 1994 to liberalize further global trade. The NG view sees the WTO as the epitome of unwelcome and unfortunate globalization, whose impact is seriously affecting the well-being of millions of people in developing countries. The NG critique rejects the consensus acceptance of market capitalism and argues that the current system is unfair, structured to benefit powerful vested interests. Proponents of the NG view, such as Gill (1993), highlight the following undesirable effects of globalization :

- Migratory and refugee movements in the developing world and the former Eastern European socialist bloc.
- Impoverishment caused by the restructuring of global production and finance.
- Growing disparities in economic and environmental conditions between the industrialized West and the rest of the world.
- War and political conflict both within and between countries.

In short, the NG view is that it is erroneous to accept the claims of the PG school at face value: globalization is a highly politicized process, based in specific conditions, that creates both winners *and* losers; and most of the latter are to be found in developing countries (Randall and Theobald 1998: 235). As we saw in chapter 1, both the International Monetary Fund (IMF) and the World Bank are seen as central to this process. Neither organization is new: both were created in the mid-1940s to supervise and oversee post-World War II global economic liberalization. Later, in the 1970s, following serious economic instability that resulted from the steep rise in global oil prices, dozens of developing countries were persuaded to accept – sometimes under duress – development strategies known as structural adjustment programs (SAPs), with the aim of integrating them further into the global(ized) economy. Recipients of loans from the IMF in the developing world were compelled to abandon national development strategies based on import substitution and nationalization and replace them with programs of economic liberalization and marketization. In the NG view, the IMF strategy was a clear example of the intensity and extensiveness of economic globalization, guided by the leading capitalist actors: the United States, Japan, and the European Union.

In sum, the PG view is strongly held by Western governments and Western-dominated IFIs, such as the IMF. The argument is that globalization is, on balance, a benign development, as it encourages more economic growth, as well as democracy and enhanced human rights. Critics, however, argue a contrary position: in a nutshell, globalization is creating a worse world than before, characterized by growing polarization between rich and poor within and between countries, as well as serious armed conflicts in various parts of the world.

The Impact of Technological, Economic, Political, and Cultural Globalization

While the PG and NG views differ radically in their assessment of the nature and characteristics of contemporary globalization, both would agree that understanding globalization and its effects is central to an understanding of the international and national relations of the developing world at the start of the twenty-first century. In a sense, the question of whether globalization is "positive" or "negative" is irrelevant. Given, as many believe, that the process is unstoppable, perhaps the key issue is how to guarantee, in the words of UN secretary general Kofi Annan, that "globalization becomes a positive force for all of the world's people, instead of leaving billions in squalor" (quoted in Wintour 2001).

Some of the confusion about globalization and its impact stems from the fact that the term is frequently used but rarely clearly defined. To be analytically useful, the term not only requires careful specification; it should also be demonstrated that globalization refers to a new, distinct phase in international relations. This is by no means self-evident: the history of imperialism and the growth of a global economic system since the seventeenth century suggest that geographical extensiveness itself is not a new phenomenon. To have analytical utility, the term should imply more than a simple geographical extension of a range of phenomena and issues for which the term "worldwide" would suffice. Globalization is about something more: it signifies a significant intensification of global interconnectedness and consciousness among peoples exposed to that intensification, and a corresponding diminution in the significance of territorial boundaries. Explication and assessment of so broad and abstract a concept is likely to be a difficult, but not impossible, task. Let's turn to it next.

When the Cold War ended in 1989, followed by the implosion of the USSR, there was much optimism that the future would be brighter than the immediate past and that globalization would result in clear progress towards a better collective future for all people. Many people believed that a benign New World Order (NWO) would start, with enhanced, beneficial interdependence between people and governments. However, feelings of disappointment and frustration quickly surfaced when progress towards a NWO ran into the sand with the Gulf War of 1990–1. Instead, for many people in the developing world, the NWO and globalization soon became synonymous: a concerted Western attempt to peddle the alleged "superiority" of its values, belief systems, and practices. It appeared that the global victory of capitalism, the extension of liberal democracy, and the implanting of Western-style human rights and environmental protection would underpin the West's global dominance, if necessary riding roughshod over alternative visions of the future.

In sum, Sen (1999: 56) suggests that three interrelated events have both underpinned and informed the process of globalization: (1) the collapse of communism and the end of the Cold War; (2) "the evident triumph of capitalism;" and (3) "the emergence of the dialectical antithesis to the triumph of capitalism" – that is, conflicts between social classes, regions, and countries – which led to novel expressions of contention both within and between countries. While Macmillan and Linklater (1995: 12) highlight the political dimensions of globalization that are "transforming the nature of political community across the world," Mittelman (1994) argues that globalization is actually a multifaceted concept. It is "a rubric for varied phenomena . . . [that] interrelates multiple levels of analysis" with political, economic, cultural, and social dimensions, including

> the spatial reorganization of production, the interpenetration of industries across borders, the spread of financial markets, the diffusion of identical consumer goods to distant countries, massive transfers of population within the South as well as from the South and the East to the West, resultant conflicts between immigrant and established communities in formerly tight-knit neighborhoods, an emerging worldwide preference for democracy. (Mittelman 1994: 429)

Taken together, these developments signify a multifaceted intensification, between governments and peoples, of global interconnectedness and consciousness of that intensification. It also implies an associated, but variable, reduction in the political and economic significance of territorial boundaries, and of the salience of state structures. Overall, globalization is a combination of processes, with four analytically discrete dimensions: (1) technological globalization, (2) economic globalization, (3) political globalization, (4) globalization of culture and ideas (Bretherton 1996: 3). Let us look at each, with a view to ascertaining their impact on the mass of developing countries.

Technological globalization

There was a gradual development – and speeding up – of technological advances during the latter part of the nineteenth century, and a par-

ticular spurt of growth in this regard after 1945. While the role of technology, especially communications technology, is widely agreed to be
very important to the progress of globalization, we should note that it
is a facilitative or enabling component. That is, technology per se is not
the determining factor: it is necessary, but not sufficient on its own to
propel globalization forward. Clark (1997) points out that technology
is essentially neutral: it can be both beneficial and hostile to globalization. For example, some governments of developing countries (e.g.
China, Iran, and Saudi Arabia) have sought in recent years to exemplify "that technology is an important source of governmental control
over its citizenry." This is because "it can be used to enhance the autar-
kic isolation of people from wider international currents. In this way,
technology made its own sinister contribution to the totalitarian fragmentation of the interwar period" (ibid: 21). On the other hand, the
increased ability of peoples, states, and organizations to communicate
has generally enhanced, and hence has been beneficial to, the processes
of globalization.

Economic globalization

Many analysts now regard economic globalization as an unstoppable
process. The term "economic globalization" refers to trends that now
seem entrenched and all but irreversible, to the point that serious questions are now raised about the relevance – and effectiveness – of individual countries in terms of what to think about, much less manage,
economic activity. Fukuyama (1992: 275) argues that, whereas nationalism once fulfilled an integrative role that met the needs of early capitalism, "those same economic forces are now encouraging the
breakdown of national barriers through the creation of a single, integrated world market." It is a process that seems to follow its own technical and economic logic, facilitated by cross-border mobility of capital,
growth in foreign direct investment, and increased economic importance of transnational business corporations (TNCs). It is often said that
economic globalization is reducing fundamentally the very possibility
of countries' pursuing national economic policies. Certainly, all states'
monetary and fiscal policies must take cognizance of the international
financial markets, with US$1.6 trillion a day passing through the for-
eign exchanges – that is, 400 percent of the collective foreign exchange
reserves of the US, Japanese, and British central banks. To this must be
added the significant amounts of employment, investment, and rev-

enue dependent on the decisions of TNCs, which choose where to invest and locate in terms primarily of profitability rather than national considerations. The overall impact is that many governments' effective capacity to pursue independent macroeconomic strategies is now tightly circumscribed.

Arguments about economic globalization tend to focus upon the following themes: (1) How territorially based are systems of manufacture and production? (2) Is international trade increasing? (3) What is the extent of international capital flows and their geographical spread? (4) What is the role of TNCs? Like other aspects of globalization, the perceived impact of economic globalization differs from observer to observer. On the one hand, Western governments and IFIs, organized around what is known as the "Washington Consensus," aver that the best framework for globalization is a worldwide free market. They argue that this form of economic globalization is both welcome and progressive, as it spreads positive economic benefits to those previously denied them by heavy-handed and damaging state policies. Critics, on the other hand, posit that economic globalization is a cipher for a Westernization of the global economy, an economic counterpart of the spread of democracy as global political ideology.

Economic globalization is different to economic internationalization in two key ways. First, the latter term implies economic interactions controlled by governments, whereas economic globalization involves movement of goods and services across national borders, for example by TNCs, to some degree beyond state control. Second, economic globalization refers to closer integration of the world economy, measured by trade/GNP ratios and international flows of foreign direct investment (FDI) and financial capital. As Sen remarks, "In contrast to *national* exports and imports of goods and services, the organization, flow and purview of FDI and global capital, undertaken by . . . TNCs, assume a global marketplace" (Sen 1999: 62).

Economic globalization can be measured both in terms of its extensiveness and, as already noted, its intensity. Expansion of the size of the global economy is probably the most obvious consequence of the end of the Cold War, as it led to the gradual, uneven, and still-continuing incorporation of the former Eastern European communist countries into the global economy and financial system. While it has not (yet) reached the extent predicted by the high expectations of the early post-Cold War period, it nevertheless seems clear that the end of the First World–Second World economic separation is, potentially, a huge step on the road to a real global economic system. In addition, the significance of the incorporation of the former Second World is added to by the steady opening to the international market, especially since the 1980s, of the economies of many developing countries. As already noted in chapter 1, and often under pressure from Western governments and the IMF and the World Bank, many governments of developing countries accepted – sometimes under considerable duress – the abandonment of national development strategies based on state-led programs and import substitution policies, and more or less rejected nationalization. SAP-based development strategies had the effect of further integrating the economies of developing countries into the global economy.

The collapse of the European communist systems in 1989–91 was an important background variable to economic liberalization: it seemed both to exonerate and galvanize market forces around the world. However, while these underlying changes in the international political economy were partly responsible for the advance of market changes in the developing world, their spread was also linked to specific local factors. Most often, the immediate reason for the adoption of economic liberalization, in many cases prior to the end of the Cold War, in the 1970s and 1980s, was a balance of payments crisis, accompanied by currency collapse, high rates of inflation, and insupportable fiscal deficit. These circumstances were usually preceded by periods of economic stagnation of variable length or declining rates of economic growth, which often led to serious social problems, including high – and growing – rates of unemployment. This factor was often exacerbated by rapidly growing work forces, galvanized by high population growth rates of 3 percent or more annually. And, as noted in chapter 1, in many cases developing countries' economic problems were further exacerbated by high levels of international indebtedness. Dozens of developing countries adopted SAPs at the insistence of Western IFIs, supported by Western governments because economic liberalization was nearly always a condition for international assistance.

But how global is economic globalization? Hirst and Thompson (1999) show that for many indices of economic globalization, notably trade and investment patterns, there is in fact a stark contrast between the economically developed OECD states – where, typically, they are high – and the mass of developing countries, where they are not. In fact, around 75 percent of total FDI is within the cluster of advanced industrial states. But, as Robinson (1998) points out, this is only one way of measuring economic globalization. He remarks that economic globalization is an ideologically directed process that is literally of worldwide importance. It is rooted in the historic spread of capitalism, a process given a fillip since the collapse of Europe's communist states, and in the now-unchallenged dominance of the West, spearheaded by the USA, Japan, and the EU. Consequently, economic globalization is now "the near culmination of the centuries-long process of the spread of capitalist production relations around the world and its displacement of all precapitalist relations (modernization)" (ibid: 4).

This process has several characteristics. First, from its inception in the seventeenth century, the global capitalist system expanded in two directions, both extensively and intensively. The most recent phase in capitalism's extensive enlargement occurred in the 100 years between the 1890s and the 1990s. This period began with Africa's colonization and ended with the reincorporation of the former Soviet bloc, as well as most communist developing countries. Second, the system simultaneously underwent a dramatic intensive expansion, with capitalist production relations superseding remaining precapitalist relations where they still existed. Thus capitalism surged on, thrusting aside preexisting institutions, paving the way, around the world, for the complete marketization of social life. Consequently, economic globalization involves not only a range of economic interactions, but is also about the triumph of the capitalist mode of production and the snuffing out of alternatives. This had not only economic, but also cultural and political, results in the developing world.

Third, internationalization of production, finance, and other economic resources is importantly expressed through and by TNCs, that managed as a result to acquire much political influence and economic clout. TNC responses to changing circumstances – including strategies of adjustment to compete with low-cost producers and/or concentration on high-value-added goods tailored to specialized markets – do not obviously favor the efficacy of national strategies of regulation. That is, states, especially in many developing countries, find it difficult to control TNCs, not least because the pace and interactions of technological and economic change means that, substantively, states' "command and control" regulations are almost impossible to apply meaningfully. Consequently, regarding regulatory strategies, governments of developing countries are faced with a stark choice: either to assist the necessary process of adjustment to attract TNCs or risk a declining tax base if TNC production facilities move elsewhere. In sum, in many cases TNC activities are seriously eroding the capacity of individual states to control their own economic futures (Schulz, Söderbaum, and Öjendal 2001: 16).

Overall, we can see that economic globalization is a multifaceted process in the developing world, with not only economic, but also political, social, and cultural results. It involves, in many cases, diminution of state autonomy in the sphere of economic policy. This implies not only a reduction in sovereignty, but also facilitates what appears to be an inexorable process of globalization of the world economy towards greater integration. Over time, the end of European colonial rule, the recent diminution of the USA's economic position and, during the last three decades, growth in the internationalization of productive capital and of finance, had a clear consequence: even powerful states had fewer options than before in relation to the range of economic policy they could use. However, this process was felt even more in weak developing economies – that is, the majority. It may not have resulted in an overt gnawing away of individual governments' legal entitlement to rule their own territories – that is, their sovereignty – but it does lay them open and exposed to networks of economic forces and relations which now ranged in and through them.

Four interrelated processes can be identified in this regard. First, the increased mobility of financial capital, making it difficult for many developing states to influence the terms on which they borrow. Second, the crucial importance of FDI as a vehicle for exports and economic growth. Third, the dramatic impact of the phenomenon of high growth rates in the East Asian "tiger" economies on the hopes and anxieties of elites elsewhere in the developing world. Fourth, East Asia's economic travails in 1997–8 increased the determination of many developing countries to speed up processes of regional economic integration as a means of becoming less vulnerable to changes in the global economy. We shall turn to this issue later in the chapter.

Political globalization

Western-supported democratization in the developing world

Economic globalization cannot be analyzed in isolation, as it helps contour the political landscape. Unlike economic globalization, political globalization – in the form of the advocacy of democracy – is a state-led project, coordinated by the American and various European governments, and expressed in what was known as the "Washington consensus" – that is, the belief that the best framework for globalization is a worldwide free market. After the Cold War, Western governments saw the spread of democracy not only as an essential adjunct to economic liberalization, but also as the final nail in the coffin of communism. It should not be overlooked, however, that the "third wave of democracy" actually began in Southern Europe in the mid-1970s, with the democratization of Greece, Spain, and Portugal. It then spread in the 1980s and 1990s to Latin America, Eastern Europe, Asia, and Africa (Haynes 2001a). The outcome was that, while in the early 1970s only a quarter of countries around the world had democratically elected governments, by the early 1990s over half did. And, by 2000, three quarters or more of governments were in power via the ballot box.

To what extent was recent democratization in the developing world influenced by globalization? While it is a basic premise for democratization that there be no hostile foreign interference in the political life of a country with the intention of subverting the political system, this is not to suggest that domestic and external factors should be treated with equal weight. Huntington (1991) suggests that foreign factors and actors can hasten or retard – but not ultimately influence fundamentally – democratic outcomes. Whitehead (1993) points out that recent democratization attempts in the developing world were influenced by, but were not the result of, international factors. In other words, in recent democratization in the developing countries, domestic elements were of prime importance and international factors of secondary significance. This can be seen in the outcome of international support for democratization – notably from Western governments – following the Cold War.

The United States was a key international actor in support of democracy: both the government, as well as state-linked bodies such as the National Endowment for Democracy, were active proponents of democracy at the global level in the 1990s (Carothers 1997). We should note that this was not an altogether new development: in the 1950s, in the early stages of the Cold War, newly democratic governments in Latin America, including those of Costa Rica, Venezuela, and Colombia, received diplomatic and financial support from the USA. Later, in the 1970s, US foreign policy under President Jimmy Carter had a prolonged focus on human rights, including democracy. During the 1980s, President Ronald Reagan promoted democracy as a counter to perceived communist expansionism. Thus, President Bill Clinton's government support for democratization and democratically elected governments in the developing world in the 1990s, seen as an integral aspect of global peace and stability, was merely the latest manifestation of a consistent US policy.

The US government was prepared to put its money where its mouth was: it provided more than $700 million to over 100 countries to aid democratization between the late 1980s and the late 1990s (Carothers

1999). Carothers argues that such assistance was provided via "a standard democracy template," involving financial support to underpin the electoral process and democratic structures: constitutions, political parties, state institutions, the rule of law, legislatures, local government structures, better civil–military relations, and civil society organizations. However, as Leftwich points out, it takes more than money to develop democracy, as it is not easy to create and embed concrete manifestations of what he calls "good governance," of which a key component is democratic, accountable government. Such an outcome is "not simply available on order," but requires "a particular kind of politics . . . to institute and sustain it" (Leftwich 1993: 612).

This raises an important issue. It suggests that external funding for democracy will be insufficient to achieve its aims if the targeted non-democratic regimes are able to "acquire democratic legitimacy internationally *without substantially changing their mode of operation*" (Lawson 1999: 23; emphasis added). Often, critics argue, international observation of elections is the only meaningful way to judge whether a democratic shift has actually occurred. Yet when external actors limit perusal of democracy and democratic processes to elections alone it is likely to result in only superficial democratization. When elections are complete, and the attention of the corpus of international observers moves on, little in the way of "democracy" may actually be achieved. Instead, the old domination of elites resurfaces, whereby political systems have only narrow bases and are characterized by "authoritarian clientelism and coercion" (Karl 1995: 74).

In sum, external actors in possession of large financial resources to encourage democracy, like the US government, were often important at the transition stage of democracy – that is, the shift from authoritarian to democratic rule – in developing countries. But they were less central to longer-term efforts both to democratize and to consolidate democracy when domestic factors are most important in political changes. This underlines the fact that democratic consolidation is always a long-term project, and dependent for success on an array of primarily domestic political, social, and economic determinants and developments. These include the spread of a pro-democracy political culture, the building of democratically accountable institutions, and sustained economic growth and general welfare provision. As we shall see in chapter 4, both democratization and democratic consolidation are fraught with difficulty and, especially in the early stages, constantly threatened with reversal.

I noted above that economic and political globalization are linked.

Burnell argues that an adverse external environment, such as a "global economic slump or international financial crisis," can help facilitate "significantly . . . chances of democratic deconsolidation, or failures to consolidate" (Burnell 1998: 12). While international pressures may help persuade economically privileged elites that democratic transition will not seriously harm their interests, and so help turn aside their opposition, "by further entrenching such groups in the economy, these same international forces are possibly dimming the longer-term prospects for greater social and political equality" (ibid: 23). This suggests that in an increasingly globalized economic system, the economic prospects and outcomes of individual states are not only the result of local decisions but are also linked to international factors. The latter can operate both to aid as well as hinder democracy. One view is that the advance of economic neoliberalism encapsulated by the Washington consensus – expressed by coordinated actions of IFIs such as the IMF and the World Bank, and through global market pressures – helps promote economic and, perhaps, political liberalization. However, it is likely to restrain democratization, because the latter encourages opposition leaders to call for social empowerment and participation by the poor in demanding fundamental political changes. This will be seen as potentially or actually destabilizing by Western governments and thus not welcomed.

"Asian values" and democracy

Some regional political leaders, such as Prime Minister Muhammad Mahathir of Malaysia and a former Singaporean prime minister, Lee Kuan Yew, claim that liberal democracy is actually "culturally alien" to the East and Southeast Asian region. This is because the countries of the region are said to have different kinds of political cultures and histories that, while differing from country to country in precise details, nevertheless reflect an important collective idea: rather than the individual, the community is of most societal significance. This claim is at the heart of the concept of a generic "(East) Asian culture," said by its proponents, such as Mahathir and Lee, to embody an array of sociopolitical values – including harmony, consensus, unity, and community – that differ significantly from those of "Western culture" and its individualistic, self-seeking values.

In Mahathir's view, Malaysia's society is richly imbued with such Asian social and political values. As a result, he claims, government is seen by society as legitimate only when it reflects values associated with the community's particular cultural contours. The political consequence is that the claimed appropriateness of Western-style liberal democracy, with its individualistic premises, is seen as misplaced because, according to Mahathir, it overlooks Malaysia's different, community-orientated, national characteristics. Instead, national political institutions and practices of democracy must necessarily be designed to "fit" local cultural and social values. The result, for Mahathir, is a national style of politics based on consensus rather than the conflictual adversarial approach characterizing Western political competition (Maravall 1995: 16).

Much of the theoretical literature would accept that, while in poor countries it is often difficult to democratize, in wealthy countries democracy has "already occurred. In between there is a 'political transition zone': countries in this middle economic stratum are most likely to transit to democracy, and most countries that transit to democracy will be in this stratum" (Huntington 1991: 31). In East and Southeast Asia, sustained economic growth, followed by economic malaise manifested in the regional financial crisis in 1997–8, encouraged opposition politicians and democrats to demand fundamental political reforms. But whereas international support for pro-democracy actors, most notably from the government of the United States, had earlier encouraged local democrats to call for reforms, the events of 1997–8 led to only muted external pressure to democratize. This was because the government of the USA, concerned with Washington consensus goals – that is, forging a free-market framework as the basis of globalization – was much more concerned to see political and economic stability than democracy.

Thus, political globalization had two main manifestations in the 1990s. On the one hand, there was a strong trend towards democratization and democracy, which was encouraged by the West. On the other hand, there was a strong rearguard action, centered in non-democratic East Asian countries such as Malaysia and Singapore, whose governments made the argument that liberal democracy might be suited to the West but it was not appropriate for their countries. The regional economic crisis in 1997–8 led to the muting of external pressure to democratize in the name of stability.

Cultural globalization

The notion of culture is central to many sociological interpretations of globalization. Much of the early theorizing about globalization focuses on what is seen as the continuing development of a global culture, dominated by the West. The media revolution and the growth of consumer-

ism are said to help erode particularistic cultures and values, to be replaced by a new "global culture" of Coca-Cola, Hollywood, Michael
Jackson, and Madonna. These developments are said to be encouraged
by a new-found global consciousness and linked to a physical com-
pression of the world, aided by technological developments that enhance ease of communications between people and groups around the
globe.

In a wide sense, culture itself becomes a potent political force that
could grow to threaten the basis of the current fragmented state system
and its structures of supporting nationalism. This is because, it is argued, "culture avoids being located and tied down to any definable
physical space" (Saurin 1995: 256). However, and somewhat paradoxi-
cally, nationalism and ethnic awareness are cultural components that
have been transmitted around the globe, to become both a globalized
and a globalizing phenomenon. As we shall see in chapter 5, one of the
causes of contemporary ethnic and religious conflict in many developing countries is said to be such groups' awareness of what other groups
around the world are doing, and with this knowledge they seek to
emulate their struggles for greater power.

A result of the spread of Western, individualistic values around the
world, cultural globalization is also apparent in the desire to spread a
Western-style human rights regime and to stimulate demands for a wide
array of rights. Anti-Western groups, including Islamists and some
Asian governments, fight against this development. Regarding human
rights and gender issues, on which we focus in chapters 6 and 7,
Bretherton identifies a growing tendency for such issues to be perceived
as "global in scope, and hence requiring global solutions." She points
to the "development of international organizations and global institutions which attempt to address such issues. More tentatively, the concept also suggests the development of a global civil society, in which
local groups and grassroots organizations from all parts of the world
interact" (Bretherton 1996: 8).

Globalization: conclusion

While still fluid and unfinished, technological, economic, political, and
cultural processes comprise globalization. In varying ways, both individually and collectively, these processes have had and continue to have
a significant impact upon developing countries. This is especially clear
since the end of the Cold War and the demise of the Second World

allowed the West to dominate the globe economically, politically and, arguably, culturally. In the first part of the chapter we looked at the domestic impacts of globalization processes on developing countries. In the next section we examine, first, how globalization undermined and significantly reduced the effectiveness and impact of the Non-Aligned Movement (NAM), until recently the main expression of the international solidarity of developing countries. Second, we examine the contemporary shift towards economic regionalization, widely seen as the best available method to deal with the economically malign effects of globalization.

The International Relations of the Developing World

The rise and fall of the Non-Aligned Movement

The developing countries constructed a vehicle to pursue their own international objectives in 1961, called the Non-Aligned Movement (NAM). For the next three decades NAM was the most important expression of the developing countries' alternative conception of the world, the primary manifestation of its proclaimed desire to project an alternative, less ideologically polarized, global vision highlighting the advantages of community over ideological polarization. In short, as Acharya notes, NAM was the chief manifestation of the developing world's "conscious and collective challenge to the dominant international order" (Acharya 1999: 89). It was the chief means by which developing countries could articulate demands and mobilize resources in response to developments involving the superpowers. However, NAM did not initially act as a uniform platform for *all* developing countries: with the exception of Cuba, few Latin American countries were early members of NAM. However, by the late 1990s NAM comprised 113 members from all parts of the developing world.

Over the years NAM pursued, at varying times, three main goals: (1) swift closure of the decolonization process; (2) "superpower non-interference in the Third World, global disarmament, and strengthening of global and regional mechanisms for conflict resolution" (ibid: 90); and (3) a New International Economic Order to benefit the developing countries. NAM developed over time to become an ambitious permanent organization for cooperation among the dozens of developing countries, which were its members. They claimed to share the aim of fundamentally redrawing the economic and political contours of the international system. Its later decline into near-irrelevance reflected the impact of the end of the Cold War, and globalization processes, especially widening economic positions.

Founded at the height of the Cold War – the institutionalized expression of ideological conflict between the liberal democratic–capitalist West and communist Eastern Europe – NAM had declined into international irrelevance by the 1990s. This development was a metaphor for the crumbling of the long-held notion that the developing countries shared common aims, which they could best pursue by working collectively. To what extent did NAM's decline and fragmentation reflect the impact of globalization on the mass of developing countries? As we shall see, the post-Cold War history of NAM is an example of how, among developing countries, globalization stimulated both political and economic fragmentation. The failure of NAM to maintain the proclaimed ideological solidarity of the developing world after the Cold War was also manifested in a new wave of economic regionalization. In sum, these developments amounted to a serious decline in the collective orientation of the developing world and reflected how its economic and political trajectories are closely linked to global developments.

Inaugurated at Bandung, Indonesia in 1955, NAM was formally launched in 1961 at a founding conference in Belgrade, Yugoslavia. Its general objective was to "increase the weight of the Third World in an increasingly bipolar world dominated by the Cold War" (Hadjor 1993: 232). The main concerns of the organization included the wholesale condemnation of Western colonialism and of foreign military installations, proclaimed at its conference in Cairo in 1964, attended by 47 developing countries. Later, in the 1970s as the numbers of still-colonized developing countries shrank, NAM's objectives were augmented by strong advocacy for occasionally radical solutions to its economic and developmental problems. When, in the late 1970s, decolonization was more or less achieved, the demand for a New International Economic Order (NIEO) increasingly took center stage in NAM demands. NAM believed that the world capitalist economy discriminated against the world's poorer countries. In pursuit of a reformist NIEO, NAM sought a thoroughgoing restructuring of the world economy in favor of the developing countries. It should be noted that at this time there was an implicit assumption that nearly all developing countries shared similar economic characteristics and, consequently, were comprehensively disadvantaged by the prevailing capitalist international economic order.

The failure to achieve a NIEO reflected the lack of influence the developing countries could collectively bring to bear compared to that of the rich, Western industrialized nations. The latter saw no compelling need to change an economic system weighted in their favor. The result of the lack of success of the NIEO campaign, as Acharya notes, was that "the process of North–South negotiations aimed at the realization of these objectives" culminated "without producing any significant break-throughs for the South as a whole" (Acharya 1999: 91). It also reflected the fact that, by the late 1970s, economic progress among developing countries was variable: some were doing well, others less so. In other words, some developing countries were doing fine without reform of the existing international economic order. A consequence of economic diversity was that the long-held notion of a bloc of developing countries, united in pursuit of shared aims, lost its efficacy. This is clear when we bear in mind what happened in the 1970s when the world price of oil rapidly increased. At that time, a number of oil-producing and exporting developing countries organized themselves into the Organization of Petroleum Exporting Countries (OPEC) and exhibited the ability to raise their revenues significantly by virtue of coordinated action in defense of oil prices. In other words, OPEC oil producers managed to transcend their poor structural status via the contingent impact of sharply increased oil prices. A second group of newly industrialized countries (NICs), including South Korea and Taiwan, were also economically successful at this time. Their governments managed consistently to raise their countries' per capita GNPs from a few hundred US dollars in the 1950s to many thousands of dollars three decades later.

These economic successes were outweighed by economic disappointments for many countries, clustered in, but not limited to, Africa. They saw their economic positions go from bad to worse in the 1970s and after. As Acharya (1999: 91) notes, "the collective institutionalized framework of the South has not contributed to, or been strengthened by, these developments." Rather, regional developmental successes – in East Asia – and regional developmental failures – in Africa and elsewhere – lessened the relevance and solidarity of the larger, and earlier, developing countries' platforms, such as NAM.

Internationally, fragmentation of the bloc of developing countries was encouraged by another factor: the divide-and-rule tactics employed by successive American governments, notably the presidencies of Ronald Reagan (1980–8) and George Bush Senior (1988–92). These regimes viewed North–South dialogue as an "annoying distraction to the administration's goal of restoring American global influence" (Acharya 1999: 92). Under American leadership, Western governments decreased the importance of North–South discourse by ignoring the latter's established negotiating channels at the United Nations, replacing this form of interaction with one-to-one talks in the capital cities of the relevant developing countries. A new economic grouping, the Group of 15 (G15), was formed in 1990. But though small and cohesive, its aim was to "promote North–South and South–South dialogue and cooperation . . . [but] it is yet to emerge as a major player in the South" (Fawcett 1999: 237). The relative failure of G15 to be a "big player" at the international level is further evidence, along with the current irrelevance of NAM, that the developing countries bloc has seriously fragmented.

This is not to suggest that NAM did not try to move with the times. After the Cold War it sought to refocus its efforts on the impact of globalization and on a more just distribution of global economic resources. The new agenda was made plain at the 1989 NAM conference held in Belgrade, Yugoslavia, which proclaimed that NAM's main aim would now be to promote a "transition from the old world order based on domination to a new order based on freedom, equality, and social justice and the well-being of all." Indonesia, chair of NAM in the late 1990s, stated that under its leadership the goal was to "address the new concerns of the world – environment and development, human rights and democratization, refugees and massive migration" (Acharya 1999: 91). It will be recalled that these issues were similar to those identified above in relation to the NG viewpoint and suggests that many of the developing countries shared such a prognosis of the post-Cold War situation.

Despite the attempt by NAM to define for itself a new role after the Cold War, it seemed moribund in the 1990s. As Roy (1999: 65) notes, by the end of the Cold War it was clear that NAM was a product of that conflict, "an attendant phenomenon of the bloc division" redolent of the late 1940s to the late 1980s. And, without the Cold War divisions, NAM no longer had a clear purpose. This is not to suggest that NAM had no lasting achievements to its credit. On the contrary, it not only led the global condemnation of apartheid in South Africa and support for the liberation of Rhodesia and Namibia, but was also instrumental in helping raise and maintain "the level of ethical concern against the doctrine of nuclear deterrence" (Acharya 1999: 90) Ultimately, however, its "effort to reshape the prevailing international order was seriously constrained," not least because of its

> poor record in international conflict-resolution. While focusing on the larger issues of global disarmament and superpower rivalry, it was un-

able to develop institutions and mechanisms for addressing local and regional conflicts such as those in the Gulf, Lebanon, Cambodia, Afghanistan, and Southern Africa . . . With the end of the Cold War, NAM faced distinct risks of further marginalization in global peace and security affairs. (Ibid)

Its second main strand – development – led NAM to call for meetings between the developed and developing countries to discuss debt relief, reduced trade barriers, increased aid for development, and increased cash flow. And, during the 1990s, NAM summit conferences were regularly held. The most recent at the time of writing (late 2001) was held in Cartagena, Colombia, in April 2000, with 98 of the organization's 115 members in attendance. But very little real progress was recorded in spreading more equitably the fruits of developments.

In conclusion, while NAM continued officially to exist after the Cold War and passed periodic resolutions about, for example, the continued desirability of a NIEO and the peaceful settlement of international disputes, it was clear that its significance was very limited. NAM's decline into near irrelevance was not only a result of the end of the Cold War but also reflected the fact that while its membership grew, serious political and economic differences became increasingly clear. This was between, on the one hand, countries enjoying sustained economic growth and those that did not and, on the other, between the new democracies and other leading NAM countries, such as Cuba, that had not democratized. In addition, NAM had proved unable to solve conflicts between its own members, a development not facilitated by the fact that members met only during its periodic summits. Over the years, NAM lacked crucial institutions, such as a budget, staff, or headquarters (Hadjor 1993: 232).

Economic regionalization and the developing world

We noted above that a key component of economic globalization is often judged to be states' loss of control of their national economic programs. We saw this in chapter 1 in relation to SAPs. The adoption of SAPs in dozens of developing countries led to the IMF and the World Bank gaining much economic influence. On the other hand, it would be incorrect to suggest that the impact of globalization has been uniform across economic sectors or societies more generally. Some countries have sought to isolate themselves from transnational economic networks by attempting to restore the boundaries or "separateness" of their markets, instituting or extending national laws to cover internationally mobile factors, and/or seeking to adopt cooperative policies with other countries for the coordination of policy. In this section, we are primarily concerned with this last strategy: the regionalization (or, as it is sometimes called, regionalism) of developing countries' economies. We should note, however, that regional economic activity clusters around a number of poles, by no means restricted to the developing countries – for example, the European Union, the North American Free Trade Association (USA, Canada, Mexico), and the Pacific Basin and Japan. The point is that the regionalization strategy is now seen by many governments as an important mechanism to try to regulate the impact of adverse global market trends.

Observers have linked regionalization to renewed interest in attempting to deal with the economic (and security) implications of globalization. "Interest in regionalism strengthened steadily from the 1950s onwards, ... practically disappeared in the 1970s," and then was reestablished after the Cold War, in the 1990s (Postel-Vinay 2001: 94). As Schulz, Söderbaum and Öjendal (2001: 1) suggest, the "return" of interest in regionalization "is undoubtedly one important trend in contemporary international relations." The trend was exemplified by the founding or rejuvenation of regional organizations devoted primarily to regional trade liberalization, including in the developing world: Latin America (MERCOSUR), Southeast Asia (ASEAN), Southern Africa (SADC), and West Africa (ECOWAS). However, the renewed interest in regionalization highlights a paradox: while many "states are strong institutions," they are also "enmeshed in networks of important regional and universal political and economic institutions" (Smith 2000: 24). During globalization this encourages them to look for regional solutions to common problems, to the extent that regionalization is likely to be a key to the success of globalization in the years to come. This is because regional agreements such as MERCOSUR and ASEAN constitute important "building blocks" in processes of making stronger and more efficacious globalization of economic and technological relations. In this regard, MERCOSUR in particular is a "fairly advanced framework of regional cooperation" (Roy 1999: 120).

Does the renewed interest in regionalism among developing countries in Latin America, Asia, and Africa constitute a step on the way to world economic integration or a hindrance? Some have argued that all developing countries need regionalization as a means to reinforce the capacity to negotiate globalization. This is a reference to the notion that producers in developing countries have long experienced pronounced difficulties in gaining access to the markets of the West. Now affected in many cases by low growth and high unemployment rates, the strengthening of regional markets among developing countries can, it is believed, play a vital role in permitting them "to adapt to the process of globalization without being excluded from it" (Heine 1999: 114). In sum, many developing countries in Latin America, Africa, and Asia have renewed or initiated interest in economic regionalization, as part of the attempt to deal with what they see as the negative consequences of globalization, especially protectionism-orientated European and North American trading blocs.

However, the problems experienced among developing countries in the 1950s, 1960s, and 1970s, when there were earlier attempts at regional integration, have resurfaced. In particular, there is difficulty in reaching agreement as to the precise format of the regional arrangements so as to ensure as equitable distribution of benefits as possible among those countries involved in the regional compact. There is also the problem of ensuring that national lobbies have an adequate voice in regional decision-making. Coussy notes that a downside of regionalization can be that "national choices are . . . devalued by making the region a means of bypassing national lobbies" (Coussy 2001: 151). In addition, regional economic integration among developing countries may well remain hostage to the political and security concerns of the participating countries. The situation will also be affected by prior interest in fuller integration with the global economy through inter-regional trade and investment linkages (Acharya 1999: 96; Grugel 2000: 124).

Conclusion: Globalization, Regionalization, and the Developing World

The implication of globalization theory is that within the developing countries distinct regions, as well as individual national and local economies, have engaged very differently with the evolving global economy. Some, such as the Asian Tigers, have consistently done very well; others, such as the OPEC countries, have done well periodically; many others, including vast swathes of Africa, have done consistently poorly in economic terms. However, as we saw above, arguments employed by the PG approach tend to overlook the fragmented impact of globalization and instead stress what is seen as its beneficial aspects. Randall and Theobald remind us that, in fact, such arguments are not altogether new. Instead, they "echo many of the presumptions of modernization theory, assuming the ongoing and broadening sweep of modernizing forces, both economic and technological" (Randall and Theobald 1998: 256). However, the PG approach, like modernization theory before it, is too unidirectional, unvariegated, and Panglossian to tell the whole story.

The alternative NG approach echoes some of the arguments of dependency theory discussed in chapter 1. The NG approach can be seen as a contemporary manifestation of the dependency idea in the sense that processes of globalization are seen as almost completely malign. Their impact goes a long way toward explaining why and how low levels of development take place in certain parts of the developing world. It is important, however, to note that dependency theory differs from contemporary globalization theory in at least two important respects. First, unlike globalization theory, in both its "positive" and "negative" manifestations, dependency theory perceived the world as divided up into discrete states and societies. The very core of globalization theory, of course, is that states and societies are being subsumed, weakened, and surpassed by global processes. Depending on which of the views we have sympathy with, this is a welcome or less than welcome development. Second, dependency theory was centered on the impact of global economic processes over long periods of time. These were determined by the structure of the global economy under the leadership of the West, and were understood to be in one direction only. That is, the economic dependence of the "periphery," that is, the developing countries, was understood to be determined by the long-term needs and initiatives of the core economies of the West. To escape from this trap it would be necessary to initiate a policy of self-sufficiency or autarky, cutting ties with the international economy. No contemporary theories of globalization would contend that such a process is either possible or desirable. Instead, economic integration via regionalization is seen as a way forward to ward off the malign effects of economic globalization. Moreover, processes of growing economic integration are not only held to be desirable at the regional level, but also in many cases inevitable. In short, there is now greater emphasis on the benefits of interdependence between developing countries, although there is less confidence that integration between the latter and the core economies is likely to be beneficial for the developing countries. Some regions – for example, Africa – are seen as even more peripheral than before.

We also examined the demise of NAM and contemporary moves to regionalization among developing countries. We noted that both developments reflected the impact not only of globalization but also the fragmenting of the idea of a unified bloc of developing countries. In the next chapter we examine in more detail an important contemporary manifestation of that fragmentation: the diverse economic and developmental outcomes among developing countries.

3

Economic Growth and Development

In this chapter we focus on economic growth and development, linked issues of great concern to all developing countries. First, we will survey the recent development literature to examine how development strategies changed between the 1950s and the early 2000s. Second, we will investigate and account for differing economic and developmental results in the five developing regions in the 1980s and 1990s. We will also see how governments of the most economically successful developing countries – found in East and Southeast Asia – managed to deal with the fallout from the region's 1997–8 economic crisis. Third, we will explore the social and economic impact of structural adjustment programs (SAPs) on developing countries. Fourth, we will briefly examine the growth of "pro-development' grassroots organizations, both within countries and transnationally. Such groups maintain that market forces alone cannot alleviate poverty sufficiently rapidly or extensively; they aim to suggest alternative development strategies which are more "people friendly" than SAPs (Leftwich 2000).

Development and Inequality at the Start of the Twenty-First Century

At the start of a new century, poverty remains a global problem of huge proportions. Of the world's 6 billion people, 2.8 billion live on less than $2 a day and 1.2 billion on less than $1 a day. Eight of every 100 infants do not live to see their fifth birthday. Nine of every 100 boys and 14 of every girls who reach school age do not attend school. Poverty is also evident in poor people's lack of political power and voice and in their extreme vulnerability to ill health, economic dislocation, personal violence, and natural disasters. And the scourge of HIV / AIDS, the frequency and brutality of civil conflicts, and rising disparities between rich countries and the developing world have increased the sense of deprivation and injustice for many.

This quotation is from the back cover of the *World Development Report 2000/2001*, the subtitle of which is "Attacking Poverty." It makes it clear that not only are development and inequality issues global in scope, but also that the measures taken to tackle them so far have fundamentally failed. As discussed in chapter 2, the current era is characterized by political, economic, cultural, and technological globalization, but it is also distinguished by deepening inequality between rich and poor, both within and between countries. To appreciate the nature and causes of developmental and economic inequalities between, on the one hand, developed and developing countries and, on the other, citizens in the latter, it is necessary to adopt a more "sophisticated analysis than the exclusive categorization of 'rich' and 'poor' states" (Thomas and Reader 2001: 76). To facilitate understanding, we focus next on a variety of relevant issues and explain how they interact with each other to produce certain results.

Approaches to reducing poverty first evolved in the 1950s in response to a growing understanding of the complexity of development. At this time, modernization theory, a "particular way of thinking about development," gained credence with many Western governments, IFIs, and analysts (ibid: 74). Initially, there was a widespread assumption that the problems of poverty and development could be solved simply by adequate investment in physical capital and infrastructure. However, despite the injection of huge quantities of foreign aid, the failure over time to make much of a dent in global poverty made it clear that developmental outcomes depended on far more than sufficient injections of capital. Of crucial importance for developmental outcomes, it appeared, was what governments did in policy terms with the fruits of economic growth. For example, it was obvious that poor people everywhere would benefit from opportunities for improved health and education, but such policy shifts would not necessarily occur unless governments were consistently and sufficiently pressurized by their own citizens; and this pressure was not necessarily forthcoming. Put another way, while improvements in, for example, health and education are important not only in their own right but also to help promote growth and development, they will be resisted by some sections of society who believe that their own positions would suffer unacceptably. In short, these kinds of decisions with major resource implications are always highly *political* decisions that vested interests will try to prevent if they regard them as unwelcome.

During the 1970s concern shifted to a "basic needs" strategy; that is, the foundation of development was seen as ensuring that all people had the necessary basics: clean water, basic health care, at least primary education, and so on. In the 1980s the aim of building what was called "human capital" was supplanted, amid much consensus among Western governments and IFIs, by the desirability of SAPs. That is, thinking shifted to believing that "market forces and economic efficiency were the best way to achieve the kind of growth which is the best antidote to poverty" (Former World Bank president, Barber Conable, quoted in Thomas and Reader 2001: 79). Conable's statement reflects the dominance in the 1980s of neoliberalism, an economic and political philosophy which underpinned the pro-market ideology and monetarist ideas of various influential governments, including those headed by Margaret Thatcher in Britain (1979–90) and Ronald Reagan in the USA (1980–8). Neoliberalism emphasized that, developmentally, the state's role should be downgraded and decreased, while the role of private capitalists and entrepreneurs should be increased and encouraged. Under pressure from Western governments and IFIs, many governments of developing countries subsequently sought to put in place neoliberal policies with variable, but mostly no success. In short, during the 1980s, and according to the tenets of neoliberal thinking, emphasis was placed in development thinking on improving economic management and allowing greater play for market forces in developing countries in the form of externally imposed SAPs.

The ideological power of neoliberalism was at its zenith in 1989–91 when the Cold War came to an end and the Eastern European communist bloc collapsed. To some observers these interlinked developments appeared to offer spectacular evidence of the superior power of liberal democracy and capitalism over its long-term rival, communism. For several years these linked events provided pro-market forces with apparently unstoppable momentum and had immense economic and sociopolitical impacts on numerous developing countries. In many developing countries, economic changes coincided with, and in many cases helped to stimulate, a shift towards democracy, a development we shall examine in chapter 4 (Sen 1999: 58).

The neoliberal development strategy became known as the "Washington consensus," reflecting the preeminence of the ideology among Washington opinion leaders, including "the IMF and the World Bank, independent think-tanks, the US government policy community, investment bankers, and so on" (Thomas and Reader 2001: 79). However, critics of the Washington consensus model pointed out that the studiously pro-market view seemed to overlook the fact that only governments have the power to alter prevailing socioeconomic realities through the application of appropriate policies and programs. In other words, the market is not very good at allocating resources fairly; only governments can do that. And whether or not they do so is strongly linked to the varying amounts of pressure put on governments by competing societal interests.

The widespread failure of SAPs to make up for developmental shortfalls was instrumental in prompting a shift in developmental thinking, reflected in the concerns of the 1990 World Development Report. It stressed the need to deal with poverty through a two-pronged strategy: (1) the promotion of labor-intensive growth through economic openness and investment in infrastructure and (2) as a result of providing basic services to poor people, including basic health and education. Moreover, as the 1990s progressed it became clear to all but the most blinkered observers that the Washington consensus could not be the whole answer to developmental shortfalls in the developing world. This was because its measures had failed to stimulate development across the board in the ways that its proponents had claimed. The result was that the international development community was faced, at the end of the 1990s, with a consistently gloomy development picture of rising global poverty and polarizing inequality. The consequence was that the international community set itself the challenge of a renewed onslaught on poverty and related dimensions of human deprivation in the developing world, with a deadline of 2015 to achieve its goals.

This reflected the fact that there was now much agreement that voluntary actions, while important, were not going to be enough on their own to reduce growing imbalances between rich and poor, both within and between countries (Thomas and Reader 2001: 77). The polarized developmental situation was reflected in an array of data and statistics, some of which are noted in the quotation at the beginning of this section. At the start of the twenty-first century, numerous developing countries collectively contained millions of people who lacked the minimum necessary for the maintenance of mere physical efficiency. These were places where thousands of children died of preventable diseases like measles and diarrhea, and life expectancy was low, no higher than it had been for the poor in Britain a century ago. Finally, across the developing world, the size of the problem was reflected in the fact that over a billion people lived on less than a dollar a day, more than 2 billion did not have access to clean water, and hundreds of millions lacked adequate healthcare and education.

To try to begin to deal with such development problems, a high-profile conference was held in London in February 2001. Its aim was to set in motion precise mechanisms to tackle the issues mentioned in the previous paragraph. The event was co-hosted by Britain's Chancellor of the Exchequer, Gordon Brown, and the Secretary of State for International Development, Clare Short. Its stated goal was to encourage the assembled country representatives to agree on concrete steps that development organizations and the states themselves believed they should adopt to achieve the UN's goal of a 50 percent reduction of poverty by 2015 (Elliot 2001a). The fact that various heavyweight figures were present – including the head of the IMF, Horst Kohler, the chief of the World Bank, James Wolfensohn, the chief executive of Unicef, Carol Bellamy, the UN secretary-general, Kofi Annan, and the former president of South Africa, Nelson Mandela (via video link) – suggested that this was an important event that might lead to significant outcomes. Reflecting the renewed developmental importance of voluntary organizations, a number of churches and other religious bodies, as well as business and non-governmental organizations, were also represented at the meeting.

The conference was important because it reflected a clear shift in developmental thinking. That is, it ended a long period of relative inactivity, during which it had been widely, if tacitly, believed that market forces acting alone could somehow significantly cut infant mortality, reduce income poverty, and give every child a primary education. Now, it appeared, there was strong agreement – between governments and voluntary organizations alike – that, left to their own devices, market forces alone could not eradicate global poverty (just as they had been unable to eradicate poverty in the now-developed countries). But it was equally clear that there was no point in simply setting ambitious goals and then sitting back and expecting them to happen. The $64,000 dollar question was: could the IMF, the World Bank, the United Nations, and the G8 group of leading industrial countries deliver the desired outcomes? Some said "no" because, historically, international "pledges are made by states who are happy to sign up to them, but then often fail to implement them" (Thomas and Reader 2001: 79).

Skepticism was engendered by the fact that, without sustained action taken by powerful actors such as the USA, Japan, and the EU, in accord with authoritative international organizations (the IMF, World

Bank, United Nations, etc.), then the goals would simply not be achieved. On the other hand, perhaps some pessimism was misplaced. It should be recalled that governments of various countries, including Britain, the USA, and France, had, with due diligence and effort, managed to pull the vast majority of their citizens from poverty during the twentieth century. And, more recently, China also achieved a similar feat in lifting millions of its people from poverty. Clearly, what was needed was both an achievable strategy and the financial means to meet ambitious developmental goals.

In short, thinking about development underwent a sea change in two ways in the late 1990s. First, it became accepted by governments and development agencies alike that beneficial developmental changes would not come about if they were left entirely to the market. Early development successes, such as that of Britain and other now-developed countries, did not come about quickly or by chance, but were the result of conscious policy decisions, taken by successive governments, in relation to (1) reducing the power of business; (2) relatively high levels of taxation to fund growth of welfare states; (3) policies for full employment; and (4) redistribution of wealth from the rich to the poor via progressive taxation policies.

To achieve development goals, the World Bank admitted in its *World Development Report 2000/2001* that adjustments would be necessary not only at the global level, but also at the national level. Nationally, the Bank believed that the goal of promoting opportunity is closely linked to increases in overall economic growth, as is the pattern or quality of growth. While market reforms can be central in expanding opportunities for poor people, reforms also need to reflect local institutional and structural conditions. And this, the Bank admitted, would be difficult because it would necessitate a significant shift in power between groups, which would be resisted by those currently enjoying a disproportionate share of wealth and power. Second, shifting its focus on how to facilitate popular capacities, the World Bank stated that the "choice and implementation of public actions that are responsive to the needs of poor people *depend on the interaction of political, social, and other institutional processes*" (World Bank 2001: 7; emphasis added). However, facilitating the abilities of ordinary citizens would not only depend on "active collaboration among poor people, the middle class [*sic*], and other groups in society," but would also be linked to wider changes in governance. These would be necessary in order to make public administration, legal institutions, and public service delivery both efficient and accountable to all citizens rather than merely a privileged few. It seems clear that achieving the general goal of enhanced participation would require bringing poor people into political processes and local decision-making.

How easy would this be to achieve? The lack of concern of elites to extend development and democracy to the mass of ordinary people is not a recent phenomenon. In his description of the ways in which vested interests in Britain denied the right of the masses even to vote because of fear of the political consequences, an opposition not finally overcome until the 1920s, Arblaster's account is reminiscent of the contemporary situation in many developing countries:

> Democracy has only become acceptable to the privileged classes because it has turned out to be less of a challenge to wealth and property than was feared, and also because democracy itself has been redefined in much narrower terms (as a method of choosing government) than it was given in the classical tradition reaching down from Pericles to John Stuart Mill and beyond. (Arblaster 1999: 33)

Third, in order to "enhance security" in various ways, the World Bank (2001) notes that effective national action would be necessary in order to manage the risk of economy-wide shocks as well as build effective mechanisms to reduce risks faced by poor people, including health- and weather-related risks. In sum, in respect of the national aspects necessary to lead to more and better development, the Bank's report explicitly refers to and discusses not only the necessity of *political* actions to achieve development gains, but also that national governments must interact with processes of globalization in order to get what they can from it.

The report admits that, on its own, "action at national and local levels will often not be enough for rapid poverty reduction" (ibid: 11). International actions are also important, including renewed focus on debt relief and moves to make development cooperation via aid more effective. "Of equal importance are actions in other areas – trade, vaccines, closing of the digital and knowledge divides – that can enhance the opportunity, empowerment, and security of poor people" (ibid). In terms of knowledge, among

> the world's 6 billion population, there are only 50 million internet users (0.833 percent), and over 90 percent of internet hosts are in North America and Western Europe. Eighty percent of people worldwide do not have access to a telephone. The point is that the majority of global citizens are not in a position to tap into the ongoing technological advance and the

associated communications revolution. This revolution, therefore, is set to increase disparities between many states and between people. (Thomas and Reader 2001: 76)

To summarize, development thinking underwent significant changes from the 1950s to the early 2000s. By the latter date it was widely agreed that measures to improve the appalling developmental position of millions of poor people in the developing countries could only happen if there was coordinated action taken at both national and international levels. Success would depend upon governments and international agencies showing willingness not only to announce policies but also to see them through with energy and verve. We shall see next that within developing regions it is precisely this combination of virtues that successful states have exhibited when drawing their countries from poverty – especially in East and Southeast Asia – while their failure elsewhere (for example, in most African countries) goes a long way to explain the region's disappointing economic and developmental results in recent years.

Economic Polarization in the Developing World: The 1980s and 1990s

There were diverse economic and development outcomes among developing countries in the 1980s and 1990s. On the one hand, a group of countries, many located in East Asia, strongly developed their economies and, as a result, managed to increase the well-being of many of their people and hence decrease the numbers of those living in poverty. On the other hand, many developing countries, mostly in Africa but also elsewhere, saw their economies consistently decline over the same period, with serious results for many of their citizens. How best to explain these diverse outcomes? To what extent were they due mainly to domestic or international factors? To answer these questions we need to start our analysis with what happened in the 1960s and 1970s, as this was significant for what occurred later in the 1980s and 1990s.

In the 1960s, economic growth rates across the developing regions – Africa, East and Southeast Asia, South Asia, Latin America, and the Middle East – were fairly uniform, averaging around 3 percent a year (Callaghy 1993: 185). In the late 1970s and early 1980s clear signs of economic and developmental polarization began to appear, largely as the result of the impact of major oil price rises in 1973 and 1979. The rise in world oil prices was highly significant, as it set in train a number of developments linked to the economic divergence among developing countries that became clearer later. During the next few years, many developing countries, with the exception of the mostly East and Southeast Asian NICs and major oil producers, experienced economic stagnation or, at best, very low growth.

"By and large it is the decade of the 1980s which remains crucial as the period of change for developing countries" (Sen 1999: 58, 63). As table 3.1 indicates, the economic positions of the developing regions fragmented. While we should remember that these were average regional performances, thus obscuring variations in individual country performances, the trend was nonetheless clear. Overall, the East and Southeast Asian region did very well, enjoying an average annual growth of GDP of 8 percent a year. South Asia also performed well, with 5.7 percent average growth a year. Despite its oil wealth, the Middle East had economic problems, not least because the world oil price fell precipitously in the early 1980s. In addition, indebted Latin America and Africa also struggled, with average annual growth in the 1980s of only 1.7 percent. Table 3.1 also shows that the broad trend towards regional economic polarization that began in the 1980s continued in the 1990s: in that decade, East and Southeast Asia and South Asia did much better than the Middle East, Latin America, and Africa, although it should be noted that the latter three regions saw some improvement.

Most developing countries that encountered serious budgetary imbalances and high, and growing, levels of foreign indebtedness in the 1980s and 1990s turned for economic assistance to the IMF and the World Bank. As we saw in chapter 2, these IFIs typically prescribed fundamental economic changes, known as structural adjustment programs

Table 3.1   GDP average annual growth by region, 1980–99

Region	GDP average annual growth,1980–9 (%)	GDP average annual growth, 1900–9 (%)
East and Southeast Asia	8	7.4
South Asia	5.7	5.7
The Middle East	2	3
Latin America	1.7	3.4
Africa	1.7	2.4

Source: World Bank (2001: 294, table 11)

(SAPs), as the price for their assistance. However, the outcome of SAPs was frequently disappointing. Although some countries, such as Ghana, saw macroeconomic improvements, the downside was a failure to reduce poverty levels. Typically, the brunt of the costs of economic adjustment were born disproportionately by the poor and underprivileged (Leftwich 2000).

Let us look next at the economic and development picture within each of the developing regions in order to highlight variations between them.

Africa

Africa had the worst economic and developmental record in the world in the 1980s and 1990s. African countries – including Angola, Benin, the Democratic Republic of the Congo (formerly Zaire), Ethiopia, Ghana, Guinea, Kenya, Liberia, Mali, Mozambique, Niger, Sierra Leone, Somalia, Uganda, and Zambia – are among the world's poorest states (World Bank 2001: 174–5). Reflecting this dire position, Africa's quality of life indicators are generally poor: in the mid-1990s, annually more than 4 million children died before they reached the age of 5 years, a third of the region's children were malnourished, one in eight was disabled, and more than 30 percent received no primary – much less secondary or tertiary – education (UNDP 1996). The seriousness of the economic and developmental problems afflicting Africa can be gauged from the fact that, starting from a low base, between 1980 and 1999, average annual growth in GDP was only around 2 percent a year. This doesn't sound too bad, but when we bear in mind that the populations of most African countries were growing by 3 percent or more annually, this meant a real annual fall in GDP of at least 1 percent a year.

The region's endemic economic weakness led to economic changes being undertaken in most countries in the 1980s and 1990s. SAPs were instituted at the behest of the IMF and the World Bank. The economic results, however, were generally disappointing. Occasionally, as in Ghana and Uganda, the programs achieved a degree of short-term macroeconomic stability and economic growth. More typically, however, such programs comprehensively failed and helped catalyse popular anti-state protests at, for example, apparent regime incapacity in Zambia, state corruption in Kenya, and Tanzania's governmental impotence.

Driven by a presumption that a prime cause of Africa's economic

weaknesses and political instability was a lack of democratic governments, Western countries sought to pressurize regional authoritarian
regimes – vulnerable to such pressure because they desperately needed
foreign aid – to democratize. Foreign aid donors made it clear that they
believed that what was needed was better governance, that is, democracy coupled with fundamental economic reforms. African regimes that
chose to disallow democracy and to deny their citizens' human and
civil rights could expect to be refused aid. Africa's economic failures, it
was believed, was to a large degree the consequence of a lack of democracy and political accountability. Without significant political
changes, economic reforms would inevitably lack impact.

In the late 1980s and early 1990s the United States Agency for International Development shifted from a traditionally single-minded concern with economic development to inaugurate "governance and
democratization" programs across Africa (Green 1999). More generally, many bilateral aid donors began to attach political conditionalities
to foreign aid programs. However, over time, observers noted that
Western support for democratization became increasingly rhetorical
rather than substantial (Lawson 1999). This was because reemerging
strategic concerns for regional order and security and deepening of
market-based economic change began to take precedence over democratization. "Presentability became the effective criterion" for African
governments to acquire "the stamp of international approval. Both African regimes and their foreign sponsors engaged in 'democracy as il-
lusion'" (Joseph 1998: 11). For example, the French government
supported decidedly undemocratic political friends, such as President
Eyadema in Togo, because it wished to retain its traditional influence
in the country (Cumming 1999). However, in Uganda there was strong
Western support for a regime that, while not conventionally democratic,
could nevertheless point to increased national integrity, social stability, regular, relatively free and fair elections, and a willingness to oversee fundamental economic reforms. In sum, foreign aid donors were
important in encouraging Africa's authoritarian governments to com-
mence democratic transitions. However, over time, foreign donors became more concerned with strategic security than democratization.

Reflecting serious difficulties in seeking to reform political and economic structures at the same time, African governments often failed to
make much progress in either respect. For example, after a quarter century of unelected, one-party rule, Zambia's President Frederick Chiluba
was democratically elected in November 1991. However, he and his
government found it impossible to turn round the country's economy,

heavily dependent on flagging copper exports, or to control state-level corruption. Instead, rising prices, partly the result of prolonged drought, led to widespread strikes and more general popular discontent. This had the effect, not only of reducing popular support for Chiluba and his government but also for multi-party democracy itself (Burnell 2000). The general point is that, even with external pressure and support, the nature of inherited economic and political structures in most African countries made political and economic reforms difficult or impossible to accomplish.

This section has showed that African countries typically had an array of structural impediments to fundamental economic reforms. Not only were there problems linked to the characteristics of long-term authoritarian regimes, characterized by a gross personalization of political power, but also the region's endemic economic weaknesses that had endured since the 1970s. Domestic pressures – principally from civil society – and external encouragement – primarily from foreign governments and IFIs – helped to galvanize both economic and political reforms, but results on the whole were disappointing.

South Asia

South Asian countries, among the poorest countries in the world, embarked on extensive economic reforms in the 1990s. As elsewhere in the developing world at this time, the key aim was to reform the economic role of the state. After many years of prevarication, the region's biggest country, India, with more than a billion inhabitants, engaged in sustained economic reforms. This turn of events was surprising because in India state control had for many years been the core of economic policy. However, like in Latin America, larger economic pressures had been building, not least the immediate cause of India's economic reform program: a foreign debt crisis. As a result of the importance of India in the South Asia region, and because its reform trajectory is a rare example of economic success in the developing world in the 1990s, we shall focus upon India in this section.

India emerged from British colonial rule in 1947 as "a continental patchwork of colonial administrations and 'princely states'" (Herring 1999: 312). The chances for economic growth were hardly encouraged by the fact that Indian capital had spread around the globe during the colonial period and was not, as a result, available to be used at home for development purposes. From independence until the late 1980s,

India was ruled by the Congress (I) Party. During this period, India had a very inward-looking, heavily statist economy whose direction was justified and defended by a dominant ideological mix of "socialism, self-reliance, nationalism and Third World pride" (Callaghy 1993: 194). While there was some economic growth in the 1980s, it rather paled into insignificance next to the thrusting economic performance of South Korea, one of the most economically successful countries at the time, whose growth rate was three times that of India. Three decades earlier, India and South Korea had had the same per capita income. However, by the early 1990s, South Korea's per capita GDP was more than ten times greater than India's. There was an important external factor in South Korea's success: in 1960 it received around 6 percent of global aid, at a time when its population was less than 1 percent of that of all developing countries. This aid was used to build up local industry, while the approval signified by relatively large resource transfers from Western donors encouraged foreign investors to risk long-term commitments.

With exports accounting for less than 5 percent of GDP, the Indian government came to the conclusion, just as the government of South Korea had done earlier, that the best course of action was to stimulate and encourage export-led growth. Until the early 1990s a succession of weak Congress (I) dominated governments had lacked the political will to attempt to reorientate the economy in this direction. However, when balance of payments imbalances and inflation grew, while foreign exchange reserves dropped and a debt crisis loomed, the government had little realistic choice but to implement far-reaching economic change. By this time India's foreign debt was US$83 billion, then the third highest in the world; only the foreign debts of Brazil and Mexico were greater. More importantly, India's debt service ratio – that is, the proportion of export earnings which had to be devoted to paying the interest on foreign debt – was over 30 percent, four times greater than South Korea's more manageable 7.1 percent on foreign debts amounting to US$35 billion (World Bank 1995: 200–1). Compounding the declining economic situation for India was the impact of the 1990–1 Gulf Crisis, which temporarily led to higher oil prices and, as a result, helped increased price inflation. India's reluctance to restructure economically was finally dispelled in mid-1991 as US$600 million of debt servicing repayments fell due which the government did not have. The result was serious economic restructuring which led to an average annual GDP growth of 6.1 percent during 1990–9 (World Bank 2001: 294).

India's successful economic reforms in the 1990s were the result of governmental decisions to reduce the role of the state and to welcome foreign investment. In these respects the Indian government followed the lead offered by South Korea and Taiwan.

East and Southeast Asia

As we saw in table 3.1, the East and Southeast Asia region recorded the best economic performance of any developing region in the 1980s and 1990s. For example, China attained average annual growth of 10 percent in 1980–99, South Korea achieved 8 percent, Singapore 7 percent, Vietnam 6 percent, Hong Kong (since 1997 part of China) 6 percent, Malaysia 6 percent, and Indonesia 5 percent (World Bank 2001: 294–5). All these countries managed, sometimes spectacularly (Vietnam managed 28 per cent *annual growth of export volumes in the 1990s*), to increase export revenues from exported manufactured goods. Strong, sustained economic growth recorded by the region's leading economies had a regional knock-on effect. This enabled weaker regional economies, such as the Philippines, to register reasonable growth rates in the 1990s – over 3 percent – following economic stagnation in the 1980s.

In short, several East and Southeast Asian countries recorded rapid economic growth in the 1980s and 1990s. However, in 1997–8 the region suffered a serious challenge, which might have thrown it off course. In the next section we see how the region dealt with the threat to its economic well-being.

East Asia's 1997–8 economic crisis and the aftermath

Optimism about the continuation of sustained economic growth took a serious knock in 1997–8, as a major financial and economic crisis rocked the region. It was triggered in July 1997 by the collapse of the Thai currency, the baht. Four years later, Aglionby (2001a) claimed, "most of the once loudly roaring tigers are still licking their wounds." The position was not helped because Japan, for long the region's economic powerhouse, was undergoing a serious and prolonged economic downturn, exemplified in early 2001 by the collapse of the Nasdaq tech-heavy index.

Earlier, during 1997–8, the region's impressive singular achievement in managing to deliver growth with relative equity had been diminished by a financial and economic crisis. Swiftly, within a matter of months, the crisis spread around the world, affecting Brazil, Russia, and, most recently, Argentina. The impact on annual GNP growth in the East and Southeast Asian region during 1997–8 was clear: it fell from over 4.3 percent in 1996–7 to *minus* 6.2 percent. A consequence was that the percentage of the region's population in poverty swiftly rose. For example, in Indonesia "the percentage in poverty rose from 11 percent to over 40 percent, and unemployment from 4.7 percent to 21 percent" (Thomas and Reader 2001: 77). The case of Indonesia indicates a close link between economic and political outcomes. Indonesia is the world's fourth most populous country, with a population in excess of 200 million people and with foreign debts of US$180 billion. As we shall see in chapter 4, analysts linked the fall of President Suharto in 1998, following serious outbreaks of popular discontent, to the country's economic crisis (Aglionby 2001a).

Indonesia's plight was not unique. Following the 1997–8 crisis, over the next few years the regional picture was mixed. At the macro level, some regional countries did well: for example, during 1998–9 Korea managed 10 percent GNP growth, Singapore 3.6 percent, and Thailand 4.1 percent. But others fared less well: Indonesia and Malaysia each attained 1.9 percent, while the Philippines did even less well: 1.4 percent (World Bank 2001: 274). The reasons for the differing impacts of the 1997–8 crisis were (1) governments' success or otherwise in dealing with the crisis and (2) countries' economic structures. For example, in Singapore, markets were badly hit by global economic problems that followed the 1997–8 crisis. In March 2001 the country's currency, the Singapore dollar, was at its lowest level since September 1999 and the stock market was at its April 1999 level. Politically, while Singapore remained extremely stable its dependence on the electronic sector seemed likely to reduce short- and medium-term economic growth by up to 40 percent. In Thailand, where the 1997–8 crisis began, attempts at economic reform soon stalled. Observers believed that the situation could deteriorate rapidly if the constitutional court upheld a corruption indictment against Prime Minister Shinawatra and he was forced from office (Aglionby 2001a). Malaysia sought to deal with the crisis with firm measures. After suffering a 6.3 percent drop in GNP per capita in 1997–8, the country managed to recover to 4.3 percent growth the following year. The government of Prime Minister Mahathir Muhammad imposed capital controls for a year during the 1997–8 financial crisis. This was done as an alternative to going to the IMF and it seems to have been fairly successful. During 1999–2001 the country's stockmarket grew by a third and the currency's value against the US dollar was fixed in September 1998 and maintained its value.

Two of the region's weaker economies, those of the Philippines and Indonesia, fared less well. In the Philippines the economy was badly affected in 2000 when President Joseph Estrada's impeachment trial began. Later, in 2001, once he had left office, the currency, the peso, began to recover from an all-time low. However, because of the close ties between the Philippines and its former colonial ruler, the USA, it seemed likely that the former would suffer from the latter's economic downturn. It was believed that the Philippines would suffer worse in this regard than any other regional country. By 2001 the picture did not look bright in Indonesia. There, the country's currency, the rupiah, hit its lowest level for three years – just prior to the fall from power of the dictator, General Suharto. With President Wahid facing impeachment in mid-2001 and the IMF withholding hundreds of millions of dollars, the outlook looked bleak. It remained to be seen whether the replacement of Wahid as president by Megawati Sukarnoputri would ameliorate the economic position.

The main lesson of the Asian Tigers' spectacular economic growth in the 1980s and 1990s was that it was crucial for governments to learn to deal expertly with actors and factors both inside and outside their country's borders if they want to oversee sustained economic growth and development. The lesson of the 1997–8 economic crash and the various regional responses to it was the same: governments had to deal with external shocks as best they could while simultaneously strengthening and diversifying their countries' economies.

Latin America and the Caribbean

As with Africa, Latin America and the Caribbean experienced both domestic and external demands for economic and political change in the 1980s. The result was that, across the region, unelected military governments were replaced by regimes chosen via the ballot box. The big question was to what extent would the new regimes be able to preside over sustained economic growth and improve the development positions of the region's poor people?

Cammack (1994: 186) notes that Latin American countries' political and economic structures are rooted in the region's peripheral capitalism and marginal position in the global economic system. Most countries do not have the necessary resources to provide steady material gains to many citizens and, as a result, struggle to bring all constituents into the political mainstream. Some prefer not to vote or to join anti-system guerrilla movements. The literature suggests that a country's chances of democratizing and sustaining democracy are linked to increasing national prosperity and a relatively equitable distribution of the fruits of growth. The continued appeal of democracy is likely to "depend . . . in part on [its] capacity to be translated into concrete meanings for the majority of the population" (O'Donnell 1992: 21). This is because economic expansion is thought to reduce conflicts arising as a result of inequality or other social cleavages and lessen the likelihood of "excessive" political alienation, societal polarization, and destabilizing social violence.

Neoliberal economic policies introduced in the 1980s did not enable Latin America to transcend its traditionally peripheral and dependent status in the global economic order, or to provide more social justice and income equity for most of its people. However, at this point contingency, including the impact of globalization and foreign pressures, must be taken into account for an understanding of regional economic outcomes. Encouraged by the United States government, virtually all Latin American countries sought to liberalize their debt-ridden and statist economies in the 1980s and 1990s under the direction of the IMF and the World Bank. The drive to construct "Washington consensus" policies – that is, to build a global trading system in the free-market image of the USA, with appropriate political and economic structures – was of considerable importance. In order to raise new capital and avoid debt defaults, Latin American governments, encouraged by the US government, engaged in successive rounds of economic marketization and privatization. Regimes sold state-owned enterprises and, in many cases, drastically curtailed social spending on education, healthcare, public transport, and subsidies for basic consumer goods. This strategy hurt the poor most, and led to yet greater social inequalities – in a region whose distribution of wealth and income is the most unequal in the world – while damaging the chances of those at the bottom of the pile to develop the human capital and/or skills most needed for accessing opportunities provided by newly marketized economies. Hilton (2001) quotes an unnamed senior US development program official as saying: "For the millions of poor, the slum dwellers, globalization now has the face of cruelty, of unemployment and marginalization . . . The rise in daily criminal violence . . . continuous drug-related problems, as well as the incidence of official corruption [are] in part, a manifestation of the unequal pattern of development." But it is an ill wind, which blows no one any good: economic liberalization and the selling of state-owned assets were highly beneficial both to incoming foreign capital as well as local elites. In various regional countries, including Brazil and Mexico, privatization, carried out by reform-minded presidents Fernando Collor de Mello and Carlos Salinas de Gortari, enabled those within the old party–state power axis suddenly to expand their already considerable wealth.

In sum, US encouragement to regional governments to introduce change often dovetailed with popular desires for reform. However, in terms of generating broad-based prosperity and enhanced welfare, while not necessarily worse than extant statist–nationalist alternatives, "Washington consensus" measures enjoyed, at best, only patchy success. As levels of societal inequality and very unequal opportunity structures in the newly liberalized and privatized economies in Latin America generally rose during the 1990s (Buxton and Phillips 1999), it raised a serious question about the long-term stability of the region's new democracies, since a high level of social polarization is surely inimical to democratic sustainability. The quandary for regional rulers was clear: while a democratic political system should allow for the articulation of popular demands for economic justice, in order to get economic recovery programs to work and to qualify for foreign aid, loans and investment, such demands must be suppressed in pursuit of economic growth. As Castañeda puts it: "a necessary condition for equity in Latin America appears to be democratic rule, but democracy seems incompatible with growth under actually existing circumstances" (Castañeda 1994: 398).

The Middle East

It is widely accepted that, around the world, countries' economic performance is closely linked to the global price of oil. Consequently, major oil-producing developing countries tend to experience a pronounced economic upturn when the price of oil rises, and downturns when it falls. Following major price rises in the 1970s – when the world price of oil rose fivefold – the price dropped in the early 1980s by 50 percent, from US$26 to US$13 a barrel. This fall led to almost immediate economic problems for Middle Eastern oil producers. Later, in the early 1990s, the price recovered modestly to around US$17 a barrel before rising strongly to more than US$30 a barrel by the end of the decade (Bill and Springborg 1994: 423).

But not all regional countries are oil rich. While some, including Saudi Arabia, Algeria, the United Arab Emirates, Libya, Qatar, Oman, Kuwait, Iran, Iraq, and a few others, have significant oil reserves and acquire significant revenues from selling oil, others – such as Yemen, Syria, Turkey, and Jordan – have little or no oil. As a result, regional per capita GNPs fluctuate widely: Turkey has a relatively low per capita GNP (US$2,900 in 1999), while oil-rich Gulf states, such as the United Arab Emirates (US$18,220, not far short of Britain's US$22,840), Saudi Arabia (US$6,790, nearly double that of Poland's US$3,960), and Oman ($4,950, higher than Hungary's US$4,650), have relative economic prosperity (World Bank 1999: 190–1; World Bank 2000: 272; World Bank 2001: 174–5). However, oil wealth has to an extent spread around the region; for example, from Egyptian workers in Saudi Arabia or Kuwait who send a proportion of their wages home. In short, it is clear that the key to the region's economic prosperity is to be found in its possession of significant oil reserves.

But this has been a two-edged sword: on the one hand, oil wealth has helped insulate some states from demands for increased political participation. In the past, when oil prices were high, authoritarian rulers could hope to buy off sociopolitical discontent through assiduous use of oil wealth. This was particularly the case when oil prices rose swiftly, as they did in the 1970s. On the other hand, when they dropped sharply, as they did in the early 1980s, regimes found it more difficult to deal with societal discontent, for example, from Islamists (Haynes 1998: 125–47). The consequence of falling oil prices was that most Middle Eastern governments were compelled to inaugurate economic reform programs in the 1980s and/or 1990s, and some, including Jordan and Kuwait, also introduced notable political changes (Haynes 2001a: 163–92). The main concern in introducing economic reforms was "to reduce the state's share of national resources consumption" (Owen 1992: 138).

Typically, these attempts – following the "standard" SAP template, involving deregulation, privatization of state-owned resources, reduction in size of state bureaucracies, modifying the exchange rate, reducing budget deficits – led to increasing hardship among ordinary people. Many employed by the state lost their jobs, while many ordinary citizens also suffered from reduction or elimination of price subsidies on basic goods. Often, economic privations associated with SAPs served to undermine a traditional state–society bargain known as khubz. Khubz was an informal pact between rulers and ruled: the former would provide the mass of ordinary people with most of their material needs, while, in return, the latter – normally implicitly – agreed to be politically passive (Sadiki 1997: 133). But growing economic hardship led to "bread uprisings" in countries across the region: people took to the streets, and protests sometimes developed into demonstrations with a wider focus against "social inequality, corruption, nepotism, authoritarianism and regime incompetence" (ibid: 138–9).

In short, across the Middle East region demands for fundamental political and economic changes became common in the 1980s and 1990s. The key cause was the failure of SAPs, which did not lead clearly to beneficial changes but rather hit the poor hardest. The latter responded by taking to the streets in protest at what they saw as their rulers' economic mismanagement.

Conclusion

Data in table 3.1 indicated that economic performances varied widely in developing regions in the 1980s and 1990s: from "highly satisfactory" in East and Southeast Asia, through "satisfactory" in South Asia and "improving" in Latin America, to "unsatisfactory" in the Middle East and "very unsatisfactory" in Africa. East and Southeast Asia's economically successful countries were good examples both of rapid industrialization and of effective adjustment to changing global factors. Apart from the ability to deal well with a variety of global factors – the external dimension – their economic success also showed how important it was for governments to exhibit clear signs of purpose and capability in relation to the domestic environment. From our survey of developing regions' economic performances in the 1980s and 1990s we can see that the most crucial issue in explaining outcomes was how *effective* was government in pushing through its policies in the face of global and domestic challenges. The more expert governments were in directing the national economy towards developmental goals then the more likely there would be (1) sustained economic growth and (2) relative equity in the distribution of resources.

Economic Reform in Developing Countries

In this section I want to examine, first, the impact of external factors and actors on developing countries' economies and, second, the domestic consequences. An array of contingent and structural external factors can be noted in relation to economic reform in developing countries in the 1980s and 1990s. Contingent factors include the impact of the oil price rises of the 1970s, the steep rise in interest rates in the early 1980s, and the international impact of the collapse of communism in

Eastern Europe. Structural factors included the growth in extent and intensiveness of a truly global economic system, whose roots were to be found in the worldwide expansion of capitalism from the seventeenth century. The dominance of the West in this system enabled both the IMF and World Bank to have a significant impact upon economic policy in numerous developing countries from the 1980s.

External actors: the IMF, the World Bank, and SAPs

From the 1980s, as already briefly discussed in chapter 1, IFIs (notably the World Bank and the IMF) encouraged dozens of seriously indebted developing countries to liberalize their economies. The important foreign aid donors, including the governments of the USA, EU, and Japan, also exerted pressures for change. It was necessary, so the argument went, that seriously indebted developing countries with serious balance of payments difficulties themselves held the key to economic turnaround. This would be achieved by fundamental economic liberalization and marketization – including a major reduction of the state's economic role – involving currency devaluation, privatization, cuts in public expenditure, slimming bureaucracies, reducing subsidies, and heavily promoting exports. While details of reform packages differed from country to country, typically the IMF made adoption of debt rescheduling programs conditional on measures in five broad areas:

1   Trade barriers were to be drastically lowered. This would expose local producers to foreign competition and make those that could compete "leaner and fitter."
2   Subsidies and price controls should be immediately reduced with the eventual aim of withdrawing them completely. This would serve to remove "distortions" in local prices for goods and services.
3   National financial systems should be restructured. This would be accomplished by withdrawing controls on international capital movements.
4   State-owned enterprises were to be privatized. In addition, private foreign investment would be strongly encouraged, not least by removing controls on remittance of profits.
5   State economic intervention was to be minimized, as was state provision of most social services. Henceforward their provision would be left largely to the private sector.

The IFIs and Western governments argued that the main purpose of liberalization and marketization packages was not to reduce the power of the state, nor to generate enough "surplus" cash so that debt could be serviced (Mosley, Harrington, and Toye 1991a: 45–51; George 1993: 63). Instead, the claim was that liberalization was objectively necessary, given the scale of economic collapse, so as to do things better in the future. They readily agreed that, in the short term, economic change would generate more pain than gain and would likely result in higher levels of unemployment and greater inequality. Over time, however, the IFIs argued that economic liberalization would lead to considerable economic and developmental gains, with reformed economies becoming largely self-regulating via more open competition between private businesses. Necessarily, the public sector would retract, while still aiming to provide sufficient services to enable private businesses to conduct their affairs efficiently and to protect society's weakest members. The aim was that, ultimately, the gap between the world's rich and poor would not continue to widen but be reduced. The result, it was hoped, would be increased development and prosperity in countries which had hitherto pursued misguided strategies of economic growth for too long. In sum, the IFIs' prescription for reform of heavily indebted developing countries' economies was dependent on the following:

- reduction of the economic role of the state;
- reform of the structure of the economy;
- liberalization of markets, with increased competition;
- construction of strong linkages to the global economy by increasing export volume and value;
- "new globalized capital markets and a reborn world trading order" (Callaghy 1993: 161).

The dependence on the IMF, the World Bank, and major Western countries for the design of economic reform packages and the resources needed to implement them was seen by some observers as a novel form of neocolonialism. Such critics argued that Western leverage converted into intensive economic policy conditionality and policy changes, in return for a strictly limited injection of financial resources. However, proponents of the reforms countered that, given the extent of prior economic collapse, projected reforms were the *only* available way to stimulate macroeconomic turnaround. However, as noted in chapter 1, the outcome of SAPs was generally disappointing. While in some cases macroeconomic imbalances were at least partially addressed, this had a serious developmental cost with, in virtually all cases, the economically vulnerable suffering the most. This helped lead, in numerous developing countries, to strong demands for political changes, an issue we shall look at in chapter 4.

Developmentally, SAPs helped to deepen the economic and developmental problems of many developing countries. The unanticipated problem, however, was that the authority of many adjusting governments was linked to the way that they dealt with the social consequences of adjustment. Demands for democracy came at the same time as attempts at adjustment: each probably helped to stimulate the other, although it is very difficult to isolate the effects stemming from SAPs from those emanating from other causes, such as the uneven distribution of wealth in society and the effects of domestic class structures. Mosley, Harrington, and Toye's (1991b) definitive study of the impact of SAPs on nine countries in the 1980s – Turkey, the Philippines, Thailand, Ghana, Malawi, Kenya, Jamaica, Guyana, and Ecuador – led to four main conclusions.

- The implementation of SAPs under World Bank guidance was nearly always favorable to export growth and the external account.
- The influence of SAPs on aggregate investment was nearly always negative.
- SAPs' impact on national income and on external financial flows was, on balance, neutral.
- Living standards of the poor fell in SAP countries, linked to cuts in public expenditure, especially withdrawal of food subsidies, and the impact of price increases on basic goods.

While it might be argued that these conclusions are now somewhat passé given the fact that they derive from data more than a decade old, a more recent example provided by the results of Argentina's current SAP indicate that little or nothing has changed in relation to the social impact. Argentina's plight led Hilton (2001) to suggest that "it is not a great moment for advocates of globalization in Latin America." Until recently, Argentina was held up as a fine example of how structural adjustment can deliver desirable results. In the late 1990s the country's president, Carlos Menem, despite initial ideological reluctance, presided over free-market policies, pegged the local currency to the dollar, controlled inflation, and oversaw a sustained privatization program. Later, however, things turned sour: by mid-2001 Argentina's foreign debt had reached US$128 billion and unemployment was at 18 percent.

The IMF, backed by the US treasury secretary, Paul O'Neill, demanded severe belt-tightening measures as the cost of an early release of new funds. In July 2001 Argentina's government was compelled to pass a "'zero deficit' plan that would limit public spending to no more than the government collects in taxes and state salaries, and some pensions were cut by up to 13 percent" (Denny 2001). This new policy of "tough love" was championed by O'Neill, who had been incensed by the IMF's bailing out of East and Southeast Asian economies following the 1997–8 crisis. In the case of Argentina, with the global economy much less vulnerable than it had been in relation to the 1997–8 Asian crisis, the US government believed that the safety net of IMF credit encouraged irresponsible borrowing and was determined to stop it. Argentina was the test case of its resolve. The finance secretary, Daniel Marx, articulated the government's response. He pointed out that Argentina had been a consistent follower of the IMF's strategy, constantly following advice on deregulating and liberalizing the economy. As Marx put it: "It would be tragic, not only for Argentina but for the global economy, if it were concluded that Argentina's experience was useless and did not work for Argentines" (quoted in Denny 2001).

Millions of Argentines seemed already to have come to this conclusion, expressed in various ways. Not only did the government come under domestic pressure from public opinion to default on the country's debts, but also demonstrations erupted led by unemployed workers against the government's rigorous policies to cut state spending, including their jobs. The *piqueteros*, as they were known, including teachers, doctors, nurses, state employees, and pensioners, devised a plan in which seven columns of protesters would march across the country to demand that the government change its policies. In early August 2001, 40,000 people filled the largest square in the capital, Buenos Aires, with similar protests in other urban centers, to show disapproval not only of the impact of structural adjustment policies generally, but also at the signs of unprecedented social crisis. This was characterized by young children begging on the streets, people sleeping under viaducts, and queues of people seeking entry visas to foreign countries in order to flee Argentina (Branford 2001)

Conclusion

SAPs were intended to open up heavily indebted developing countries' economies to new internal and external capital investment by making them more attractive to investors. This would be facilitated by a reduction in the economic role of the state, long seen as an impediment to investment. However, economic liberalization, at least initially, was undertaken as though it was "merely" a technical fix, without taking it sufficiently into account that sensitive policy changes needed firmly to take cognizance of state–society relations. That is, efforts to deal with developing countries' debt crises and macroeconomic problems more generally, were undertaken by Western actors attempting to apply the monoeconomics of the then-dominant neoclassical orthodoxy, neoliberalism. However, despite the avowed good intentions of the IFIs, the result of sometimes insensitively applied conditionality was not what they intended. SAPs forced affected developing countries to adjust to full orthodox liberalism without allowing the pace or thrust of liberalization to be tempered by the singularities of local state–society relations. And, crucially, in the 1990s and early 2000s, when numerous SAPs were being applied, global economic conditions were unhelpful: governments of developing countries, seeking to use deflationary policies to deal with economic crisis, found that, in the absence of strong demand for exports from rich countries, they were unable to prise their economies out of recession. The main developmental consequence, as noted in Argentina, was that poor and unemployed people experienced serious economic hardships, which led in some cases to social upheaval.

Domestic responses to SAPs: bottom-up demands for development

We saw that in Argentina the failure of its SAP led to a growing demand for a different approach to tackle economic and developmental problems The country is not unique in this regard: numerous developing countries have developed national and local groups similar to the *piqueteros* (Haynes 1997). In addition, there are many transnational and/or global organizations, such as Oxfam (campaigning for poverty reduction and development), Jubilee Plus (the successor to Jubilee 2000, a major champion of debt relief for severely indebted developing countries), and Greenpeace International (environmental protection and sustainable development). In addition, there are numerous citizen groups, part of what is known as global (or transnational) civil society (Risse, Ropp, and Sikkink 1999; Florini 2000). In short, at both country and global levels dedicated organizations have recently evolved to tackle the developmental problems which SAPs have by and large failed to resolve.

Focusing on domestic initiatives and global civil society efforts serves to highlight the crucial role which non-state organizations and interest groups can play in pursuit of developmental outcomes. Especially since the 1990s, numerous ideas, advanced by miscellaneous individuals, community groups, and private foundations at country level, have coalesced with those advanced by the UN and other organizations. Thomas and Reader (2001) refer to such initiatives as a "broadly critical alternative approach" in contrast to those emanating from bodies like the World Bank. Although varying in their core concerns, "bottom-up" initiatives tend to share a similar developmental approach, built on "equitable satisfaction of basic material and non-material needs, self-sufficiency, self-reliance, diversity, appropriate (often local) knowledge, community participation, local ownership and control of policies and projects which are predominantly small scale, and cultural, economic and environmental sustainability" (ibid: 75). While welcoming the goal of a 50 percent reduction in the number of absolute poor by 2015, proponents of the critical alternative approach are often "skeptical of the ability of current development policies, based on the market, to deliver the required results" (ibid).

Conclusion

While the clout of bottom-up movements is often linked to their global profile, what, more generally, is the role of globalization in development in developing countries? We saw in this chapter that, until recently, there was a perceived lack of ideological alternatives to the apparently omnipotent global market. During the Cold War, at least three alternative development models were extant: Western-style liberal democracy/capitalism, Soviet-style communism, and state-led strategies pursued by many African and Asian governments. However, the end of the Cold War led to the preeminence of one model that became dominant: the liberal democratic/capitalist model championed by the most influential international actors: Western governments, the IMF, the World Bank, the market, and big business, including TNCs.

With the importance of globalization to the fore, development strategies later underwent a significant change. Two goals were proclaimed at an important international get-together held in London in February 2001: first, generally to increase economic well-being and, second, to bring the swathe of poor countries and people into the development mainstream. The background to the meeting was that, despite some clear successes, overall the share of the poorest countries in world trade had halved in 20 years: from 0.8 percent in 1980 to 0.4 percent in 2001. Reflecting this unfortunate development, Clare Short, the British international development secretary, averred that "marginalization rather than globalization poses the greatest threat to the economies of impoverished countries" (Elliot 2001b). In an attempt to reverse this trend, Short, in tandem with the head of the World Trade Organization, Mike Moore, put forward a three-pronged argument: (1) debt relief on its own would be insufficient to put the poorest countries on the road to sustained prosperity; (2) further trade liberalization would help boost export growth and overall economic performance; and (3) enhanced global economic integration – via free trade – was the key to the reduction of global poverty and hunger. In an argument first encountered in chapter 2 in the examination of the "positive globalization" position, Short and Moore expected, through this strategy, to achieve the greatest possible global economic growth which, in turn, was expected to result in the greatest possible contribution to enhanced global economic welfare. However, critics argued that a key problem in this formulation was that it did not contain a clear strategy to secure a necessary and equitable distribution of the claimed benefits.

The stated concern in the Moore/Short plan – to bring the poorest countries and people into the development mainstream – clearly reflected the growing importance of the bottom-up, critical alternative approach and acceptance and utilization of some of its terminology. Increasingly high-profile "anti-globalization" protests – the first was at Seattle in 1998 at the WTO's millennium conference – focused inter alia on development concerns. As we noted, compared to a decade or so ago, there was a changed emphasis in the *World Development Report 2000/2001*. The report built on earlier strategies in light of the cumulative evidence and experiences of the 1990s – not least of the impact of globalization and its developmental impact. To deal with the malign effects of globalization, the report proposed a strategy to attack poverty in three ways: promoting opportunity, facilitating empowerment, and enhancing security.

It was cautiously optimistic in tone and argument, with a basic presumption that, for millions of impoverished people in the developing countries, major reductions in dimensions of poverty were now theoretically possible; it was also notable for the adoption of some of the critical alternative approach's concerns. Whereas the World Bank's chief concern in the 1980s and early 1990s was to reduce the role of the state in development and leave it to the market, its 2000/2001 report emphasized that desirable development goals could be achieved by a three-way effort by domestic markets, state institutions, and civil society. However, the report also accepted that to attain these "international development goals will require actions to spur economic growth and reduce income inequality, but even equitable growth will not be enough to achieve the goals for health and education (World Bank 2001: 6). Whether actors could actually work together to harness globalization, via economic integration and technological changes, in order to serve the interests of poor people and increase their share of society's prosperity, remained to be seen.

4

Democratization and Democracy

Until recently there were few democratically elected governments in the countries of the developing world. Instead, various kinds of unelected regimes – including military, one-party, no-party, and personalist dictatorships – were the norm. We noted in chapter 3 that, developmentally speaking, one of the key outcomes of the 1980s and 1990s was growing division between richer and poorer developing countries. Those decades were also notable for the spread of democratically elected governments to numerous developing countries. Democratization, many observers agree, was the result of the interaction of various domestic and external factors, with the former normally most important. At the domestic level, a shift to democracy – that is, democratization – was typically linked to expressions of popular dissatisfaction with the often-abysmal development and political records of unelected governments. Internationally, Western "political conditionality" was an important factor in the shift to elected regimes in many developing countries. Aid-donating governments, such as those of the USA and Britain, sought to promote democracy by linking moves in that direction to the granting of foreign aid. Political conditionality has two dimensions: "positive" assistance to encourage democratic development and "negative" aid sanctions to leverage reform in recipient countries.

So widespread was the move to democracy in the developing world in the 1980s and 1990s that Huntington (1991) gave it a name: the "third wave of democracy." The third wave followed two earlier waves (the first was in the late nineteenth century and the second directly after World War II) and began with the shift from authoritarian to democratically elected governments in Greece, Portugal, and Spain in the mid-1970s. In the 1980s and 1990s democracy spread to numerous Latin

American, Eastern European, Asian, and African countries. The extent of the changes in this regard can be gauged from the fact that in 1973 only a quarter of countries had democratically elected governments. Twenty years later the proportion of democracies had grown to more than half and, by 2001, it had reached about 75 percent, that is around 150 countries. In this chapter I define democracy as follows: it refers to the holding of relatively free and fair elections, following which a victorious party or parties takes power.

The structure of the chapter is as follows. First, we investigate the circumstances surrounding the third wave of democracy in the developing world. Second, we assess the regional picture, among developing countries, in relation to democracy. Third, we examine the relative importance of domestic and external factors to democratic outcomes. Fourth, we look at two interesting and topical examples of developing countries – South Africa and Indonesia – that recently made democratic transitions from authoritarian rule.

The Third Wave of Democracy in the Developing World

From authoritarian to elected regimes

Transition from authoritarian regimes to democracy can occur in four reasonably clear-cut stages: (1) political liberalization, (2) collapse of authoritarian regime, (3) democratic transition, (4) democratic consolidation. Liberalization is the political process of reforming authoritarian rule, while the stage of collapse of the authoritarian regime refers to when a dictatorship falls apart. Democratic transition is the material shift to democracy, normally characterized by the accession to power of a democratically elected government, via free and fair elections. Democratic consolidation involves the construction of the institutions of divided power. It can take much time to reach, and by no means all new democracies in the developing world had managed it by 2001.

The four stages are complementary and can overlap. For example, liberalization and transition can happen simultaneously. Aspects of democratic consolidation can appear when certain elements of transition are barely in place or remain incomplete, or they may even be showing signs of retreating. However, it is nearly always possible to observe a concluded transition to democracy. This is when a pattern of behavior developed on an ad hoc basis during the change in regimes becomes a stable structure in the new system, and when the admittance of political actors into the system – as well as the process of political decision-making – proceeds according to previously established and legitimately coded procedures.

Before then, absence of predictable "rules of the democratic game" makes it difficult to be sure about eventual outcomes. This is because the dynamics of the transition revolve around strategic interactions and tentative arrangements between actors with uncertain power resources. This involves (1) defining who will legitimately be entitled to play the political game; (2) what criteria determines who wins and loses; and (3) what limits are placed on the issues at stake. What chiefly differentiates the four stages of democratization is the degree of uncertainty prevailing at each moment. For example, during regime transition all political calculations and interactions are highly uncertain. This is because political actors find it difficult to know what their precise interests are and which groups and individuals would most usefully be allies or opponents. During transition, powerful, often inherently undemocratic political players, such as the armed forces and/or elite civilian supporters of the incumbent authoritarian regime, characteristically divide into what Huntington (1991) calls "hardline" and "softline" factions. "Softliners" are more willing to find a middle way with opponents to negotiate a political solution, but "hardliners" are less inclined. The eventual outcome is linked to which faction predominates. Democratic consolidation is thought most likely when "softliners" triumph because they are more likely than "hardliners" to find a compromise position.

Democratic consolidation is said to have occurred when contending social classes and political groups accept both formal rules and informal understandings determining political outcomes: that is, "who gets what, where, when, and how." If achieved, it signifies that groups are settling into relatively predictable positions involving politically legitimate behavior according to generally acceptable rules. More generally, a consolidated democracy is characterized by normative limits and established patterns of power distribution. Political parties emerge as privileged in this context because, despite their divisions over strategies and their uncertainties about partisan identities, the logic of electoral competition focuses public attention on them and compels them to appeal to the widest possible clientele. In addition, a strong civil society – that is, the aggregate of non-state groups who collectively keep an eye on the power of the state – is crucial for chances of democratic consolidation. In sum, democratic consolidation is said to be present when all major political actors take for granted the fact that democratic processes dictate governmental renewal.

Observers have noted that, despite numerous relatively free and fair elections over the last two decades, ordinary people often seem to lack the ability to influence political outcomes in many developing countries (Haynes 2001a). This is largely because small groups of elites – they can be civilians, military personnel, or a combination – usually remain in control of important political processes. That is, despite relatively free and fair elections, the power of urban-based elites and their rural allies is often not seriously diminished. Instead, the elites manage to solve the conundrum of how to remain in power while simultaneously giving the appearance of allowing democratizing. In many developing countries, groups of elites have managed to acquire at least some democratic legitimacy – both internationally and domestically – but without substantively changing their mode of operation. As power is still focused in relatively few elite hands, it is hardly surprising that political systems often have narrow bases from which most ordinary people are, or feel, excluded. This is a concern because, by definition, a democracy should not be run by and for the few, but instead should signify popularly elected government operating in the broad public interest.

To summarize the points made so far:

- Western pressure – known as political conditionality – encouraged the shift from authoritarian to elected governments in many developing countries.
- Democratization produced many elected regimes but many do not have strong democratic credentials.
- Despite democratization, power often remains broadly in the hands of the same groups of elites that held it during the authoritarian period.
- Strong civil societies are crucial to healthy democracies, but developing countries often lack them.

The third wave of democracy

While dozens of developing countries held at least one relatively free and fair national-level election in the 1990s, there were significant regional differences. Latin America had a comprehensive shift to elected governments: in 2001, all 23 Latin American countries, with the exception of Cuba, had elected governments. Several Asian countries – including Bangladesh, Mongolia, Nepal, the Philippines, South Korea, and Taiwan – registered a shift to democracy in the 1990s, as did a large number of African states: over half the region's nearly 50 countries were democracies in 2001. In contrast, few Middle Eastern countries – with the exceptions of Turkey, Jordan, Morocco, and Kuwait – made the shift from authoritarian to popularly elected governments during the third wave.

Overall, there were 45 new democracies in the developing world in 2000. Regionally, the breakdown was as follows: Asia had 7 new democracies, Latin America 16, Africa 18, and the Middle East 4. Of the 8 in Asia, the US organization Freedom House (FH) classified 5 (57 percent) "free" (Mongolia, the Philippines, South Korea, Taiwan, and Thailand), and the remaining 3 (43 percent) – Bangladesh, Nepal, and Indonesia – "partly free." Of the 16 in Latin America, FH judged 7 (44 percent) "free" and 9 (56 percent), "partly free." Africa had 5 (28 percent) new democracies rated "free" and 13 (72 percent) "partly free," while all of the democracies in the Middle East were "partly free." (See the Freedom House website for details: http://www.freedomhouse.org/survey00/method/). In sum, as table 4.1 shows, in 2000 FH rated 16 of the 45 new developing world democracies (36 percent) "free" and the remaining 29 (64 percent), "partly free." Table 4.1 also indicates that the percentage of "free" states (57 percent) among new Asian democracies was higher than in Latin America (44 percent) and considerably better than in Africa (28 percent) or the Middle East (0 percent).

Democracy in the Developing World: The Regional Picture

Why were democratic outcomes patchy? Why were there proportionately more "free" states in Asia than in Latin America or Africa? It is difficult to argue that time is the main factor, as shifts to democracy in all three regions occurred at the same time, the 1980s and 1990s. However, it should be noted that, historically, democratic consolidation is a slow process. Most first and second wave democracies – such as Britain, the United States, and Japan – took decades or longer to achieve it. This is because developing democratic institutions takes much time and continuous effort. The eventual chances of success depend upon certain key factors, discussed above. To explain and account for the variable democratic picture in the developing world we turn next to a regional survey.

Table 4.1 Regional breakdown of "free" and "partly free" countries in the developing world, 2000

Region	Total "free" new democracies	Percentage "free"	Total "partly free" new democracies	Percentage "partly free"	Overall total of "free" and "partly free" democracies
Asia	4	57	3	43	7
Latin America	7	44	9	56	16
Africa	5	28	13	72	18
The Middle East	0	0	4	100	4
Total	16		29		45

Africa

Africa is a culturally and religiously diverse, politically complex region of nearly 50 countries. The impetus for political reforms came from a combination of domestic and international sources. However, the background to Africa's recent democratic transitions was an array of unpropitious structural characteristics, which, according to many observers, made it surprising that the region has democratized to the extent it has. That is, beset by endemic economic problems and growing societal strife, African countries seemed "somehow [to have] 'gone wrong' since independence" (Villalón 1998: 3).

Observers expressed strong doubts that the democratic trend in Africa would last for long. Many African countries seemed unlikely to consolidate democracy because relevant indicators for democratic success were lacking: ethnic and religious homogeneity; robust party systems; a professional national bureaucracy; a relatively tolerant society; a reasonably equitable economic system with a certain degree of prosperity for all; and modern agrarian relations. The democratic success of South Africa was, for many, especially unlikely. Later in the chapter we shall see how South Africa managed it. The overall regional picture regarding new democracies is given in table 4.2. Note that only countries rated by FH as "free" or "partly free" are included: those judged "not free" are omitted.

Table 4.2   Democracy in Africa, 2000

Country	Political rights	Civil liberties	"Freedom status"
Cape Verde	1	2	Free
Sao Tomé e Principe	1	2	Free
South Africa	1	2	Free
Benin	2	3	Free
Namibia	2	3	Free
Mali	3	3	Partly Free
Malawi	3	3	Partly Free
Seychelles	3	3	Partly Free
Ghana	3	3	Partly Free
Mozambique	3	4	Partly Free
Central African Republic	3	4	Partly Free
Burkina Faso	4	4	Partly Free
Guinea-Bissau	3	5	Partly Free
Lesotho	4	4	Partly Free
Tanzania	4	4	Partly Free
Madagascar	5	3	Partly Free
Gabon	5	4	Partly Free
Zambia	5	4	Partly Free

1 = most free, 7 = least free. "Free" = combined political rights and civil liberties
total of 2–5; "Partly Free" = 6–9; "Not Free" =10–17.
Source: http://www.freedomhouse.org/research/freeworld/2000/
countryratings/

Table 4.3   New democracies in South Asia, 2000

Country	Political rights	Civil liberties	"Freedom status"
Bangladesh	3	4	Partly Free
Nepal	3	4	Partly Free

1 = most free, 7= least free. "Free" = combined political rights and civil liberties
total of 2–5; "Partly Free" = 6–9; "Not Free" = 10–17.
Source: http://www.freedomhouse.org/research/freeworld/2000/
countryratings/

South Asia

South Asian countries differ greatly in terms of size, geography, economic structures, political traditions, forms of rule, relations with external powers, and cultures. Following independence from colonial rule in the late 1940s, the region had a history of political diversity: undemocratic monarchical rule in Nepal; a civil war since the early 1980s in Sri Lanka between the majority Sinhalese and the minority Tamils; a democratic system in India since independence in 1947; and alternating military and civilian regimes in Bangladesh and Pakistan. However, both Bangladesh and Nepal democratized in the early 1990s. This followed an earlier move to democratic rule from military rule in Pakistan in 1988, following pressure from the American government. Later, however, in October 1999, a military government returned to power following a coup d'état. Despite this setback, regional democratic progress was clear: during 1988–99, South Asia witnessed over 20 governments and, most unusually, all (except the military regime in Pakistan) came to power via democratic processes. But, like Africa, the region's countries had many factors unpropitious for democracy, including poverty and underdevelopment and widespread ethnic and religious strife. The overall regional picture regarding new democracies is given in table 4.3. Note that only countries rated by FH as "free" or "partly free" are included: those judged "not free" are omitted

East and Southeast Asia

In the 1980s and 1990s there were shifts to democracy in several regional countries, including South Korea, Taiwan, Thailand, the Philippines, and Indonesia. In the Philippines a "People Power" movement forced President Ferdinand Marcos and his government from power in 1986 while, nearly at the same time, South Korea and Taiwan moved from unelected to elected rulers. Popular pressure was also notable in two other recent regional examples of democratization: (1) the "May 1992 events" in Thailand which led to the ousting of the government of Suchinda Kraprayoon and replacement by a new regime, and (2) student-led protests in Indonesia in 1998 which helped catalyse wide societal unrest culminating in the downfall of President Suharto and his regime. Generally, across the region, pro-democracy campaigners – focused in a variety of civil society groups and encouraged by external actors including the government of the United States – helped undermine the legitimacy of unelected governments. The overall regional picture regarding new democracies is given in table 4.4. Note that only countries rated by FH as "free" or "partly free" are included: those judged "not free" are omitted.

We noted in chapter 2 that certain political leaders, including Malaysia's prime minister, Muhammad Mahathir, and a former Singaporean leader, Lee Kuan Yew, have claimed that liberal democracy is "culturally alien" to their peoples. They argue that their countries have political cultures and histories that, while differing from country to country in precise details, nevertheless reflect an important collective idea: not the individual but the community is of most societal and political significance. We saw that this claim is at the heart of the concept of a generic "(East) Asian culture" said to embody an array of sociopolitical values, including harmony, consensus, unity, and community, that differ significantly from those of "Western culture" and its individualistic, self-seeking values. Given the importance of this debate for democracy in the East and Southeast Asian region it seems appropriate to return to it now.

Contrary to the claims of some regional leaders that pro-democracy groups were instigated by foreign actors, Hewison points out that "demands for the opening of political space, with calls for increased democracy in Southeast Asia, are not originating in the West or among Western-influenced actors, but have domestic causes" (Hewison 1999: 231). Authoritarianism and suppression of political opposition had long been justified and legitimized by governments as a price for often impressive economic growth. But that legitimation took a major knock in

Table 4.4   New democracies in East and Southeast Asia, 2000

Country	Political rights	Civil liberties	"Freedom status"
South Korea	2	2	Free
Taiwan	2	2	Free
The Philippines	2	3	Free
Thailand	2	3	Free
Indonesia	4	4	Partly Free

1 = most free, 7 = least free. "Free" = combined political rights and civil liberties total of 2–5; "Partly Free" = 6–9; "Not Free" = 10–17.
Source: http://www.freedomhouse.org/research/freeworld/2000/countryratings/

1997–8 when many regional economies experienced serious economic downturn that began with a collapse of the Thai currency which, as we saw in chapter 3, triggered a regional domino effect of collapsing currencies and economic problems. The regional economic malaise in 1997–8 made it plain that authoritarian development models were fallible. This was also consequential for the claimed trade off – economic growth and prosperity, but little political freedom – which regional governments had explicitly or implicitly invoked as justification for their styles of rule. In sum, the economic and financial crisis in the region in the late 1990s revealed new weaknesses in regional authoritarian developmental models and helped strengthen the legitimacy of pro-democracy discourses.

Analysis of recent political changes in East and Southeast Asia are made complex by the fact that, while a large number of countries are conventionally identified as belonging to the region, other than in the sense of countries' physical proximity to each other, they share few characteristics. There is no obvious way to delimit the East and Southeast Asia region in terms of geography, politics, economy, history, or culture. Unlike Africa with its common, colonially derived European languages, English and French, or Latin America with Spanish and Portuguese, East and Southeast Asia has no common language to bind together the diversity. Instead, it has many very different regional languages written in different scripts. In addition, unlike the ubiquitous Christianity of Latin America, East and Southeast Asia has a variety of profoundly different religious traditions. Finally, unlike Africa or South Asia, the East and Southeast Asia region does not share colonial histories. While many regional countries were colonized at one time or the other by various powers (including Britain, France, Spain, the Netherlands, the United States, Japan), not all were. For example, there was a distinctive non-colonial form of authoritarianism – royal absolutism – in Thailand. The overall point is that East and Southeast Asia is marked by more political, historical, and cultural diversity than perhaps any other region examined in this book. A consequence, it seems plausible to suggest, is that this factor will have implications for political outcomes. Not least, it is likely to make them variable.

The region's political diversity is manifested in the fact that, apart from various examples of (mostly limited) democracies, East and Southeast Asia also has sundry kinds of non-democratic political systems. These include communist governments (Vietnam, North Korea, Laos, China), non-communist authoritarian regimes (Cambodia), a military administration (Burma), civilian absolutist rule (Brunei), a restricted "communitarian" democracy (Singapore), and a dominant-party system (Malaysia). Freedom House categorizes these countries' political systems as either "not free" or at the interface between "not free" and "partly free." Various kinds of political structures and processes underpinned authoritarian rule; often strongly centralized regional states developed various measures for societal control, including hegemonic single-party systems (Indonesia, Malaysia), vote-buying (Thailand), ethnic affirmative action (Malaysia), restrictions on the right to organize, debate, and voice opinions (*inter alia*, Singapore, Malaysia), and cooption of civil society activists and emergency laws to restrict opposition activities (most of the region's countries at various times).

Taiwan and South Korea are important regional democratic success stories. From the mid-1980s both moved – independently and consistently – from authoritarian to democratically elected rule. It seems unlikely that either country would soon revert to non-democratic rule as in both countries democratic progress is apparently linked to several factors: (1) growing cultures of tolerance; (2) strong desire for consensus-seeking by both those in power and the political opposition; (3) continued economic growth, despite the 1997–8 economic crisis; (4) relatively equitably distributed wealth; (5) an increasingly politically quietist military; and (6) increasingly solid civil societies. In sum, both countries had clear signs of democratic consolidation in the early 2000s. The contrast with Indonesia, a regional neighbor, was clear. As we shall see later in the chapter, Indonesia was characterized by ethnic and religious conflict, a declining economy, and a continued high political profile for the military despite democratization starting in 1998.

Latin America and the Caribbean

The background to the recent regional wave of democratization was the widespread assumption of power by military rulers in most Latin American countries in the 1960s and 1970s, which took a particular form, known as bureaucratic authoritarianism. While specific characteristics of military rule differed from country to country, what they all had in common was a political scene where civil and political societies were comprehensively repressed. Prior to the recent regional wave of democracy, regime legitimacy had plummeted in many Latin American countries, consequential to political repression and poor economic performances. Encouraged by the government of the United States, and pressurized by rejuvenated civil and political societies, democratically elected leaders came to power proclaiming a willingness to try to make democracy work. Allegations of fraud in the June 2000 presidential poll in Peru, which led to the ousting of President Fujimori, coup attempts in Ecuador and Paraguay, declaration of martial law to quell a popular uprising in Bolivia, and Colombia's continuing civil war, all combined to suggest that overall regional progress towards democracy was problematic. Nevertheless, by 2001, all 35 members of the Organization of American States, except Cuba, were ruled by popularly elected leaders. The regional democratic picture in 2000 is given in table 4.5. Note that only regional countries rated by FH in 2000 as "free" or "partly free" are included: those judged "not free" are omitted.

One of the most significant changes of regime was in Mexico, where presidential elections in mid-2000 brought to an end more than seven decades of single-party rule by the Institutional Revolutionary Party. The main question asked was this: would the new Mexican president, Vicente Fox, an avowed democrat strongly encouraged by the USA to democratize and liberalize the economy as part of the continuing development of the NAFTA

Table 4.5 New democracies in Latin America, 2000

Country	Political rights	Civil liberties	"Freedom status"
Uruguay	1	2	Free
Panama	1	2	Free
Bolivia	1	3	Free
Chile	2	2	Free
Argentina	2	3	Free
Dominican Republic	2	3	Free
Ecuador	2	3	Free
El Salvador	3	3	Partly Free
Honduras	3	3	Partly Free
Nicaragua	3	3	Partly Free
Brazil	3	4	Partly Free
Guatemala	3	4	Partly Free
Mexico	3	4	Partly Free
Paraguay	4	3	Partly Free
Colombia	4	4	Partly Free
Peru	5	4	Partly Free

1 = most free, 7 = least free. "Free" = combined political rights and civil liberties total of 2–5; "Partly Free" = 6–9; "Not Free" = 10–17.
Source: http://www.freedomhouse.org/research/freeworld/2000/countryratings/

regional economic grouping, be able to overcome the entrenched anti-democratic structural characteristics of Mexico's political system?

The region also provides another interesting example of an unconventional political system. Unlike Mexico, Venezuela has been a democracy for over four decades, since 1958, and is, as a result, a regional rarity. Many observers long believed that it had successfully consolidated its democracy. However, it became increasingly clear over time that its democratic position was problematic. This was because power was firmly in the hands of two main political parties, AD and COPEI, which developed a cosy system of power rotation effectively denying the possibility of alternative parties achieving power. The election to president of a former military officer and anti-system politician, Hugo Chavez, in December 1998 suggested that significant political changes would occur. Enjoying much popular support, especially among the poor, Chavez pledged that he would fundamentally reform Venezuela's political and economic system to the benefit of the less privileged. However, it remains to be seen how far Chavez is able or willing to overcome the entrenched structural characteristics of the country's political system, which ensured that power remained in the same hands for decades.

The Middle East

It is often suggested not only that the Middle East region is filled with countries that have few structural characteristics conducive to democracy, but also that things have been that way for a long time. Others assert that in fact the countries of the region do not comprise an unchanging, undemocratic monolith and point to three periods of profound political changes in the region during the late nineteenth and early twentieth centuries. The first major political change occurred when national assemblies were created in North Africa and the Arabian peninsular between the 1860s and the 1930s. The second took place after Ottoman (Turkish) colonial rule collapsed during World War I. Parliamentary regimes were created in a number of regional countries, for example in Egypt (during 1924–58), Iraq (1936–58), and Lebanon (1946–75). A third period of political change occurred in the late 1950s and early 1960s, when radical, youthful army officers overthrew conservative governments in Egypt, Iraq, Libya, and Syria. Their goal was to get rid of their countries' traditionalist political systems, manifested by unrepresentative governments regarded as unforgivably subservient to the West. However, over time, it appeared that the new rulers had no real intention of convention-

Table 4.6 New democracies in the Middle East, 2000

Country	Political rights	Civil liberties	"Freedom status"
Jordan	4	4	Partly Free
Kuwait	4	5	Partly Free
Morocco	5	4	Partly Free
Turkey	4	5	Partly Free

1 = most free, 7 = least free. "Free" = combined political rights and civil liberties total of 2–5; "Partly Free" = 6–9; "Not Free" = 10–17.
Source: http://www.freedomhouse.org/research/freeworld/2000/countryratings/

ally democratizing their political systems. Instead, they installed a variety of authoritarian regimes whose rulers regularly win presidential elections with a huge proportion – typically, over 90 percent – of the popular vote. The overall point is that there is a variety of kinds of regime in the Middle East region, which developed in the wake of three periods of political upheaval over the last hundred years or so. Significantly, many existing regimes – whether monarchical, military, or single-party dominated – are characterized by a lack of democracy: they tend to be both authoritarian and unrepresentative, closely supported by the armed forces, often buoyed by significant oil revenues. The regional picture in relation to new democracies in 2000 is given in table 4.6. Note that only regional countries rated by FH in 2000 as "free" or "partly free" are included: those judged "not free" are omitted.

Why is the Middle East, a region of nearly 20 countries, so uncongenial for democracy? Apart from those of Kuwait, Jordan, Morocco, and Turkey, democratic systems are lacking in the region. Waterbury (1994: 23) contends that "the Arab Middle East is exceptional in its resistance to political liberalization, respect for human rights, and formal democratic practice." Karl (1995: 79) suggests that the reason is that regional countries suffer "a culture of repression and passivity that is antithetical to democratic citizenship." On the other hand, Ibrahim asserts that significant political changes are now taking place, resulting in political elites in a number of regional countries "beginning a [democratic] march from which ultimately there may be no retreat" (Ibrahim 1995: 43). A question often asked is to what extent can Middle Eastern countries reconcile their largely undemocratic political backgrounds with popular desire for democracy?

Ibrahim appears to be suggesting that in fact the Middle East region is not entirely different to the other democratizing developing regions, as he detects some movement towards democracy. But Karl and Waterbury see things differently: they highlight what they see as the structural drawbacks to regional democratization. If a polity has more anti-democracy than pro-democracy structures, then this will be a powerful inhibitory factor making the achievement of democracy very difficult. We also noted the importance of contingency factors in chapter 1, such as the personal preferences of powerful political leaders and the impact of a range of sometimes one-off external factors, such as significant oil price rises and falls.

External actors did not clearly encourage democracy in the Middle East in recent times. Instead, the collapse of the Soviet Union and the contemporaneous regional fallout from the Gulf War of 1991 led to tentative moves towards democracy in some countries of the region, but greater repression in others. It is also difficult to detect in the recent political histories of Middle Eastern countries the kind of pro-democracy figure – such as Nelson Mandela – that was so important to democratic progress in South Africa.

Accounting for Democracy: The Comparative Importance of Domestic and External Factors

Our regional surveys suggest that we need to take into account a range of domestic and international factors when seeking to account for democratization and democracy in the countries of the developing world. However, while external encouragement can be important, domestic circumstances are of primary importance.

Domestic factors

Democratic advances are likely to be facilitated when three sets of domestic factors are in place:

1   comparatively unfragmented civil societies;
2   a reasonable amount of social capital;
3   cohesive party systems.

Civil society

There were many demands for democracy in numerous developing countries in the 1980s and 1990s. But there was only real and sustained democratic progress when there was consistent pressure from "below," focused in and through a strong civil society (Rueschemeyer, Stephens, and Stephens 1992; Haynes 1997, 2001a; Törnquist 1999). Yet civil society organizations do not only help push the limits of newly created political space. When capable of linking up with representative political parties they can be instrumental in helping to deliver democracy. Such pressure was often instrumental in encouraging authoritarian governments to announce programs of democratic reform, articulate political reform agendas and, eventually, allow relatively free and fair multi-party elections.

The term "civil society" not only crept quietly and largely unexamined into the literature on political economy in the 1980s, but also began to be heard in the discourse of many opposition leaders in developing countries. However, civil society is not a new term. Often associated with the German philosopher Hegel (1770–1831), it appeared in the literature on Western political philosophy from the time of the emergence of the modern nation-state in the eighteenth century. It is significant that it has reappeared at a point in history when the capabilities of existing governments even minimally to satisfy the political and economic aspirations of nationalities and ethnic communities are increasingly called into question.

At the present time, the expression "civil society" is often "used to describe associations and other organized bodies which are intermediate between the state and the family" (Bealey 1999: 59), including labor unions, peasant organizations, grassroots movements, professional associations, student groups, religious bodies, and the media. Collectively, such entities help maintain a check on states' power and totalizing tendency; ideally, they amount to an ensemble of arrangements to advance the sociopolitical interests of society, with the state and civil society forming mutually effective counterweights (Stepan 1988). Sturdy civil societies nearly always stem from strong societies. For Risse-Kappen, "'strong societies' are characterized by a comparative lack of ideological and class cleavages, by rather 'politicized' civil societies which can be easily mobilized for political causes, and by centralized social organizations such as business, labor or churches" (Risse-Kappen 1995: 22). In sum, civil society is a key defender of society's interests against state (over-)dominance.

Civil society organizations are not directly involved in the business of government or in overt political management, but it does not prevent them from exercising sometimes profound political influence on various matters, from single issues to the characteristics of national constitutions. Shown by recent events, such as in Eastern Europe in 1989–91 when seemingly strong communist regimes swiftly toppled like dominoes, well-organized and determined civil society can destroy an authoritarian regime. But to take the next steps, from the collapse of authoritarianism, through a democratic transition to a consolidated democracy, additionally requires the active involvement of *political society*. Political society is the "arena in which the polity specifically arranges itself for political contestation to gain control over public power and the state apparatus" (Stepan 1988: 3). The construction and development of a democratic polity requires a great deal of serious thought and action about its core institutions – including political parties, elections, electoral rules, political leadership, intra-party alliances, and legislatures – and most work in this regard will come from political society. In sum, both conceptually and empirically civil society is linked to, but separate from, political society. Through the latter, civil society can constitute itself politically to help select and monitor government performance. However, the conception of civil society discussed above is an ideal one, most reflective of the situation in mature democracies, such as those in Germany, Sweden, or France.

Three broad categories of civil society can be identified in the countries of the developing world:

1 Weak civil societies (found in most African and Middle Eastern countries).
2 Maturing civil societies (found in some East and Southeast Asian countries, such as South Korea, Taiwan, and the Philippines).
3 Relatively strong civil societies (located, for example, in India and several Latin American countries, such as Argentina and Chile).

Most African and Middle Eastern countries have weak and fragmented civil societies, ineffective as counterweights to state power. Regarding Africa, Robert McNamara, a former president of the World Bank, puts the problem of civil society thus: "Africa faces problems of governance which are . . . far more severe than those of other regions" (quoted in Harsch 1996: 24), with inadequate popular participation and transparency and accountability in government operations. Villalón argues that failure or inability "of social groups to organize in such a way as to defend and promote their interests" seriously reduces the capacity to "counter the state's hegemonic drives" (Villalón 1995: 24).

Like most African governments, regimes in the Middle East have often shown themselves adept at buying off or, if necessary, crushing expressions of discontent. Bromley (1994: 166) links this power to the region's weak and divided civil societies, likely to be an important problem in the "future process of democratization." Said (1996) asks rhetorically why "real" – that is, effective – civil societies are lacking in the Arab societies of the Middle East. For him, civil society is frail for reasons similar to those found in Africa: there are often strong states, while civil societies are fragmented because of ethnic and/or religious divisions.

Turning to Asia, several countries, notably India, are said to have strong civil societies. India's civil society is both vibrant and robust, with many civil rights organizations and local protest movements, while that of Pakistan is relatively underdeveloped. In the Philippines, the turn to democracy in 1986, delivered by "popular power," not only reflected societal outrage at the incompetence and corruption of the Marcos regime, but also a relatively strong civil society. Democratization occurred in the Philippines as a result of (1) an active civil society, with a high degree of associational activity; (2) emerging democratic institutions (despite serious economic setbacks in the late 1990s, the country's democratic institutions were said to have stood up "robustly" (Putzel 1999: 214)); (3) a flourishing, critical media, with dozens of Manila-based newspapers, as well as provincial newspapers; and (4) public opinion favoring democracy over other imaginable political systems: large percentages have regularly turned out to vote, averaging around 70 percent in presidential and legislative polls since 1986 (IDEA 1998). Elsewhere in Asia, for example in Taiwan and South Korea, recent democratic advances are linked to gradual maturing and strengthening of civil society (Shin 1999)

Compared to many Asian and most African and Middle Eastern nations, Latin American countries tend to have stronger civil societies, for three reasons: (1) they have had longer to develop: most Latin American countries gained independence nearly 200 years ago; (2) they are typically less divided by ethnic and religious schisms than, for example, many African, Asian, and Middle Eastern nations; (3) many are relatively industrialized and urbanized: this encourages politically active working classes and well-organized trade unions

In sum, the effectiveness of civil society varies according to four main factors:

1   The degree of societal cohesiveness, linked to the amount of social capital.
2   The level of economic development and industrialization.
3   The length of independence from colonial rule.
4   The degree of societal – especially ethnic and religious – diversity.

Social capital

Civil society is most effective when it builds upon society's store of social connections, that is, its *social capital*. Whereas *human* capital comprises formal education and training, and *economic* capital is material and financial resources, *social* capital is defined by Törnquist as the "interpersonal trust that makes it easier for people to do things together, neutralize free riders, and . . . agree on sanctions against nonperforming governments" (Törnquist 1999: 95). Robert Putnam (1993, 1999), an American political scientist, has analyzed the importance of social capital in helping build and sustain democracy. He argues that the level of trust in a society varies according to the vibrancy of associational life. "As done in Italy and Spain, the stock of social capital from both extensive and growing membership in voluntary associations is likely to promote the deepening of . . . democracy" (Shin 1999: 132). Portes and Zhou (1992) identify two main relational characteristics of social capital: first, what they call "bonded solidarity," that is, the sense of common nationhood and cultural identity which helps focus group resources. Second, the "enforceable trust" that controls the mutual assistance supplied and demanded, permitting a higher degree of resource sharing than would be conceivable through more informal channels.

Creation of social capital in developing countries is often undermined by the presence of some or all of the following factors.

●   inefficient government performance;
●   authoritarian regimes that frown on the growth of societal solidarity;
●   widespread societal hardship;
●   social disintegration, due in part to development shortfalls.

Under such circumstances, it will normally be very difficult to build recognizably democratic political systems.

Political parties

The chances of democracy taking root, Sartori (1991) argues, are bolstered when there are relatively few, not ideologically polarized, political parties competing for power. In addition, autonomous, democratically organized political parties can help to keep the personal power aspirations of political leaders in check. Morlino (1998) argues that such political parties are crucial to democratic consolidation, especially when a pervasive pro-democracy legitimacy does not prevail during democratic transition. He also contends that the more rapidly the party spectrum forms during transition, then the more likely is eventual democratic consolidation. When party systems become institutionalized in this way, parties typically orient themselves toward the goal of winning elections through choate appeals to voters. But when the party structure is only slowly established, then citizens may respond better to personalistic appeals from populist leaders rather than to those of parties. This scenario tends to favor the former, who may attempt to govern without bothering to establish and develop solid institutions underpinning their rule. The point is that institutionalizing party systems matters a great deal, as they are much more likely to help sustain democracy and to promote effective governance than the alternative: amorphous party systems dominated by populist leaders. An institutionalized party system can help engender confidence in the democratic process in four main ways. First, it can help moderate and channel societal demands into an institutionalized environment of conflict resolution. For example, in both India and Costa Rica the party system helped over time to prevent "landed upper class[es] from using the state to repress protests" (Rueschemeyer, Stephens, and Stephens 1992: 281). Second, it can serve to lengthen the time horizons of actors because it provides electoral losers with the means periodically to mobilize resources for later rounds of political competition. Third, an effective party system can help prevent disenchanted groups' grievances from spilling over into mass street protests, likely to antagonize elites and their military allies and help facilitate a return to authoritarian rule ("the need for strong government"). Fourth, an effective party system, linked to a capable state, can be important in helping imbue the mass of ordinary people with the idea that the political system is democratically accountable.

External factors

It is often suggested that three sets of external factors were of importance in recent shifts to democracy in the developing world:

1　Background factors
2　State actors
3　Non-state actors

Let us look at each in turn.

Background factors

Background factors, such as a favorable or unfavorable geostrategic circumstances, can be important to democratization and democracy. This can be seen in relation to earlier periods of attempted democratization in the developing world. For example, in the 1930s, tentative democratization in Latin America could not make headway against a background of regional and global economic depression. In the 1960s and 1970s, fears of the Cuban revolution spreading led to a regional crackdown on calls for democracy.

Suddenly, in the 1980s, global circumstances became more advantageous for democracy, particularly with the unforeseen collapse of European communist states. However, as we have seen, not all developing regions moved to democracy at the same pace and with the same enthusiasm. For example, in the Middle East, where the influence of the USSR had long facilitated the continuity of the region's centralized control models of government, there was no shift to widespread democracy (Nonneman 2001). Part of the reason was that many non-democratic Middle Eastern countries are major oil producers: for example, Saudi Arabia, the Gulf Emirates, Libya. State control of oil wealth helped governments ignore any popular demands for democracy and, in addition, Western calls for political reforms in the Middle East tended to be muted. This was partly due to the already destabilizing effect of the continuing Arab–Israeli conflict and the desire to maintain a fragile political stability.

State actors

Prospects for democracy, already improved with the collapse of the European communist systems, were encouraged further by Western governments, including the largest aid donors in quantitative terms: the USA, Japan, France, and Britain. Many Western governments introduced "political conditionalities" linked to the provision of foreign aid. There were two sides to this policy: "positive" assistance, to encourage democratic development with promises of increased aid, and "negative" aid sanctions to leverage reform from unwilling recipient governments. However, as Crawford (2001) discovered, aid sanctions undertaken by Sweden, Britain, the US, and the EU in the early 1990s helped promote political reform in only 11 of the 29 cases where they were applied. Crawford finds that aid penalties were most effective where governments were also subject to internal pressures for reform. He also found that aid penalties failed where they met strong resistance from recipient governments or where they threatened the strategic or commercial interests of donors.

Non-state actors

Cross-border, non-state actors make up what is known as "transnational (or 'global') civil society." The concept has three main components. First, like domestic civil society, the term encompasses neither governmental groups nor profit-seeking private entities, like transnational corporations (TNCs). Second, such groups are transnational – that is, they interact across state boundaries, often beyond the control of governments. Third, transnational civil society can take a variety of forms, for example, a single international nongovernmental organization (INGO) with individual members or chapters in several countries, such as Transparency International. Or it can be a more ad hoc border-crossing coalition of organizations and associations, such as the International Campaign to Ban Land mines, formed to campaign on a certain issue. Several questions are commonly asked in relation to transnational civil society. *Why* does transnational civil society exist? *How* does it manage to influence powerful states and rich TNCs? *Why* should people scattered around the globe bother to use their unpaid time and energy to work together with other individuals and groups with whom they share neither history nor culture?

To answer such questions we must note, first, that transnational civil society differs both from states and TNCs in key respects. For example, states have sovereignty: they exist within clearly defined physical territories; they have the power to elicit resources from the territory and populations they control; they command legal recognition from other states; and at least theoretically they can appeal to citizens' patriotism to cement loyalties to the state. Transnational civil society also differs from transnational corporations, whose constituent parts are linked by common economic interests and legal obligations. Why then does it exist? Transnational civil society networks – which some contend are an emerging "third force" in international politics – typically aim for broader goals based on their conceptions of the public good. Consequently, such groups are bound together not primarily by self-interest but by shared values. However, the values they embrace differ considerably, ranging from a belief in animals rights, through conviction that democracy is a global right of all peoples, to the inherent superiority of some ethnic groups over others.

We have seen in this section that a variety of domestic and external factors are linked to democratization and democracy in the countries of the developing world. Next, we move to an assessment of these factors in two very different democratizing countries: South Africa and Indonesia.

Case Studies: South Africa and Indonesia

South Africa and Indonesia have been selected for the following reasons. First, both are very much in the news. Second, they each represent very different democratic trajectories: since democratization in 1994, South Africa has been a *cause célèbre*. While the legacy of apartheid was expected to be a huge impediment to democratization, there are indications of democracy taking root in inauspicious surroundings. Indonesia, on the other hand, is more typical of democratization outcomes in the third wave: it has been inconclusive. Third, both country examples not only show the importance of internal and external actors but highlight that outcomes differ from country to country according to a range of structural and contingent factors. In the case of South Africa, apparently unhelpful structural factors – especially half a century of white-dominated, apartheid rule – seemed to be overcome, not least due to the commitment of individual political leaders, especially Nelson Mandela and F. W. de Klerk. In Indonesia, on the other hand, Abdurrhaman Wahid, democratically elected president in 1999 but deposed in mid-2001, claimed to be a democrat, but he was unable to overcome the negative structural impact of three decades of authoritarian rule, the influential anti-democracy political role of the military, and the country's ethnic fragmentation. It remains to be seen whether his successor, Megawati Sukarnoputri, will fare any better.

South Africa

We examine two main issues in this section. First, we look at the crucial roles in South Africa's democratization of Nelson Mandela, anti-apartheid hero and, from 1994 until his retirement in 1999, national president, and the last apartheid-era leader, F. W. de Klerk. However, the second issue highlights the relatively fleeting impact of contingent factors in South Africa's medium- and long-term democratic outcome. Once the democratic transition was over, characterized by the initial post-apartheid elections in 1994, the country's structural characteristics reasserted themselves. It appeared to some observers that democratization had in fact changed little in terms of the distribution of power. We examine the issues under the following headings, which are of importance when assessing democratic progress in a country:

- political culture and regime legitimacy;
- democratic transition;
- political participation and institutions;
- external and economic factors.

South Africa is a country of more than 40 million people. About 10 percent are white and of European origin, a similar proportion to "coloreds" – that is, people of mixed white European and black African racial characteristics. The remainder, over 30 million, are black Africans. This unusual racial mix is one of the reasons why South Africa is not a "typical" African country. Another is that the country is very wealthy in African terms: its GNP per capita of US$3,160 in 1999 made it the richest regional nation (World Bank 2001: 275). However, there has traditionally been an extreme polarization in wealth between black South Africans and most whites, while the former enjoyed few political rights until 1994.

Political culture and regime legitimacy

South Africa was ruled by exclusively white governments for decades prior to a shift to democracy in 1994. The change to democracy came in three swift stages: collapse of apartheid rule; democratic transition; attempts to consolidate democracy. The collapse of the apartheid system and the democratic transition were encouraged by both domestic and international factors.

Domestically, apartheid had long been embraced by many white South Africans as a way, they believed, to ensure political order and their domination over blacks and coloreds. But this justification began to evaporate following a serious black insurrection in the mid-1980s. This suggested that the apartheid system, rather than providing order, instead led to serious opposition and unrest, including civil disobedience, strikes, and riots. Further, pressure from civil society organizations encouraged democratization, while the declining economic situation also encouraged demands for change. Adding to the pressure were various external factors, including direct (governmental, non-governmental, moral, economic, diplomatic, military) pressures, the indirect influence of global economic relations, and diffusion and demonstration effects – especially the collapse of communist rule in Eastern Europe.

McGarry suggests that democratic transition occurred not because the dominant white group "came to [its] senses, but because it became sensible for [it], because of the changing environments [it] faced, to reach agreement" (McGarry 1998: 855). Guelke (1999) argues that President de Klerk's National Party (NP) government calculated that Mandela's African National Congress (ANC) was seriously weakened by the demise of the USSR and the associated loss of support to the extent that it would be anxious to negotiate a settlement to the political conflict. Another interpretation is that the government reached a settlement in 1994, not so much because it became persuaded by the activities of liberal civil society activists (as President de Klerk's consistent refusal to apologize for apartheid appeared to indicate), but principally because of changing circumstances at home and abroad. That is, interrelated external and internal pressures were pivotal in persuading the de Klerk government to seek and secure a negotiated settlement.

De Klerk was well aware that the proportion of whites among South Africa's population, which held steady at around 20 percent between 1910 and 1960, had dropped to 15 percent by 1985, and was projected to fall to 11 percent by 2010. The belief was that this waning demographic presence ultimately would endanger the ability of the white minority to occupy strategic positions in the state apparatus and economy, and to run and staff the institutions of apartheid. McGarry suggests that the looming demographic crisis was an important factor encouraging President de Klerk to put forward the prospect of a negotiated settlement that would be "indispensable for the survival of the whites as a shrinking minority" (McGarry 1998: 863). In sum, "South African whites were brought together to negotiate because of a range of domestic crises and diffuse international pressures" (ibid: 855).

Democratic transition

It was a surprise to many that South Africa's turn to democracy was accompanied without the feared racial conflagration threatened by dissident groups, such as Eugene Terre' Blanche's Afrikaner Resistance Movement or Chief Buthelezi's Inkatha Freedom Party. The threat was dissipated, it is suggested, in part because of the strong desire of mainstream politicians, both black and white, to make the new democracy work.

Democratic reforms were, unusually for Africa, the result of what is known as a "pacted" transition. South Africa's transition could be described as a textbook example of the situation outlined by Huntington: conflicting political groupings "can neither do without each other nor unilaterally impose their preferred solution on each other if they are to satisfy their respective divergent interests" (Huntington 1991: 141–2). The terms of the pact between the two sides – black and white – involved, at least in the short term, not a majoritarian democracy but a power-sharing agreement preserving many of the institutions of the former regime and, critics allege, avoiding a meaningful redistribution of economic resources. In addition, transition theory suggests that a precondition for elite-pacted democratization is the preservation of capitalist institutions through the public suppression of "extremists" and radicals and the incorporation and cooption of political leaders who, if left outside the negotiations, might disturb the balance of the agreement the "moderates" were attempting to construct (Przeworski 1991). Once agreement on the political way forward was reached, however, it proved impossible for the ANC and the NP together to impose their terms on the other interest groups that had been involved in the negotiations. As Kiloh remarks, "for a pact to be successful it is necessary for the parties to it to guarantee the support of their followers by buying off or disciplining extremist wings. In South Africa this was not possible as opposition to the agreement came from those excluded by it who had already spun out of control of the two main protagonists" (Kiloh 1997: 318).

Contingency was important for the democratic transition in South Africa and, central to this, was the almost unparalleled statesmanship of Nelson Mandela, a man incarcerated for nearly three decades in one of the country's most notorious jails until his release in 1990. The mod-

erate stance of the most important opposition group – Mandela's ANC
– was crucial to the government's willingness to negotiate. Although
Mandela had suspended the ANC's "armed struggle" only *after* the
start of negotiations, this struggle had actually been rather tame, hardly
ever directed against the white population per se. And, unlike the more
radical Pan-African Congress, leading ANC figures went out of their
way to assuage white fears, reassuring the white community that South
Africa belonged to *all* of its citizens. Mandela's moderation also encouraged the development of a desire for limited change among many
whites: not only was he a supremely important, although aging politician; there were also fears that his anointed successor, Thabo Mbeki,
would be distinctly less accommodating to the white constituency. And
while the ANC insisted on and ultimately achieved majority rule, it
reassured many whites, including even some among the most conservative Afrikaners, that their culture would be accommodated in the new
order. Finally, the ANC's movement away from socialist economics in
the late 1980s helped to reassure whites that they could retain private
power while releasing their grip on the public variety.

In sum, the pacted transition to democracy in South Africa assuaged
fears among many whites that a Mandela-led regime would be "too
radical"; the settlement with the ANC posed little or no existential threat,
whether physically or culturally. Taylor (n.d.: 9) argues that white and
black elites cooperated in helping create a political climate wherein radical changes were impossible.

Political participation and institutions

We noted earlier in the chapter the positive role of a consolidated party
system for democratic progress: it provides a forum for political actors
to compete legitimately to exercise the right to control power and the
state apparatus (Linz and Stepan 1996). In addition, autonomous political parties can help keep power holders in check. It is for this reason
that political parties are sometimes seen as *the* key to democratic consolidation, especially when, as in South Africa, a pervasive legitimacy
has not prevailed during the process of democratization. The point is
that the more rapidly the party spectrum forms during transition, then
the more likely is progress towards democratic consolidation. In inchoate – that is, not consolidated – party systems voters tend to respond to
personalistic appeals rather than party affiliation, favoring populist leaders who govern without attempting to establish solid institutional foundations for their rule.

Following transition, South Africa quickly consolidated its party system under the hegemony of the ANC. The ANC won an emphatic electoral victory in the 1994 elections, winning nearly 63 percent of the vote on a massive turnout: more than 85 percent of the voting-age population cast their ballots. Mandela was voted president by a unanimous vote of the new Assembly. The ANC underlined its dominance five years later, when, in the 1999 elections, it gained just under two-thirds (66.4 percent) of the vote. Its dominance was made clear when no other party could muster even 10 percent of the vote: the leading opposition party, the Democratic Party, achieved slightly more than 9 percent; the Inkatha Freedom Party managed 8.6 percent; and the erstwhile governing party, the National Party, gained under 6 percent. While the result of the second elections appeared to confirm that South Africa had a party system conducive to democratic consolidation, there were also fears that the dominance of the ANC might lead it to rewrite the constitution – which it could do if it gained two-thirds of the popular vote – and proceed to rule in a manner unhelpful to the well-being of the white minority.

External and economic factors

Apartheid's collapse was facilitated by South Africa's increasingly serious economic position. Strong economic growth in the 1960s and 1970s gave way, in the 1980s and early 1990s, to stagnation and then decline. The declining economic situation was reflected in an average annual *negative* GNP growth rate during 1985–95 of 1.1 percent (World Bank 1997: 215). Economic decline, which many believed was linked to the continuation of the apartheid system – because it discouraged both external and domestic investors – threatened whites' material privileges while narrowing governmental options. It not only affected the state's ability to buy off the emerging black middle class but also, given the rising cost of defense expenditures, threw into increasing question the state's ability to defend itself. Finally, international economic sanctions, reinforced by cultural, academic, and sporting boycotts, effectively cut whites off from the Western community with which they identified. This made many feel very isolated.

Once in power, ANC plans for large-scale nationalization and redistribution of resources were abandoned and more moderate liberalization of the highly protected South African economy substituted. It soon became clear that, following the democratic transition and the installation of the ANC government, many leading figures within the government, including President Mandela, were strongly in favor of a mixed economy. Some observers argue that this strategy was chosen because the "pro-capitalism" strand within the ANC had become dominant within the party, the spearhead of an emerging black bourgeoisie. Enthusiastically accepting the basic tenets of economic neoliberalism, the main goal of such people was to acquire a larger slice of the economic cake. However, while a capitalist development strategy suited a powerful group in and close to the ANC, who materially benefited from the strategy, it was less clear that many poor black South Africans benefited economically under the arrangements. Skeptics argued that the government's economic policies, with their emphasis on business and the free market, encouraged both corruption and a culture of acquisitiveness at the apex of the government. Such a development, it was feared, was unlikely to be conducive to democratic consolidation, not only reliant on a perception that economic gains were being shared relatively equitably but also on the institutionalization of a representative political system able to channel and regulate societal demands.

Rather than narrowing the gap between the majority of poor South Africans and the minority rich elite, commentators suggest that democratization led to an increased wealth imbalance in the country. This is most clearly seen in the polarization between a new black elite and the poor black majority: by the early 2000s, more than half a decade after democratization, the richest 20 percent of blacks acquired nearly two-thirds of all the income brought in by black workers. This led to growing concern, especially among trade union activists, that the government had done too little to redress the legacies of apartheid rule. The government responded, however, that to increase the size of the economic cake so that all South Africans would benefit necessitated a strategy which looked to the global picture: to compete, South Africa had to offer an attractive economic context to potential and current foreign investors.

The concern was that, nearly a decade after apartheid rule came to an end, the enormous hopes generated by the country's political transition had given way for many poor South Africans to the disappointing realities of frustrated change. The government's response was that nothing would be gained by radical policies of wealth redistribution that would frighten off potential foreign and domestic investors. Mandela's presidential successor, Thabo Mbeki, pointed out that, whatever government was in power, the nature of the country's involvement in the global economy would severely constrain governmental ability to bring about a significant shift in economic resources from the rich minority to the poor majority. South Africa had to compete internationally, which meant that its economy had to be competitive. The problem for political stability, however, was that although South Africa is the richest African country, at least a quarter of the population – nearly all non-whites – lives below the poverty line. But to provide necessary conditions for large increases in wages and employment which the influential trade union confederation COSATU demanded, it would have been necessary for the economy to grow substantially year-on-year; and this, the government argued, could only be accomplished if businesses and investors remained in the country, and new ones came in.

South Africa's democratic transition in 1994 was the result of both domestic and external pressures. The motivation of the apartheid government to allow democratization, involving the enfranchisement of non-whites, was partly an acknowledgment of the importance of the global economy and South Africa's place within it. But to compete within the global economy it was necessary, the Mandela and Mbeki governments claimed, to put in place conservative economic policies that did not seek to redistribute wealth. Given the skewed nature of the South African economy – with whites receiving the lion's share of available resources – the government's failure to redress the situation led to a growing collapse in support for the ANC regime from its crucially important trade union ally, COSATU, which claimed that its conservative policies risked a political crisis.

Indonesia

Indonesia is the most populous country in East and Southeast Asia, with over 200 million people. It comprises over 13,500 islands fringing the equator for a distance of 5,000 kilometers, stretching from the Asian mainland to Australia. Java, Sumatra, and Borneo are the principal islands and contain most of the population, mostly of Malay stock but also including around 4 million ethnic Chinese. Following independence in 1947 from Dutch colonial rule the country endured nearly two decades of political instability before power was seized in 1965 by General Suharto. From then, until the latter stood down in 1998, Indonesia experienced decades of political stability, albeit under a regime which, Putzel (1997) claimed, was among the most authoritarian in the world. But things eventually began to fall apart politically. By 1998, as Suharto aged and his personal power declined, Hewison characterized Indonesia's political system as *"crumbling* authoritarianism" (Hewison 1999:

224; emphasis added). Later that year, Suharto's regime crashed, ushering in a period of both instability and tentative democratization. As in the case of South Africa, we examine the issues under the following headings:

- political culture and regime legitimacy;
- democratic transition;
- political participation and institutions;
- external and economic factors.

Political culture and regime legitimacy

For three decades prior to Suharto's fall, Indonesia had been regarded as a prime example of an East Asian "developmental state": that is, economically successful, and with a stable political system, under the control of an authoritarian government (Leftwich 2000). The political changes of 1998 were preceded the year before by a serious economic upheaval, which most observers regarded as pivotal to the fall of Suharto. The outcome was that he was forced to stand down following popular pressure, including street demonstrations in the capital, Jakarta. His temporary successor, B. J.Habibie, tried to make piecemeal reforms, but was soon replaced in 1999 by a popularly elected president, Abdurrhaman Wahid.

The decline and demise of Suharto's authoritarian rule encouraged the rise of an increasingly confident, yet fragmented, civil society, temporarily united only by the demand for fundamental political changes. By 2001, three years after Suharto's downfall, the situation was stalemate between, on the one hand, a regime apparently unwilling to countenance fundamental reforms and, on the other, a vibrant civil society seeking to accomplish major political changes but stymied by serious urban–rural, class, regional, ethnic, and religious divisions. The possibilities for democratic consolidation in Indonesia seemed to depend very much on whether the idea of democracy could take hold, incorporated into the criteria by which government in Indonesia is popularly regarded as legitimate.

Democratic transition

After seizing power in 1965, General Suharto and his regime spent much time and effort on the consolidation of power; by the 1980s the government had managed to entrench itself in power. This was accomplished in part by restricting the activities of already tame opposition political parties. In addition, the security and political role of the armed forces, known as *dwifungsi* ("dual function") was reinforced. Election victories were efficiently organized both for Suharto's political party, Golkar, and for the president himself. In 1983 he was authorized as president for a fourth term. Suharto seemed to be unchallenged, at the pinnacle of his power. However, as Hewison notes, the downfall both of Suharto and his regime can be traced to this period. Although political control was constantly asserted, "economic problems were forcing economic change, including liberalization and market-oriented reforms. These reforms had a remarkable impact on economic power, and provided considerable impetus to political opposition" (Hewison 1999: 235) Not that this was clear at the time. In the late 1980s the regime seemed not only to have weathered the economic problems but also to be maintaining a tight political control, reflected in the fact that Golkar continued to win elections with huge majorities and, for the first time, to move beyond its long-term reliance on the armed forces. However, signs of limited political competition were reflected in the fact that there was a sudden move to limited competition among the political elites and a destabilizing discussion regarding the post-Suharto succession and political arrangements. More concretely, pressure for change began to surface among certain groups, including students and intellectuals, the press, and some Islamic organizations.

Surprising many, Suharto responded to these demands by speaking of the need for political reform and more open debate. This led to a brief opening of political space, but did not immediately lead to democratization. Instead, perhaps troubled by the eruption of criticism of his rule, Suharto soon moved to reinstate tight control, declaring that the existing system would not change. However, the political space, once granted, could not be entirely regained. This was partly because the opposition became increasingly heterogeneous, with critical groups found among both the middle and working classes, and, gradually, protests began to hot up: 1994 saw not only a series of protests in urban centers across the country but also financial scandals involving state figures, and labor unrest. The overall result was that the government's control was increasingly challenged (Törnquist 2001).

While the government sought to continue to limit the political space available to the opposition, its various elements were collectively undermining the foundations of the state's control. From the regime's point of view, the unwelcome situation was exacerbated not only by emerging rebellions in the islands of Aceh, East Timor, and Irian Jaya, but also by international criticism of the government's human rights record in these and other parts of the country. Overall, by the mid-1990s the available political space had been expanded, primarily by the actions of the opposition, and a slow democratic transition had begun.

The elections in 1997 coincided with another serious economic downturn which gave further impetus not only to demands for Suharto to resign but also an outburst of resentment against the entire Suharto family and the government. Suharto's survival strategy – gradually to oversee political reforms – was contemptuously rejected by the main opposition groups. Students and Muslim activists led the opposition to demand his resignation and – eventually – got it: on May 19, 1998 Suharto resigned, handing over to B. J. Habibie. Hewison (1999: 238) notes that the transition from Suharto's rule "may have had considerable orchestration by elements within the elite," but this did not prevent reform and the further expansion of political space. There was the release of some political prisoners, eventually concessions on independence for East Timor (but not for Aceh), investigations of human rights abuses, and greater freedom for the activities of trade unions, non-governmental organizations, and opposition parties. However, over the next three years there was political confusion as regimes rose and fell, while conditions close to civil war were felt throughout several parts of the country. This suggests that Indonesians may have had more political space than for three decades but the potential for further democratization is unclear.

Political participation and institutions: the political clout of the military

The case of Indonesia illustrates that to achieve democratic stability the important issue is not what religious or cultural system is in place; rather it is this: is there an "appropriate" civic culture – one characterized by relatively high levels of mutual trust among citizens, with societal tolerance of diversity, and an accompanying propensity for accommodation and compromise? When such factors are present, as some would argue is the case increasingly in South Africa, then they are likely to be encouraged by the work of democratic institutions over time, as they serve to encourage appropriately democratic values and beliefs among ordinary citizens and members of the political class.

There remain two main stumbling blocks to increased political participation and democratization in Indonesia: (1) the attitude of the politically powerful military, and (2) difficulties in achieving national integration incorporating the country's hundreds of ethnic groups. Since Indonesia's independence from the Netherlands in 1947, its military has regarded itself as the guardian of the nation-state and, despite democratization, has retained enormous power within state organizations. In short, the military played a powerful, perhaps dominant political role in the Suharto regime, and while it is clear that the aim is to reduce its political role, it is not certain how or when this would be managed.

During Suharto's rule the military was adept at crushing dissenting voices and separatist movements, as well as appointing active or retired officers to hold government jobs, from cabinet members to district heads. Golkar was set up by military officers in 1967; relying largely on intimidation and coercion, it won every election for the next 30 years. While the regime of Abdurrhaman Wahid (known as Gus Dur) elected to power in 1999 acted to advance civilian control, the military (and police) were still represented in the parliament (in both lower and upper houses). An act of parliament in January 1999 stipulated that the military's seats should be cut by half: from 75 to 38. It was anticipated that by 2009 neither group would have any representation in parliament. However, while Wahid moved to control the military, the results were mixed. So-called "rogue elements" were believed to be trying to destabilize Indonesia, as there were mysterious bombings and trouble, including in the rebellious island of Aceh and newly independent East Timor.

External and economic factors

Suharto's fall was welcomed by both the IMF – which blamed him for the country's serious economic slump – and the government of the USA – which saw his regime dragging Indonesia, and perhaps the region, into political turmoil. Later, the campaign to "impeach" (dismiss from office) the Wahid government, which saw success in July 2001, was tacitly supported by the US government, which did not believe that he could arrest the national decline. Wahid's successor, Megawati Sukarnoputri, enjoyed some support from the USA, although it was not convinced that she possessed the ability to turn things around.

This was not only because Indonesia's economic future remained cloudy but also because both civil society and the state were weak – hardly surprising in the case of the former, as many civil society organizations were parented by the state. Prior to the economic crisis of 1997, authoritarian politics had been dominant in Indonesia, a position maintained to a considerable degree by the fact that most ordinary citizens placed a high value on political stability and economic growth. This conservatism was facilitated by the fact that during the mid-1960s half a million or more Indonesians had been killed in a civil war between communist and non-communists. Memories of the violence and unrest characterizing that period, the time of rule by President Sukarno, continued to have considerable societal resonance decades later.

It is often suggested that problems of national integration are a serious impediment to the creation of a consensual political culture so important to democratization and democratic consolidation. In Indonesia, subnational identities – including religious, ethnic, linguistic, and "tribal" divisions – have had enormous "staying power." For decades, backed by the military, Indonesian authorities consistently alluded to separatist and ethnic divisions as a key justification for the perpetuation of authoritarian rule. Indeed, as Putzel presciently noted prior to the fall of Suharto in 1998, it was not "unimaginable that a quick transition to democratic politics could make Indonesia the Yugoslavia of Southeast Asia" (Putzel 1997: 264).

External support for democratization in Indonesia was undoubtedly significant in bringing pressure on its recalcitrant incumbent regime and helped to provide a favorable international setting for the newly elected government of Abdurrhaman Wahid in 1999. However, while Western pressure was an important catalyst in undermining Indonesia's authoritarian regime, following founding elections the West's impact on political outcomes diminished over time. But the overall point is that the importance of Western political conditionality declined, not only in Indonesia, but also more widely. This is because, generally speaking, Western governments became more interested in stability than democracy in most developing countries.

Conclusion

This chapter has suggested that, far from being a straightforward process, attempts to consolidate democratic systems are tied up politically with a number of issues. These include the ruling elite's control over society, the nature of a polity's political culture, the strength and effectiveness of civil society as a counterweight to state power, the political role of the military, and the overall impact of external factors and actors. We saw that while many formerly authoritarian developing countries democratized to some degree, overall, the impact of the third wave of democracy was patchy. In some countries, democratically dubious governments managed to stay in power – for example, those in Côte d'Ivoire, Cameroon, and Burkina Faso – by transforming themselves, via the ballot box in tightly controlled elections, into "democratic" governments. Elsewhere, some unelected rulers simply refused to budge and did not allow meaningful elections. Overall, in the developing world, over 40 countries – concentrated in the Middle East and Africa – were devoid of most democratic characteristics at the end of the 1990s (Karatnycky 1999: 124–5).

Democratization and democratic consolidation, once perceived as a fairly straightforward set of processes and structures, is actually a highly complex issue. There is not only the question of the relationship between economic and democratic progress – does the latter depend on the former? – but also the issue of the nature of interactions between state and civil society: how much political space does the former allow the latter? To what extent can civil society organizations collectively pressurize the state to deliver democracy?

To be democratically relevant, civil society will not merely be an ordering of elite groups, but will actively encourage involvement from those traditionally lacking political influence: the poor, women, the young, certain minority ethnic and religious groups. But, because such an extension and deepening of democracy will normally be resisted by those in power, legal guarantees and extensive protections for individual and group freedoms and associational life are crucial, to be secured by and through an independent, impartial judiciary. To increase welfare to those that need it, redistribution of scarce resources is both politically necessary and economically appropriate, while the military must be neutralized as political actors. Put another way, the consolidation of democracy necessarily implies a conscious effort to redress past imbalances, a course of action necessary so that the mass of ordinary people come to believe that democracy is a better system than alternative ones, such as benign dictatorship.

5

Religious and Ethnic Conflict

We have seen that the 1980s and 1990s were a time of major political, social, and economic change. These included the consolidation of what many see as a truly global economy and the steady, yet uneven, advance of democracy. These changes were linked to social and political instability in many developing countries, including new – or renewed – ethnic and religious conflicts.

The focus of chapter 5 is on religious and ethnic conflicts and is structured as follows. First, I offer a brief survey of religious and/or ethnic ("religio-ethnic") conflicts in the contemporary developing world. Second, I define religion and ethnicity and highlight their political and social salience in many developing countries. Third, I examine the importance of both domestic and external factors in conflicts characterized by religio-ethnic concerns. Fourth, I present a survey of contemporary religious and ethnic challenges to the state in the regions of the developing world.

In the early years of the twenty-first century it is difficult to find a developing region where religion or ethnicity are not somewhere near the top of social or political concerns. For example, in the Middle East Islamic fundamentalist groups – many of which draw inspiration both from Iran's Islamic revolution of 1978–80 and from the continuing Palestinian Intifada against Israel – fight the state.

Turning to South Asia, in Sri Lanka a three-decade civil war – between Buddhist Sinhalese and Hindu Tamils – has cost thousands of lives. Next door, in officially secular India, an explosion of militant Hinduism, focused on, but not confined to, the Babri Masjid mosque incident at Ayodhya in the early 1990s, served to transform India's political landscape. From that time, Hindu fundamentalists, mainly in the Bharatiya Janata Party (BJP), have achieved significant political gains.

Currently (late 2001), the BJP is the dominant party in the ruling coalition government.

Turning to East and Southeast Asia, in Thailand a Buddhist orientated political party emerged in the early 1990s, while in both Indonesia and the Philippines restive ethnic and religious minority groups have fought the state for years. In Indonesia the people of East Timor managed to acquire their independence in 1999, while their counterparts in Aceh seek the same objective.

Many African countries are also beset by religio-ethnic conflicts. For example, Nigeria is politically and socially polarized between Muslims and Christians, while some ethnic groups, such as the Ogonis, are in dispute with the government over the ownership of oil revenues. In addition, Sudan is now in its third decade of religio-ethnic conflict. In Sierra Leone, Liberia, Uganda, and the Democratic Republic of the Congo civil wars characterized by ethnic conflict continue.

Finally, Latin America has also seen ethnic conflicts, notably in Mexico, where the Zapatistas have been in conflict with the government since 1994, and in Brazil where indigenous Indians seek to fight the encroachment of outsiders on their land.

Defining Religion and Ethnicity

Religion

Religion has two analytically distinct yet related meanings. In a spiritual sense, religion pertains in three ways to models of social and individual behavior that help believers to organize their everyday lives. First, it is to do with the idea of transcendence; that is, it relates to supernatural realities. Second, it is concerned with sacredness; that is, it is a system of language and practice that organizes the world in terms of what is deemed holy. Third, it refers to ultimacy; that is, it relates people to the ultimate conditions of existence.

In a material sense, religion can motivate groups and individuals to act in pursuit of social or political goals. Very few – if any – religious groups have an absolute lack of concern for social and political issues. Consequently, religion can be "a mobilizer of masses, a controller of mass action . . . an excuse for repression [or] an ideological basis for dissent" (Calvert and Calvert 2001: 140). So numerous are recent examples of the interaction of religion and politics around the world, both within and between countries, that the American commentator, George Weigel, has claimed that there is a global religious revitalization: an "unsecularization of the world" (quoted in Huntington 1993: 26). In sum, religion is an important source of basic value orientations, often with social and/or political connotations.

How best to account for Weigel's claim of global "unsecularization"? The first thing to note is that there is no simple, clear-cut reason, no single theoretical explanation to cover all cases. But what does seem clear is that modernization – a period of historically unprecedented, diverse, massive change, characterized by urbanization, industrialization, and abrupt technological developments – has the ability to undermine traditional value systems. The result of modernization is that groups of people get allocated opportunities – both within and between countries – in highly unequal ways. Modernization also seems to have led in recent times to a diminishing belief in secular ideologies of change, such as socialism and communism. The overall result of modernization is that, in many countries, people feel increasingly disorientated and troubled and, as a result, turn or return to religion, perhaps with the aim of achieving a new or renewed feeling of identity, something to give their lives meaning and purpose.

A recent example that has attracted much attention are the various forms of what is often called religious fundamentalism. While it differs from place to place, and from religion to religion, all religious fundamentalist groups have in common the use of a "set of strategies, by which beleaguered believers attempt to preserve their distinctive identity as a people or group" in response to real or imagined attacks from non-believers who, it appears, are trying to draw them into a "syncretistic, areligious, or irreligious cultural milieu" (Marty and Appleby 1993: 3). Such a defense of religion can easily develop into a social or political offensive seeking to alter what is seen as an unacceptably anti-religious environment.

Religious beliefs can also reinforce ethnic consciousness and inform inter-ethnic conflict, not just in the developing world (think of Northern Ireland, Cyprus, or former Yugoslavia). A recent example of the link between ethnicity and religion comes from East Timor. There, popular resistance to Indonesian rule was reflected in a religious statistic: hundreds of thousands of ethnic Timorese converted to Catholicism after Indonesia's takeover in 1974. For many Timorese this was in order to differentiate themselves from the invader's Muslim culture, as more than 90 percent of Indonesians are followers of Islam.

Ethnicity

Bealey (1999: 123) defines ethnicity as "the characteristic of belonging to an ethnic group," involving identification "with people one sees as similar to one's self." But what makes ethnicity politically salient? Some commentators have posited a causal link between the end of the Cold War and an intensification of ethnopolitical conflicts in many parts of the world. This is said to be because the demise of the Soviet Union allowed dormant conflicts to resurface. Others contend that such conflicts were more a backlash against a cultural threat of global Americanization. However, data compiled by Gurr and Harff show that the number of ethnic conflicts grew fourfold between 1950–5 and 1985–90, that is, during the Cold War (Gurr 1994). Their data show

> that ethnopolitical conflicts were relatively common, and increased steadily, throughout the cold war . . . [T]he greatest absolute and proportional increase in numbers of groups involved in serious ethnopolitical conflicts occurred between the 1960s and 1970s, from 36 groups to 55. From the 1980s to the early 1990s the tally increased only by eight, from 62 to 70. Moreover, ongoing ethnopolitical conflicts that began [after the Cold War] are not appreciably more intense than those that began earlier. (MacFarlane 1999: 28)

This indicates that the end of the Cold War did not give the green light for ethnic groups to embark upon conflict, not least because many had already done so, often years earlier. Three conclusions can be drawn at this point: (1) ethnopolitical conflicts have been a significant feature of the global scene for half a century; (2) absolute numbers of such conflicts rose only slowly after the Cold War; and (3) among developing countries "the incidence of conflict has [not] increased (or decreased) since the end of the Cold War" (ibid: 26).

Let us next examine the political salience of ethnicity and religion in the developing world.

The Political Salience of Ethnicity and Religion in the Developing World: Domestic and International Factors

First, I present a typology of types of groups informed by religio-ethnic concerns. Second, I examine the influence on them of various domestic factors, by focusing upon, on the one hand, the difficulties of forging national identities in postcolonial developing countries and, on the other, the political consequences for developing countries of significant religious and/or ethnic fragmentation. I then examine the claim that the main threat to global order comes from Muslim and Confucian countries.

Domestic factors

While religio-ethnic groups take a variety of forms in the developing world, we can identify four broad types: (1) culturalist; (2) fundamentalist; (3) community-orientated; and (4) syncretistic. While differing in what they seek to achieve, what they have in common is that their leaders use religious and/or ethnic appeals to put forward a message of hope and a program of action, and seek to gain popular support to express and direct dissatisfaction with the status quo. Two types of groups – the fundamentalist and the culturalist – are often most antipathetic to the state, while syncretistic groups are defensive, seeking to counter outside interference to their way of life. Finally, community-orientated groups concern themselves primarily with self-help efforts rather than political issues. Similarities and differences between the groups are presented in table 5.1.

Culturalist groups

Culturalist groups are formed by minority peoples who believe they have particular ethnic and/or religious characteristics and are powerless as they are repressed by a dominant group in control of both political and economic resources. Culturalist groups organize for various reasons, including the pursuit of development goals, political autonomy, or even self-government. Examples come from many parts of the developing world, including the East Timorese, the Muslim minority in the Philippines, India's Sikhs, southern Sudanese Christian peoples (fighting the state's attempts to Islamicize and Arabize), Tibetan Buddhists in China, and the mostly Muslim Palestinians of Israel's occupied territories. In each case, the religion followed by the ethnic minority provides an important ideological aspect of what they do to rebuff attempts at domination by a dominant group.

Whether culturalist groups seek autonomy or independence depends largely on what appears to be possible as much as what is desirable. Achievement of autonomy within a state may be a good platform for eventual secession. The possibility of separatism obviously depends upon the existence of a specific territory that a secessionist group can call its own. However, particular problems exist when, as with the Kurds, their land lies across several countries (Iran, Iraq, Syria, and Turkey).

Separatist culturalist groups are not confined to Asia and Africa, but are also found in Latin America among indigenous Indians. Comprising about 10 percent of the region's population, most Indians are poor and uneducated, exist on the margins of society, and are politically powerless. Lately, however, such groups have begun to press for what they see as their rights, including the defense of their land, culture, and language. Across the region, as populations grow and the amount of vacant land fit for agriculture diminishes, pressure on the land occupied by indigenous peoples increases. Typically, the latter control land which outside interests – for example, the state, farmers, national or transnational corporations – want. In some cases, the Indians work with other, non-Indian groups to press for land redistribution, as well as enhanced economic opportunities and civil rights. For example, rubber tappers and Indians have joined forces in Brazil to defend forests against logging companies, while in Chiapas, Mexico, and on Nicaragua's eastern Pacific coast, Indians have taken part in armed uprisings against the state to press for political and economic reforms (Haynes 1997).

Syncretistic groups

Syncretistic groups are typically found among rural dwellers in several African and Latin American countries. Ethnic differentiation may form a component of syncretism, which refers primarily to systems of premodern religious belief, such as ancestor worship, healing, and shamanistic practices. A syncretistic community group will use religious beliefs and rituals to help defend their individuality and way of life in the face of threats from hostile outside forces – often, but not invariably, the state. Examples include the cult of Olivorismo in the Dominican Republic and Sendero Luminoso in Peru, whose ideology, a variant of Maoism, utilizes aspects of indigenous (i.e., pre-Christian) cultural–religious belief to attract peasants in Ayacucho. In addition, the *Napramas* of northeastern Mozambique have both premodern and Roman Catholic beliefs, which, in the early 1990s, helped them temporarily to defeat a South African-supported guerrilla movement, the Mozambique National Resistance (RENAMO). Other syncretistic groups are found elsewhere in Africa, including Uganda (The Lord's Resistance Army) and

Table 5.1   Types of religio-ethnic groups in developing countries and their political interaction with the state

	Culturalist	Fundamentalist	Community-orientated	Syncretistic
Objective	To use cultural separateness to seek to achieve autonomy in relation to centralized state (for example, Sikhs, Tibetans)	To protect self-proclaimed groups of "religiously pure" against state attempts to belittle religion (for example, HAMAS, FIS)	To direct community activities for enhancement of local groups' self-interest (for example, Basic Christian Communities, Latin American Indians)	To achieve higher political standing within national culture of diverse groups (for example, *Napramas* of Mozambique)
Perceptions of state and society	Aggregation of diverse groups with state structures dominated by one particular group	Society is dichotomized between believers and non-believers. State aims to extend its power to the cost of believers	Society comprises diverse interest groups. Local groups need to be aided so that self-interest can be protected and furthered	Society comprises diverse groups with one or several often dominating at state level
Perception of role of government	To prevent the full flowering of diversity	Regarded as seeking to undermine religion's societal roles	Seen as indifferent to plight of local communities	Seen as hostile or indifferent
Role in political process	May use vehicle of political party if government permits; if not, non-constitutional methods are likely	May fight elections if allowed. In addition, a wide range of other means may be employed to achieve political ends	Formally uninvolved, but activists may ally with political parties judged to be "progressive"	Will often remain outside formal political process and pursue goals via direct action, lobbying, negotiation with the state

Table 5.1 (*cont'd*)

	Culturalist	Fundamentalist	Community-orientated	Syncretistic
Citizen participation	Active participation of group members will be encouraged in pursuit of political goals	Individual interests seen as subordinate to interests of group	Popular participation essential to offset elite dominance	Individual interests seen as synonymous with community goals
Tactics to achieve goals	Any necessary means considered	Any necessary means considered	Lobbying of political elites and popular mobilization	Lobbying of political elites and popular mobilization

Zambia. Charismatic females, who lead struggles against the state in pursuit of various political goals, often head such groups (Haynes 1996).

Religious fundamentalists

In the developing world, religious fundamentalists are to be found among Buddhists, Christians, Hindus, and Muslims (Haynes 1993, 1996, 1998). Such people tend to live in population centers, or at least are closely linked with each other by electronic media. What they all have in common, irrespective of religious belief, is that they perceive their way of life to be under serious threat from hostile outside forces. What they seek to achieve is a reformation of society in accordance with religious tenets: to change laws, morality, social norms and, sometimes, political configurations to create a more tradition-orientated, less modern(ized) society.

As we shall see below when we examine Islamic fundamentalism, religious fundamentalists often struggle against governments because the latter's jurisdiction encompasses areas which the former hold as integral to the building of an appropriate society, including education, employment policy, and the nature of society's moral climate. They may also attack both "nominal" co-religionists, whom they perceive as lax in their religious duties, and members of "ungodly" religions and belief systems.

Community-orientated groups

Whereas each of the groups we have discussed so far target governments and other power holders, community-orientated groups, in contrast, principally work towards material improvements for their members. Usually, this does not involve conflict with the state because often the groups undertake to provide themselves with services that are officially the responsibility of government. The most prominent example of community-oriented groups in the developing world are the tens of thousands of Basic Christian Communities (BCCs) which developed since the late 1960s in predominantly Roman Catholic areas, including Latin America, parts of East Asia, and Africa. Typically, BCCs undertake a range of self-help projects – including literacy campaigns, environmental improvement efforts, and basic health endeavors. Although they are often apolitical, the basic idea behind the BCCs comes from the radical tenets of liberation theology. First articulated in Brazil in the early 1960s, liberation theology is an ideology that grew as a response to poor social and economic conditions. It is a radical form of Christianity that exhorts the dispossessed to take their futures into their own hands rather than relying on governments to change things for them (Haynes 1993: 95–121).

In conclusion, each of the four broad types of religio-ethnic groups are primarily concerned with the well-being and solidarity of communities who feel themselves under threat, whether from the state or from a lack of development. It is necessary to bear in mind, however, that the characteristics of the groups described are not necessarily exclusive to each. For example, fundamentalist groups may also be community orientated, while culturalist groups can also be syncretistic (Haynes 1995).

What does emerge from the analysis is that group perceptions of ethnic and/or religious separateness may lead to conflict with the state. We might expect it to follow from this that the political stability of a country with extensive religious and/or ethnic schisms will be low. Many countries in Latin America, South Asia, East and Southeast Asia, Africa, and the Middle East have pronounced religious fragmentation and/or multiple ethnic cleavages. Table 5.2 indicates developing countries with high levels of ethnic and religious fragmentation.

Cameroon, Chad, Côte d'Ivoire, Democratic Republic of Congo, India, Kenya, Liberia, Mali, Nigeria, Tanzania, and Uganda – score very high (0.8 or more) on the ethnic fragmentation index. Religious divisions, on the other hand, are pronounced in Cameroon, Central

African Republic, Chad, Côte d'Ivoire, Kenya, Liberia, Malawi, Mozambique, Rwanda, Tanzania, Togo, Trinidad & Tobago, and Uganda. Overall, table 5.2 indicates that 18 African countries, plus Indonesia and Malaysia, have to accommodate serious ethnic *and* religious cleavages. However, the data do not make it easy to give a clear response to the following question: does ethnic and/or religious fragmentation in a country lead to violent political conflict? The answer is: sometimes.

Of the 20 countries in table 5.2 that score highly on both ethnic and religious fragmentation indices, only six, all in Africa – Angola, Chad, Ethiopia, Liberia, Mozambique, and Uganda – have experienced civil wars since the early 1970s. More recently, in the mid-1990s, there was serious civil conflict in Burundi, Rwanda, and Somalia. In the first two countries the cause was ethnic rivalry – Hutu versus Tutsi – while in Somalia it was a result of inter-clan discord, rather than a more generalized ethnic or religious antagonism. Finally, it should be noted that none of these three countries appears in table 5.2 in relation to the ethnicity fragmentation criterion, and only Rwanda has a relatively high level of religious fragmentation.

Kaplan (1994: 44–76) has sought to explain religio-ethnic conflicts in Africa and Asia in relation to three main factors: (1) "cultural dysfunction"; (2) "loose family structures"; and (3) "communalism and animism." Kaplan portrays Africa's recent civil wars, including those in Liberia and Sierra Leone, as anarchic and primitive. He claims they are primarily caused by fixed ethnic and cultural realities, which make them beyond the reach of Western understanding and help. However, in failing to provide any meaningful analysis of the causes of the conflicts, Kaplan is content to focus upon the allegedly "uncivilized" and bizarre methods of the fighters in Liberia and Sierra Leone, including claims of cannibalism (Atkinson 1999: 106).

The anthropologist Paul Richards (1996) claims that Kaplan's analysis is an example of what Richards calls the "New Barbarism (NB) thesis." This is a type of analysis that works to mask or make unclear the actual power relations that inform and underpin most war situations. As Atkinson points out, a prominent omission in NB analyses in developing countries is the lack of material analysis of the postcolonial state (Atkinson 1999: 106). That is, NB analysis tends to overlook the primary role of states in many such conflicts. The state is important here because it is the location of concentrated competition for access to power and resources, as well as the place where the nature of links with the international economy are determined. Two points are worth underlining: (1) given the ethnic, religious, and/or regional divisions in many

Table 5.2   Ethnic and religious fragmentation in the developing world

Country	Ethnic fragmentation[a]	Religious fragmentation[b]
Africa		
Angola	0.80	0.49
Benin	0.75	0.53
Botswana	0.72	0.59
Cameroon	0.86	0.73
Central African Republic	0.74	0.63
Chad	0.80	0.70
Côte d'Ivoire	0.87	0.67
Democratic Republic of		
Congo	0.80	Low
Ethiopia	0.70	0.61
Kenya	0.86	0.69
Liberia	0.86	0.64
Malawi	0.65	0.73
Mozambique	0.75	0.62
Nigeria	0.88	Low
Rwanda	Low	0.64
Sierra Leone	0.78	0.57
South Africa	0.68	0.48
Tanzania	0.95	0.73
Togo	0.72	0.64
Uganda	0.92	0.66
East/Southeast Asia		
Indonesia	0.77	0.59
Laos	0.61	Low
Malaysia	0.71	0.55
Philippines	0.79	Low
South Asia		
India	0.90	Low
Nepal	0.69	Low
Pakistan	0.63	Low
Latin America		
Bolivia	0.70	Low
Ecuador	0.60	Low
Guatemala	0.58	Low
Peru	0.63	Low
Trinidad & Tobago	0.61	0.70
Uruguay	Low	0.49
Venezuela	0.54	Low

Table 5.2 (*cont'd*)

Country	Ethnic fragmentation[a]	Religious fragmentation[b]
The Middle East		
Afghanistan	0.63	Low
Iran	0.76	Low
Jordan	0.52	Low
Lebanon	Low	0.51
Morocco	0.53	Low

[a] Ethnic fragmentation index over 0.55 signifies a high level of ethnic fragmentation

[b] Religious fragmentation index over 0.45 signifies a high level of ethnic fragmentation

Source: adapted from data in Lane and Ersson (1994: 134–5)

developing countries, it is an extremely difficult task to build nation-states, and (2) seeking to expand underdeveloped economies to the point that economic growth becomes self-sustaining has also been problematic. It is for these reasons, rather than their allegedly anarchic and primitive characteristics, that many developing countries have experienced civil conflicts that have been expressed via religio-ethnic concerns.

However, as table 5.2 indicates, developing countries with theoretically glaring ethnic and/or religious divisions have not necessarily seen serious civil conflicts. Rather, their propensity in this regard may well depend on the extent to which the state is able to deal with popular concerns, especially the massive, rapid social and economic changes that characterize modernization. For example, postcolonial India had several factors apparently conducive to societal conflict: ethnic, caste, and religious diversity (Hinduism, Islam, Sikhism, Christianity, Jainism, and Buddhism). Yet the country inherited – and managed to maintain – Western-style democracy, while rapidly industrializing. Despite occasional ethnic and religious conflict, the Indian state has, since independence in 1947, managed to maintain the country's integrity and, apart from the 1975–7 "Emergency", a democratic political system. This suggests successive governments have managed adequately to deal with factors conducive to social conflict.

Religiously and ethnically diverse East Africa presents a different picture. After decades of European colonialism, following centuries of Arab and Islamic influence, East Africa's postcolonial states were, like

India's, based on Western models. However, governmental skill in dealing with potential societal schisms was much less apparent in East Africa than in India. After independence in the early 1960s no East African state managed to retain a democratic system for long. In addition, several countries saw religio-ethnic conflicts, including Somalia (where civil war broke out in the early 1990s, resulting in the creation of two separate states) and Kenya, where ethnic riots in October 1995 left five people dead.

Regarding East and Southeast Asia, religious and cultural determinants – especially Buddhism and Confucianism – were, after independence from colonial rule, juxtaposed with the Western idea of statehood and accompanying institutions: centralized government, monopoly of use of force, and comprehensive administrative structure. This was not sufficient, however, to eliminate ethnic and religious challenges to governments in several regional countries, including the Philippines, Thailand, and Indonesia. Finally, certain Latin American countries, including Brazil, Nicaragua, Peru, Bolivia, and Mexico, have important religio-ethnic minorities whose influence on national-level politics has already been noted.

In conclusion, modernization has contributed to a resurgence of religious and ethnic identity in many parts of the developing world. But it did not impinge upon an otherwise blank or uniform cultural and political situation; rather, the struggle to develop modern political institutions and a developed economy often conflicted with premodern social norms and traditions. Sometimes, but by no means invariably, ethnic and/or religious schisms led to serious political and societal conflicts. We saw, however, that it is difficult accurately to predict where or when ethnic or religious conflict will erupt by reference to a simple fragmentation model. Sometimes civil war has erupted in a religiously and ethnically homogeneous country – such as Somalia – but not in a neighboring state – Tanzania – with apparently higher levels of religious and ethnic fragmentation. What seems to be important is the level of governmental skill in achieving and maintaining a fair level of social solidarity able to transcend potentially serious cultural schisms.

International factors

The reemergence of religion as an international political actor in the late 1970s took many people by surprise. At that time Iran's Islamic revolution went against the conventional wisdom that societies would invariably secularize as they modernized and, as a consequence, religion would lose its sociopolitical importance. A decade later, the collapse of the Soviet Union and its communist empire encouraged the US president, George Bush, to speak confidently about the birth of a benign "new world order." But is was short-lived: the Gulf War of 1990–1 quickly dashed such optimism, to the extent that the West no longer strove for a qualitatively better world order but sought primarily to rebuild global stability. Many Western observers saw the brand of Muslim radicalism espoused by Iraq's leader, Saddam Hussein, as a significant threat to Western security. Further, the aggression of Muslim Iraq against Kuwait, a strong ally of the West, seemed to some to crystallize the new threat to global order: Islamic fundamentalism.

Huntington (1993) advanced the argument that the main threat to global peace in the future would be clashing "civilizations." That is, religiously and culturally distinct blocs of countries would fight each other. The main civilizational division Huntington alluded to was the "Christian democratic West" pitted against the Muslim and Confucian countries, with their different religious and social values. For Huntington, the invasion of Kuwait by Iraq in 1990 – and the ensuing struggle of Muslim Iraq's armed forces with United Nations troops – was a highly significant event, a catalyst in the emerging battle lines between the (Arab) Muslim world and the (Christian) West.

Huntington describes the West in religious–cultural terms, with its Christianity and democratic political cultures characterized by tolerance, belief in moderation, and consensus. Huntington sees Christianity as a religion spawning cultures highly efficacious to the growth of liberal democracy and, by extension, global peace and security. Huntington sees the collapse of dictatorships in Southern Europe and Latin America in the 1970s and 1980s, followed by the development of liberal democratic political norms (rule of law, free elections, civil rights), as conclusive proof not only of the synergy between Christianity and liberal democracy but also of their importance as foundations of global order.

In sum, for Huntington, the post-Cold War order was characterized by cultural and religious competition between the "Christian" West and authoritarian challengers, especially Islamic fundamentalism. Israel, with its dominant Jewish population, was seen as a staunch Western ally, while Hindu and Buddhist countries – such as India and Thailand – dismissed by Huntington as anti-democratic, were nevertheless seen as irrelevant in the coming "battle." Africa, economically marginalized and culturally inchoate, was also seen as peripheral.

Let us look next at the claim that the Confucian and Muslim countries pose a serious threat to global security and the well-being of the West.

Is Confucianism a threat to global order?

We saw in chapter 2 that several East Asian governments, including those of Malaysia and Singapore, argue that individualistic liberal democracy might be suited to the West but is not appropriate for their countries, allegedly characterized by a collective ethos. Are the Confucian countries (named after Confucius, a Chinese philosopher who lived from 551–479 BC) – and by extension those espousing "Asian values" – a threat to the West's security and well-being? Confucianism is often perceived by Western scholars as a "value system most congruent with Oriental authoritarianism" (King 1993: 141). Fukuyama, who suggests that Confucianism is "hierarchical and inegalitarian," highlights "the community-orientedness of Asian cultures" which can "originate in doctrines like Confucianism that have acquired the status of religion from being handed down through centuries of tradition" (Fukuyama 1992: 217, 325).

Many East Asian countries – including Singapore, China, Japan, South and North Korea, Taiwan, and Vietnam – have cultures rooted in Confucianism. China, North Korea, and Vietnam are, of course, three of the few remaining communist countries, while during the Cold War Japan, South Korea, Singapore, and Taiwan were all staunch ideological allies of the West. What seems to be the chief shared cultural characteristic of such countries is that they are community orientated rather than individualistic.

Weber noted that, in China, "Confucianism was the status ethic of prebendaries, of men with literary educations who were characterized by a secular rationalism" (Weber 1969: 21). It was important to belong to the cultured stratum; if one did not, he (much less she) did not count. The result was that the Confucian status ethic of this stratum not only determined the way of life in China itself, but also in those areas which came under Chinese influence, including the East Asian countries mentioned in the paragraph above. For example, Confucianism grew in Korea between the seventh and tenth centuries AD to become not only the ideological root of the system of government, but also "a religious or philosophical system which affected the social and cultural aspects of the nation's life" (Grayson 1989: 153).

Two of the most economically important Confucian countries, Taiwan and South Korea, recently democratized, while enjoying not only improved human rights records but also meaningful competition for state power through regular elections. In both countries there are now significant opposition parties and considerable civil and political liberties, with multiple freedoms: of expression, the press, to form organizations, and the right to demonstrate and to strike. Thus, three of the "Confucian" countries – South Korea, Taiwan, and Japan – have democratic systems and good human rights records. In addition, the tiny island state of Singapore, while claiming the appropriateness of its "Asian values," is nevertheless heavily pro-Western, although by no means fully democratic. On the other hand, both Vietnam and China are still officially communist countries, although increasingly opening up to Western influences. Only North Korea retains its communist aloofness, although things may be changing, as the country's increasingly dire poverty compels its leaders to deepen dialogue with former enemies in both South Korea and more widely. Overall, differences between "Confucian" states are more important than their alleged authoritarian similarities. There is very little – if anything – in the specter of a "Confucian" threat to global order.

In conclusion, the topic of "Confucian" values has been the subject of much critical discussion. Far from underpinning a culturally attuned and dynamic form of local democracy, critics see the Asian values debate as little more than an attempt by an influential set of authoritarian leaders to legitimate their own authority in the face of challenges from within, and criticisms from without. On the other hand, there is very little evidence that the continuing debate about the nature of Asian/Confucian values is set to erupt into a major international relations divide, as Huntington believes. Of much greater concern to many East and Southeast Asian leaders – for example, in Malaysia, the Philippines, and Indonesia – is the specter of Islamic radicalism. On this issue they are as one with Western governments; it also unites otherwise confrontational regimes in a shared fear of Islamic fundamentalism.

Islamic fundamentalism and global order

For Fukuyama (1992: 236), Islamic fundamentalism, with its "more than superficial resemblance to European fascism," is a serious threat to the West. However, it is one thing to argue that Islam has a different belief system to Christianity, but quite another to claim that Muslim countries *en masse* are about to enter into a period of international conflict. In fact, it has been argued that perceiving a collective Muslim threat to the West crucially overlooks one of its most salient characteristics: the Muslim world is neither united nor overwhelmingly enthused by the tenets of Islamic fundamentalism. This can be illustrated by what occurred after 1991 in Algeria.

In December 1991 Algeria held legislative elections which most independent observers characterized as among the freest ever held in the Arab Middle East. The following January, however, Algeria's armed forces seized power to prevent a probable electoral victory by an Islamic party, the Islamic Salvation Front (FIS). The assumption was that if the FIS achieved power it would summarily close down Algeria's newly refreshed democratic institutions and political system. A respected London-based weekly news magazine posed the question on many people's lips: "What is the point of an experiment in democracy if the first people it delivers to power are intent on dismantling it?" (The *Economist*, January 2, 1992). The answer might well be: as the electoral outcome is the popular will, it must be respected whatever the outcome. But Algeria's army had its own ideas. The FIS was summarily banned, thousands of its activists and supporters were thrown into prison without trial. But this did not prevent a civil war from breaking out between the state and the armed wing of FIS, *la groupe armée islamique* (GIA). Over the next decade, official figures indicate that more than 100,000 people died in a conflict which spilled over onto the streets of Paris. During the mid-1990s a brief bombing campaign was carried out in Paris by the GIA (Webster 1995). Despite Western fears, the struggle in the Islamic world of groups like the FIS was directed primarily against their own rulers rather than against the West *per se*. The bombing campaign in Paris by the GIA was justified by the FIS leaders because of France's support for the military junta in Algeria.

It is important to realize that, since the beginning of Islam over 1,000 years ago, Muslim critics of the status quo have periodically emerged to oppose what they perceive as unjust rule (Haynes 1998: 125–45). Contemporary Islamic fundamentalists see themselves as the most recent example in a long line of anti-ruler critics, and characterize themselves as the "just" involved in struggle against the "unjust." The dichotomy between "just" and "unjust" in the promotion of social change throughout Islamic history parallels the historic tension in the West between "state" and "civil society." The implication is that the "unjust" inhabit the state while the "just" look in from the outside, aching to reform the corrupt system.

Historically, the goal of the Islamically "just" was to form popular consultative mechanisms in line with the idea that the Muslim ruler was legitimately open to popular pressure and, as a result, would seek to settle problems brought to him by ordinary citizens. However, this concept of *shura* (consultation) should not be closely equated with the Western notion of popular sovereignty because, in the Muslim worldview, sovereignty resides not with any earthly ruler but with God alone. Instead, shura is a way of ensuring unanimity from the community of Muslims, "which allows for no legitimate minority position. The goal of the 'just' is an Islamically based society" (Dorr 1993: 151). Some – but not all – Islamists oppose Western interpretations of democracy, where sovereignty resides with the people, because it is seen as a system that negates God's own sovereignty. It is partly for this reason that Islamists (often in conflict with conservative "unjust" Islamic establishments) have been conspicuous by their absence in demands for Western-style democratic change in the Muslim world. Yet, despite an unwillingness to accept any sovereignty other than God's, some Islamic radicals have accepted the need for earthly rulers to seek a mandate from the people. For example, Dr Abdeslam Harras, leader of the Moroccan radical Islamic movement, Jama'at al-Da'wa al-Islamiyah, has asserted that rulers of Muslim countries should be elected by a majority of the population (ibid: 152).

The recent emergence of Islamic fundamentalism in many Muslim countries was primarily the result of the failure of modernization to deliver on its promises. Etienne and Tozy argue that Islamic resurgence carries within it "the disillusionment with progress and the disenchantments of the first 20 years of independence" (Etienne and Tozy 1981: 251). Faced with state power, which seeks to destroy or control the former communitarian structures and to replace them with an idea of a national citizenry based on the link between state and individual, popular (as opposed to state-controlled) Islam frequently emerges as a vehicle of citizens' political aspirations. Consequently, Coulon argues, the Muslim awakening should be seen primarily in relation to its *domestic* capacity to oppose the state: "It is primarily in civil society that one sees Islam at work" (Coulon 1983: 49). It does not translate into a wider threat to *global* order, except in isolated incidents, such as the bombing of the World Trade Center (WTC) in New York or the brief GIA bombing campaign in Paris in the mid-1990s. (This was written before the September 11, 2001 attacks on the WTC and the Pentagon.)

However, to many people in the West, Islam is perceived

monolithically as the undifferentiated "house of Islam" (*dar-Isam*), while
the rest of the world is understood as "the house of war," meaning that
Islam is at war with everything outside it. But this by no means describes current realities within Muslim societies where there are ener-
getic debates over the question of what Islam *is* and how it should
express itself in fast-changing societies. In short, there is a battle over
the definition of Islam and over who or what represents the voice of
"authentic" Muslims. For example, governments in Saudi Arabia, Algeria, and Egypt have for years been persecuting Islamic fundamentalists – in the name of Islam! "Official" Islam – comprising the leading
figures in national Muslim religious establishments – are in alliance
with these governments. In sum, there are at least two broad interpretations of Islam: on the one hand, that of the official pro-establishment
voice and, on the other, that of its challengers, focused in Islamic fundamentalist groups. Because the latter primarily challenge those in
power *within* their countries, their activities do not amount to a global
Islamic threat against the West.

The issue of the role of Islamic fundamentalism in international politics brings us to a further controversial issue linked to religion's recent
global political involvement: its association with democratization and
democracy. When we look at the roles of non-Christian religious leaders in recent demands for democracy in the developing world, a complex picture emerges. Huntington argues correctly that democracy is a
trait often associated with Christian political cultures – both in the developing world and elsewhere; democracy, as we noted in chapter 4, is
much less prominent in the Muslim world (Huntington 1991: 73). In
addition, Fukuyama contends that both Hinduism and Buddhism, like
Islam, are rooted in "hierarchical and inegalitarian" religious teachings
(Fukuyama 1992: 217). Consequently, he avers, Hindus have a decidedly ambivalent attitude towards democracy, while Buddhism, said to
"confine itself to a domain of private worship centering around the
family," also results in political passivity (ibid).

Huntington and Fukuyama see non-Christian political cultures in the
developing world as both cause and consequence of non-democratic
political systems. This is a familiar "chicken or egg first?" argument.
Are Buddhist, Hindu, and Muslim political cultures allegedly undemocratic because their followers live in authoritarian political systems? Or
are they that way because religious beliefs dictate that is how they should
behave? Do authoritarian leaders in non-Christian countries not need
to be concerned about democratic challenges because their subjects
adhere to religions making them politically passive? Does the separa-

tion of religious from political imperatives cohere with the fundamentals of spiritual cultures, thus precluding involvement in demands for political changes? While the answers to such questions are contested, it is important to understand that the claims of Huntington and Fukuyama relating to the interrelationship between a lack of democracy and certain religious cultures are empirically untrue. For example, India, a nation of more than a billion people, over 80 percent Hindu and 11 percent Muslim, has been a democracy – except for a two-year period, 1975–7 – since 1947. In addition, Muslim-majority countries such as Jordan, Kuwait, Morocco, and Turkey, and most recently Indonesia, the largest Muslim country in the world, recently emerged as democratizing countries. Moreover, Hindu/Buddhist Nepal has an elected government, while Buddhist-majority Thailand and Confucian Taiwan and South Korea also have democratically elected governments after decades of military rule. The point is it is empirically impossible to defend the claim that all non-Christian cultures are lukewarm or worse about democracy and that, by extension, their political cultures are always destined to be authoritarian.

However, we cannot just leave it there. To further complicate matters, the impact of religion on democracy is variable in another important way. There is rarely consensus among co-religionists as to the precise nature or form of a desirable political regime. Gehad Auda outlines the nature of the broad Islamist political consensus in Egypt (Auda 1993: 379–407). He notes that there is widespread agreement that liberal democracy is anathema – and this despite years of de facto one-party rule – but there is equally strong disagreement about the precise nature not only of a desirable Islamic state but also how to get there: is it to be *à la* Iran, Saudi Arabia, Sudan, Afghanistan, or *sui generis*? Would it be won by violent revolution, the ballot box, or by a mix of tactics and strategies? On the other hand, it should be noted that millions of middle-class *Muslim* Egyptians would regard the notion of *any* form of Islamic state with horror, and would probably prefer a modern, Western-oriented polity where religion is politically unimportant.

The same kind of dichotomy is evident in Thailand. Religious activists in the Palang Tham party were unable, via the ballot box in the 1990s, to deliver their goal of a state where Buddhist values would be to the fore. This was because so few Thais – 95 percent Buddhist – supported their goal. As in Egypt, many among the burgeoning middle classes in Thailand seemed to prefer a Western-style and Western-oriented political system. Another example comes from India. There Hindu nationalist parties, especially the electorally successful BJP, were able to win many millions of votes – and not only from poor, alienated people, but also from middle-class urbanites – by claiming that groups outside the Hindu "family" – especially Muslims and Christians – benefited disproportionately from the state's secular policies. By targeting non-Hindus as scapegoats, the BJP and its allies were able to gain impressive electoral successes, convincing many Hindu voters that Muslims and Christians were progressing "too fast" because of overly sympathetic state policies (Haynes 1998).

In conclusion, neither Confucian nor Muslim countries provide a realistic threat to global security. In addition, it is not only Western "Christian" countries that have democratic systems.

Regional Analysis: Religio-Ethnic Conflict in the Developing World

Africa

Unlike the Arab Middle East, largely populated by Muslims, Africa is filled with numerous and diverse religious and ethnic groups. Ethnic and religious conflicts are common in the region, but it would not be correct to assume that they are necessarily primordial, ages-old phenomena, firmly entrenched at the time of European colonization in the late nineteenth century. In fact, "most situations where the structuring of the contemporary political arena seems to be enunciated in terms of ethnicity relate to identities which did not exist a century ago, or, at least, were then not as clearly defined" (Bayart 1993: 46). This suggests that contemporary ethnic – and religious – rivalry is a manufactured phenomenon, linked to postcolonial modernization.

While it would be going too far to argue that every manifestation of contemporary ethnicity is a product of the colonial period, the speed of the formation of ethnic identity in Africa is incomprehensible if divorced from the circumstances of European rule. While colonizers regarded their – nearly always arbitrarily carved out – colonies, peopled with myriad groups, as embryonic nation-states, the European authorities created and then maintained their dominance by mostly coercive means. To do this, they controlled migratory movements and imposed ethnic details on people via birth certificates and identity cards. This is not to suggest that colonial rulers imposed ethnic identity only for their own convenience. Of equal importance was that many Africans sought to adjust to prevailing circumstances by using the Europeans' rules to their own advantage. That is, many African communities did not traditionally have "chiefs," but because Europeans believed that *all* societies naturally had such leaders, then many chiefless communities, when required, produced their "leader."

For example, in the Belgian Congo (now the Democratic Republic of Congo) the chief's function was adopted by a community elder who then drew an administrative salary from the Belgian authorities – as well as "customary" tribute from "his" people. Such payments, proportional to the population and number of subchiefs over which the chief had jurisdiction, led over time to chiefs seeking to augment the numbers of people under their rule. Over time, as they grew in size, communities became "ethnic groups." Focused in the chief, political power became linked both to ruling structures and to allocation of material resources. The size of the latter was tied to the size of communities under a chief's control.

For example, in both Uganda and northern Nigeria, Kasfir (1998) has argued that communities were organized by their traditional (or neo-traditional) leaders for the latter's pecuniary benefit as "ethnic groups." Bayart notes the case of the Aïzi, a small group of about 9,000 people living in 13 villages by the lagoons of the Côte d'Ivoire. Each of the groups of Aïzi was different from each other, with a distinct language, divergent traditions of origin and so on, while each Aïzi village had an original configuration. Nevertheless, during the colonial era "Aïzitude" emerged and grew into a sense of Aïzi ethnicity based both on cultural similarity as well as fear of outsiders (Bayart 1993: 52–3). Bayart's point is that since the notion of "ethnic group" was one of the ideological premises of the colonial administration, it became useful for groups to affirm their existence in this way. This was the case both in relation to other (rival) groups as well as regards the colonial administration. Over time, these ethnically orientated divisions became the languages of the relationships between the subject peoples themselves.

Such examples could be extended but hopefully the point is clear: before European colonialism, Africans worked out their own ways of community life, of living together and governing themselves, over the course of many centuries. The result was that they managed to create a very large number of different communities and, in some cases, states. Each of the communities had its own territory, language, beliefs, and loyalties. European colonizers understood little or nothing about the long and complex development of African sociopolitical units. To them,

Africans lived in "tribes" or larger, self-contained ethnic groups. As-suming control, the Europeans asked themselves a key question: how could Africans be controlled as cheaply as possible? The answer was that each tribe must have its own chief; if there was none one must be created. The cultivation or invention of chiefs had two results: (1) sev-eral communities would unite under a single chief, and (2) combined communities would be regarded as comprising a single people or "eth-nic group." Concocting chiefs led, in many cases, to "inventing" eth-nicity and much modern ethnic conflict in Africa has roots in colonial foundations.

South Asia

Religio-ethnic conflicts are common in South Asia. For example, Paki-stan's capital, Karachi, is frequently rent by ethnic conflict between Pathans and Mohajirs, many of whom are relatively recent migrants from India. Nationally, the regions of Sind and Baluchistan have long challenged traditional Punjabi dominance. Further south, Sri Lanka has endured a two-decade civil war between the majority Buddhist Sinhalese and minority Tamil Hindus, with the latter fighting to achieve their own state. Bangladesh too has endured religio-ethnic conflict be-tween Buddhist Chakmas from the hill tracts and Muslim Bengalis from the crowded plains. Finally, in India, clashes have taken place between indigenous, non-Hindu "tribals" and Hindus in Bihar, while in Assam autochthonous peoples have sought to defend their land and jobs against what they see as an "invasion" of outsiders from Bangladesh, Bihar, and West Bengal (Hettne 1995: 7).

One of the most serious and long-running challenges to the state in India has involved the Sikh minority. The assassination of Prime Min-ister Indira Gandhi in October 1984 followed "Operation Bluestar," an assault by security agents and soldiers to end the occupation of the Golden Temple, Amritsar, by the Sikh extremist, Jernail Singh Bhindranwale and a large number of his followers. In the process more than 2,000 people were killed. This catastrophic event focused atten-tion on Sikh designs for an independent state, Khalistan. Over time, however, Sikh unity has fractured in a struggle for dominance among a number of competing groups, whose ideologies range from "extrem-ist," that is, they are willing to use terrorism in pursuit of political aims, to "moderates," whose chief tactic is negotiation with the state and the ballot box. However, although the Sikhs, like their counterparts, the mostly Muslim Kashmiris, have failed so far to gain their state, their exemplary opposition to what both groups perceived as "Hinduization" of India has helped to stimulate other religio-ethnic separatist movements in the country.

East and Southeast Asia

A number of East and Southeast Asian countries, including Indonesia, Burma, the Philippines, and Thailand, have minority religio-ethnic groups who seek autonomy or independence. In these countries, as elsewhere in the developing world, governments have sought to build nation-states, in which all ethnic and religious minority groups feel a strong sense of national identity. As we shall see, however, most regional governments have failed in their goal. To illustrate this and to explain the reasons why, we focus upon culturalist groups in Burma, Thailand, and the Philippines.

Until the mid-1990s rebel religio-ethnic groups were active in 12 areas of mostly Buddhist Burma. Most dynamic were the Karens and Shans. The mainly Christian Karens had fought for independence since 1947, when the Karen National Union (KNU) was formed. This followed the granting of independence to Burma by the colonial rulers, the British. After independence it was a common characteristic of the groups fighting central government that they considered themselves excluded from power in a state dominated by the Buddhist Burmese. In other words, the marginality of minority groups in Burma was exacerbated by their religious distinctiveness from the dominant group in the country (Encarnacion and Tadem 1993: 150). While most insurgent groups signed ceasefires with the government in 1988, the Karens continued to fight for another decade. However, in 2000, under pressure from its main backer, the government of Thailand, the KNU changed its leader, but the KNU's military wing, the Karen National Liberation Army, pledged to fight on.

Like Burma, the Philippines is home to many ethnic groups, in the case of the latter, more than 100. While most Filipinos are Christians, the country's Muslim minority is concentrated in the southern islands, and amounts to more than 4 million people in the southern population of over 14 million; that is, about 5 per cent overall. Thirteen ethnolinguistic groups comprise the country's Muslim population; among them are the Tausugs, Maranaos, and Maguindanaos; all are active in a Muslim secessionist movement. The Muslim separatists contend that their people have been forcibly included in a state that is dominated by foreign and domestic capitalists (Encarnacion and Tadem 1993: 152). But the Muslims are divided among themselves in relation both to tactics and organizational matters. The largest separatist group, the Moro Islamic Liberation Front (MILF), has had "to contend with other groups with differing agendas" (Mehden 1989b: 217). During the 1980s the conflict became internationalized: Muslim Libya allegedly supplied military equipment to the MILF. Later, in the 1990s, the MILF adopted an effective ceasefire and maintained it until 2000 when renewed heavy fighting broke out. However, in 2001 the MILF signed a ceasefire with the authorities, leaving only the Abu Sayyaf group still fighting.

Abu Sayyaf ("the sword bearer") was formed in 1990 in the southern Philippines and quickly attracted between 250 and 600 recruits. The Philippines authorities suspected that Abu Sayyaf receives funds from Islamic fundamentalist groups in the Middle East. From April 1992 the group unleashed a number of terrorist assaults beginning with a hand grenade attack on the Roman Catholic cathedral in Iligan city, killing five and wounding 80 people. In 1995, 200 alleged Abu Sayyaf activists attacked the southern town of Ipil, killing 53 people. Later, in 2000, Abu Sayyaf militants were implicated in the kidnapping of a party of foreign tourists, most of whom were freed by the end of the year following the payment of large ransoms.

As in the Philippines, religion and ethnicity have played a crucial political role in southern Thailand. Many among the Malay–Muslim minority – about 4 percent of the national population of nearly 65 million – were alienated from the mainstream of predominantly Buddhist Thailand because of their "strict adherence to Islam" (Encarnacion and Tadem 1993: 153). Alienation also made many among the Malay–Muslim minority resentful of what they saw as Buddhist state chauvinism. Their estrangement was exacerbated by the fact that many among the Malay–Muslim minority engage in non-lucrative small-scale farming which serves to marginalize and impoverish them in a national economic situation dominated by Thai Buddhists and ethnic Chinese.

One result of Muslim alienation was armed conflict with the state. Muslim rebels have fought Thai authorities for more than 40 years in a conflict which has nevertheless failed to deliver the results the Muslims desired. Two groups, the Pattani National Liberation Movement and the Path of God, were at the forefront of separatist demands (Encarnacion and Tadem 1993: 154; Mehden 1989a: 265). However, by the late 1980s about 200 cadres of the two main Muslim separatist groups were serving long prison sentences. Ten years later, in the late 1990s, the Thai authorities claimed that there were less than 200 Muslim fighters in the field compared to around 2,000 20 years earlier. The government claimed that it had tried to meet the Muslim demands by increasing government services and by greater local participation in state political activities, but that its attempts were thwarted by aid from Iran and Libya to the Muslim separatists which helped to keep the flame of revolt alive.

In conclusion, minority groups in Burma, the Philippines, and Thailand justified their anti-state struggle by arguing that that they were coerced into conforming to the requirements of the dominant national groups in each country. That is, the separatists did not see themselves as part of the nation, believing their ethnic, religious, political, and economic rights were being violated. However, none of the separatist groups were powerful enough to achieve their objectives and were eventually encouraged to seek their peace with the state authorities.

Latin America and the Caribbean

As we saw above, Basic Christian Communities (BCCs) in Latin America represent attempts by predominantly poor communities to improve their material situations. Yet, whereas thousands of BCCs emerged in Latin America they were much less common in the islands of the Caribbean. Part of the reason for this may be that for decades many Caribbean governments were democratically elected, unlike Latin America where most regimes, until recently, were not elected. The result was that the former had to be concerned with winning – and maintaining – the support of a large proportion of the poor if they wanted to ensure reelection. One way of achieving this was to make as certain as possible that living standards were as high as possible, with reasonable community amenities provided by government. However, in the 1990s, due to downturns in the global economy, many Caribbean countries experienced economic problems that encouraged religio-ethnic tensions to surface. For example, there was an attempted takeover of power, a coup d'état, by a splinter Muslim group, the Jamaat al Muslimeenin, in Trinidad in 1990. In neighboring Jamaica, economic downturn and political polarization are less recent phenomena. There a syncretistic religious cult, Rastafarianism, was born in the 1930s. It focused the desire of many Jamaicans for redemption from, first, colonial rule and, second, an enduring poor postcolonial socioeconomic situation.

Jamaica's 2.7 million people, mostly descendants of West African slaves, are predominantly Christian, although more than 100,000 describe themselves as Rastafarians (Wiebe 1989). The emergence of Rastafarianism in the 1930s was fueled by the unacceptability for many Jamaicans of the image of a white-skinned God promulgated by the British Christian colonists. Rastafarians regard the last Ethiopian emperor, Haile Selassie ("Ras Tafari"), who ruled from 1932 until his overthrow and death in 1974, as God, and Marcus Garvey, who died in 1942, the religion's chief prophet (Hall 1985; Haynes 1993: 58–9). The militant message of liberation preached by Garvey was influential in helping to spread Rastafarianism as the route to emancipation for Jamaicans from British rule.

Following independence in 1962, serious riots occurred in 1965 and 1968 which reflected a polarization of society between a numerically tiny rich elite and the mass of poor Jamaicans. For many, the Rastafarian vision of a new type of society based on equality and communitarian ideals offered an attractive and radical alternative to the status quo. Over the next decades Rastafarianism enjoyed growing popularity, encouraged for many by the popularity of the great reggae artist, Bob Marley, a Rastafarian. However, following the death of Marley in 1980, the influence of the Rastafarian movement declined, losing much of its direct political influence.

Just as Rastafarianism was initially only a marginal creed that later found a short-lived political influence, so Islam in Trinidad went through a series of developments. A line of the national anthem of Trinidad & Tobago – "Here every creed and race finds an equal place" – illustrates the country's desire for religious and ethnic tolerance. The two islands of more than 1.3 million people have a racially and religiously diverse culture: about 40 percent of people trace their ancestry to Africa, while the same proportion have cultural roots in the Indian subcontinent. There are also small communities of Lebanese, Syrians, Chinese, Portuguese, and Jews. Racial complexity is paralleled by religious diversity, with Christianity, Hinduism, Islam, and a variety of Afro-Caribbean religions present. About 60 percent of the population are Christian, 25 percent Hindu, and around 5 percent Muslim.

The country prospered in the oil boom of the 1970s, but during the 1980s real GNP per capita, i.e. purchasing power, fell by more than a third to US\$3,830 (World Bank 1995: 163). At the same time, GNP per capita declined by an annual rate of 2.8 percent, one of the worse performances in the Caribbean at the time. Further, unemployment rose to 22 percent, while crime and violence increased as living standards and job availability dropped (Rueschemeyer, Stephens, and Stephens 1992: 250–2).

The deteriorating socioeconomic position was the background for an armed Muslim insurrection. On July 27, 1990 a group of about 100 members of a radical Muslim group, Jamaat al Muslimeen, burned down Trinidad's main police headquarters, occupied the television station, took over parliament, and held the prime minister A. N. R. Robinson and most of his cabinet hostage. The Muslimeen were black converts to Islam who acted, according to their leader, "for the sake of our community and the good of Trinidad" (Mullin 1995). The Muslims' leader, Yasin Abu Bakr, demanded an amnesty from arrest for his followers, an interim government to be formed to include him, and elections within 90 days of the coup d'état. Five days later the Muslim insurrectionists gave themselves up, convinced that they would go free and that their leader's demands would be met. Instead, they were arrested. The government claimed that an amnesty promised during the siege was invalid because it was obtained under duress.

Abu Bakr, an ex-policeman and former goalkeeper for the national football team, believed that his group's action would precipitate a popular uprising. Instead, widespread looting ensued, with 20 people killed and 500 injured in the violence, most of them wounded by gunshots allegedly fired by police. For their pains the members of the Jamaat al Muslimeen involved in the coup attempt spent two years in prison (ibid). The attempted takeover did, however, have some popular support. An unpopular coalition government, the National Alliance for Reconstruction (NAR), had swept to power in 1986, but had been unable to tackle the country's increasingly pressing socioeconomic problems. Later, in elections in early 1992, the NAR lost all of its 31 seats. Abu Bakr formed a political party at this time, the New National Vision (NNV), whose chief aim was to build an Islamic state in Trinidad. However, he and his followers soon found that his electoral appeal, as well as that of the NNV, was very limited. The party came a poor third in a by-election in early 1994 in Laventille, a poor area of the capital, Port of Spain, which might have been expected to be natural territory for his anti-establishment message. After this humiliating setback, the NNV faded away. For the rest of the 1990s the People's National Movement (PNM) and the United National Congress (UNC), who shared power in coalition governments, dominated the political scene.

In sum, while the Islamic message of deliverance preached by the NNV failed, its coup attempt not only exemplified how serious were the social divisions in the country, but also illustrated the failure of the traditional parties to integrate and articulate effectively the interests of all sections of society. Like Jamaica's Rastafarians, the NNV of Trinidad showed, albeit temporarily, an alternative to the poor based on a message of religious deliverance and redemption.

The Middle East

While the radical Islamic message of Trinidad's Jamaat al Muslimeen was directed to a relatively small Muslim minority, the political importance of Islam in the Middle East reflects the faith's predominant cultural and demographic significance. But like Trinidad's Jamaat al Muslimeen, the widespread emergence of Islamic fundamentalist groups, as we have already seen, was symptomatic of the failure of many governments to institute mechanisms of accountability, to spread the fruits of economic growth or, in some cases, to stimulate development. Such failures were reflected in extensive internal migration from rural to urban areas, high levels of unemployment and, in many cases, declining living standards for many people.

Who joins the Islamic fundamentalist groups in the Middle East? While little sustained research has yet been completed, it seems clear that they attract recruits from across society. What little hard information there is relating to membership of the Islamic fundamentalist groups mostly comes from Egypt. Egypt has been beset by conflict between the state and Islamic fundamentalists since the early 1980s. Five members of al Jihad ("Holy War") were responsible for the assassination of President Anwar Sadat in 1981, and were sentenced to death in March 1982. In 1984 over 300 al Jihad members were arrested, and some were executed for their alleged involvement in the murder of state security forces in the town of Asyût. From the late 1980s the group engaged in sporadic guerrilla war with the authorities, turning its attentions in the 1990s to foreign tourists and the Christian minority, some of whom were murdered. A second group, the Muslim Brotherhood, was also in conflict with the state. In 2000 hundreds of its members were arrested and detained in custody for long periods without trial.

The goal for both the Muslim Brotherhood and al Jihad is to create a state in Egypt run according to the tenets of *sharia* (Islamic) law (Dessouki 1982: 10–13). However, despite their shared aims, different groups of Islamic fundamentalists in Egypt have varying ideas regarding tactics, leaders and, to an extent, the precise vision of an Islamic society. But what they have in common is a strong desire, as they see it, to put society back on a religious straight and narrow path. To achieve this it is necessary to remove from power modernizing elites and replace them with certain Muslim leaders. This involves achieving power not only in order to introduce *sharia* law for moral and religious reasons, but also to achieve necessary political goals in order to create an Islamically orientated society.

Ayubi asserts that Islamist movements appear to be stronger in countries such as Egypt, "that have openly discarded some of the symbols of 'traditionalism' and have clearly declared a schema for Western-style modernization" (Ayubi 1991: 118). Modernizing governments have been in power for years in several regional countries, including Algeria, Tunisia, Syria, and Libya. However, unlike the other three countries, Algeria has had a strong Islamist movement since the 1980s. This suggests that the relative weakness of Islamist movements in some of the region's modernizing countries is more to do with the ability of the state to create a political system which has the support – or at minimum the quiescence – of most people. Libya achieved this by the shrewd use of its massive oil revenues, Syria by the control of a single-party state, and Tunisia by gradual, yet discernible, increases in living standards for most citizens. Neither Algeria nor Egypt, on the other hand, has had governments able to maintain societal support, whether through authoritarian tactics or use of oil revenues.

In sum, Islamic fundamentalist groups in the Middle East have as their goal the creation of an Islamic society to replace what they see as a modernizing one whose aim is to destroy the social and political presence of Islam. In other words, the division between secular and Islamist forces amounts to a comprehensive conflict between two different conceptions of society and social change. The division is manifested in the fields of politics, economy, religion, and social affairs. The success or otherwise of the fundamentalists in achieving their goals is to a large extent a function of the ability of incumbent governments to deflect them by societal control or palpable amounts of development, or a mixture of the two.

Conclusion

In this chapter we have focused on two main issues: the political impact of religio-ethnicity (1) within developing countries, and (2) between the West and, on the one hand, Islamic fundamentalists and, on the other, Confucian countries. In relation to the first issue, we saw that many developing countries in all five regions have experienced religio-ethnic conflict linked to instabilities associated with modernization. That is, confidence that the spread of urbanization, modern education, and technological developments would combine to diminish significantly the sociopolitical position of religion and ethnicity was not well founded. Instead, religio-ethnic concerns – reflected in culturalist, "fundamentalist," and syncretistic entities in the developing world – served as vehicles of opposition for numerous groups. Attacks from powerful outsider groups or the unwelcome symptoms of modernization (such as the perceived breakdown of suitably moral behavior and an unacceptable liberalization of education and social habits) helped encourage such responses. Further failure of governments to push through successfully programs of social improvement encouraged community-orientated groups aiming to develop religion-based solidarity and community development.

Overall, what do the findings of this chapter tell us about the nature of contemporary interactions in relation to religion and ethnicity? We have seen that the end of the Cold War was followed by concern that "civilizational" conflicts between the West and certain non-Western belief systems would throw off course the pursuit of peace, prosperity, and cooperation. Specifically, new threats to global order were, some suggested, to be found in both Confucianism and Islam. We have seen, however, that such fears did not have strong foundations. In the case of Islamic fundamentalism, we saw that in the Middle East, the Muslim heartland, Islamist groups – for example, in Egypt and Algeria – primarily target their own domestic rulers, not the West or global stability. As for Confucianism, we saw that the differences between the "Confucian" states are more important than their alleged authoritarian similarities. In sum, fears of Confucian or Islamic fundamentalist threats either to the West or to global order do not seem to be well founded.

While contemporary religious and ethnic movements display a number of broadly similar features across cultural and state boundaries, there are also differences both between and within them. But this should not surprise us. The world religions have always functioned as "terrains of meaning," subject to radically different interpretations and conflicts, often with profound social and political implications. Islam, Hinduism, Christianity, and Buddhism all have long traditions of reformers, populists, and "protestants" seeking to give their religion contemporary meaning and social salience. The contemporary era is a period both of religious reinterpretation and ethnicity-linked political concerns, galvanized by changes at both the national and global levels. It is, however, by no means clear what will be the eventual outcome. What is clearer is that to neglect either religion or ethnicity in analyses of global and domestic politics is to miss highly dynamic features of the contemporary global scene.

6

Human Rights

So far we have examined the interaction of states and societies in relation to democratization and democracy, economic development, and religio-ethnic conflict. In this chapter we move on to human rights. Like other topics we have examined, human rights issues are highly controversial – and not only in relation to individual countries and the realm of international relations. In addition, in the academic world, various disciplines such as area studies, international law, and political theory have all produced conflicting interpretations of human rights theory and practice as well as profound definitional disagreements over what human rights are.

Reflecting these concerns the structure of this chapter is as follows: (1) discussion of the concept of human rights; (2) the relative importance of external and domestic factors in the state of human rights in the developing world in the early 2000s; (3) individual and collective interpretations of human rights; (4) how to measure states" human rights records: we do this primarily by assessing the veracity of Mitchell and McCormick's (1988) statement that "Countries that enjoy higher levels of economic well-being have . . . better human rights records than those that do not"; and (4) the regional picture among developing countries. We do not examine the social, political, and economic position of women in developing countries in the current chapter, but devote chapter 7 to that purpose.

What are Human Rights?

Bealey suggests that human rights include not only "freedom from want and freedom from fear" but also a right to "life, liberty and property"

(Bealey 1999: 140). Fukuyama (1992: 42–3) offers a list of what he terms "fundamental" rights, falling into three categories:

1 Civil rights: these involve "exemption from control of the citizen in respect of his person and property."
2 Religious rights: these amount to "exemption from control in the expression of religious opinions and the practice of worship."
3 Political rights: these focus on "exemption from control in matters which do not so plainly affect the welfare of the whole community as to render control necessary," including the right of press freedom.

Note that, unlike Bealey, Fukuyama does not identify positive economic and social rights, such as "freedom from want" but, instead, focuses upon what individual citizens should be allowed to do free from state interference. Ajami offers a further interpretation. He identifies three human rights which, if one is to allow for cultural diversity, amount, he argues, to the "maximum feasible consensus" (Ajami 1978: 28–9). The first two are civil and political rights, the third is an economic and social right:

1 The right to survive.
2 The right not to be subjected to torture.
3 The right to food.

Ferguson (1986) also seeks to identify "universally accepted . . . basic or primary rights, which apply regardless of cultural differences or social order." Like that of Ajami, Ferguson's list includes the right to life and the right to freedom from torture, slavery, or summary execution. In addition, he contends that *if* a state has the resources, further rights would include freedom from hunger, a minimum standard of living, and basic education and healthcare for all (ibid: 211).

Bealey, Ajami, and Ferguson all agree that the right to food and the right to life are interdependent human rights, necessary for people to live a minimally satisfactory human life. Fukuyama, on the other hand, seems to deny the veracity of this interdependence. But what all four commentators have in common is an agreement that human rights, whether "positive" (for example, freedom from want) or "negative" (for example, preventing the state from doing something that curtails individual rights), are both inherent in the individual as well as socially derived by development. This is a way of saying that, for example, certain political freedoms are not possible without some reasonable degree of economic and social development.

However, such concepts are notoriously subjective and we shall see later that their interpretation is at the core of recent human rights controversies, not least in the developing world. Despite lapses, in general Western governments are usually judged to have better human rights observance records than states in most developing countries. Why should this be the case? When charged with poor human rights records, governments of developing countries often argue that because their society's conception of rights is different from that of the West, it is difficult, if not impossible, to compare like with like. Individualistic conceptions of human rights have long been dominant in the West (exemplified by Fukuyama's list above), while collective interpretations were long privileged in socialist and many developing countries (shades of this are inherent in Ferguson's interpretation). The result was that many governments of developing countries sought to defend their apparently arbitrary or harsh treatment of individuals by arguing that such actions were justified in the name of the collective or national good.

Human Rights in the Developing World: Domestic and External Factors

Emerson suggests that most governments of developing countries routinely abuse their citizens' human rights. He notes that the

> intricate set of provisions outlawing arbitrary arrest or detention, asserting the right of anyone arrested or detained to take proceedings before a court, and seeking to guarantee humane treatment, presumption of innocence till proved guilty, and fair and speedy trial are remote from a world in which . . . preventive detention without right of access to any court is a standard part of the procedure. In much of the Third World . . . recourse to torture is so common as to attract little attention. (Emerson 1975: 207)

Writing more recently, Jackson portrays a similarly bleak picture of human rights abuses in the developing world, with many governments a serious threat to citizens' well-being (Jackson 1990: 139). Underlining such accounts, independent non-governmental organizations (NGOs) devoted to human rights, such as Amnesty International and Human Rights Watch, have long cataloged myriad examples of human rights abuses in every developing region. In their annual reports they typically note the following: political prisoners, abductions, arbitrary detentions, beatings, torture, political killings, massacres, terror, disappearances, refugees, death squads, and wanton destruction of people's livelihood. Let us look next at the relative importance of external and domestic factors.

External factors

We have already noted that the end of the Cold War and associated international changes altered the global picture both politically and economically. What was the impact upon human rights in the developing world? Given the current importance attached to concepts like "democracy" and "good governance," it might be expected that there would be a new set of conditions more favorable to increased respect for human rights after the Cold War. We saw in chapters 3 and 4 that two of the most pressing issues for many people in the developing world were a lack of democracy and insufficient economic growth. Each is associated with a basic human right: the right to choose one's government and the right to have a sufficiency to live on ("freedom from want"). We also saw that, in the 1980s and 1990s, these two issues became central to political debates and economic struggles throughout the developing world. Important here was that increasing numbers of governments were democratically elected, while both domestic groups (civil society) and international NGOs (such as Amnesty International and Human Rights Watch) checked on what governments were doing in relation to human rights. As Bealey put it: "Any country's claim that the way it treats its subjects is no one else's business has now become a relic of a past age" (Bealey 1999: 141). The overall result was that it became less easy than before for many governments routinely to deprive their citizens of basic human rights.

The notion of fundamental human rights has a long history, dating from the seventeenth century. However, the concept of *universal* human rights is of more recent origin, stemming from the San Francisco Charter of the United Nations proclaimed in 1945. The Charter not only affirmed its faith in "fundamental human rights" for all people, but also declared that discrimination on the grounds of sex, religion, and race was repugnant. The Universal Declaration of Human Rights (UDHR), which followed in 1948, proclaimed traditional rights and freedoms, as well as new economic, social, and cultural liberties.

The UDHR itself is an intricate document expressed at three separate levels. The first sets out the basic principles every government should satisfy. The second reduces these principles into the language of rights and lists different kinds of rights. The third lays out which institutions and practices, in its view, can guarantee and safeguard these rights. Parts 2 and 3 have a liberal democratic bias. In the second part this is because of its use of the language of rights and the kinds of rights it stresses, while in the third it is because the suggested kinds of institutions and procedures both presume and are specific to liberal democracy. The general philosophy of the declaration falls into two types. The first groups a number of principles, both liberal and culturally specific, including a declaration that marriages should be rooted in the "free and full consent" of the putative partners. There is also mention of a right to freedom of expression and the importance of private property. The second group relates to vital human interests, said to be objectively valued in all societies, regardless of culture, including respect for human life and dignity, equality before the law, equal protection of the law, fair trial and, less certainly, the protection of minorities. Such concerns are emphasized as core themes of the world's great religions, and commonly practiced in both Western and non-Western societies.

Following the promulgation of the UDHR, the United Nations (UN) Commission on Human Rights was established as the UN's watchdog. The latter sought to ensure that UN guidelines were observed by all member states. However, during the Cold War the relative lack of power of the UN in relation to its leading states was reflected in the fact that both of the superpowers – the USA and the USSR – cultivated allies whose observance of basic human rights was, to say the least, sketchy. Later, in the early 1990s, New World Order rhetoric reflected renewed international concern with human rights. Concretely, the changed mood was reflected in the international community's determination to implement war-crime tribunals following the Gulf War (1990–1) and the conflicts in former Yugoslavia (1993–2001). This development seemed symptomatic of a rediscovered universalism that had first surfaced in the aftermath of World War II. The *Zeitgeist* was also reflected in renewed emphasis on human rights issues in North–South relations, especially in terms of the right of people to choose their governments. Western governments, as well as the European Union, championed liberal democracy and better human rights observances, a policy known as "political conditionality." Consequently, if they had not already done so, foreign aid recipients in the developing world were encouraged to improve their human rights records. It is sometimes argued that political conditionality was no more than an attempt by the West to impose its values in order to spread and entrench its global influence.

As a result of the higher international profile for human rights after the Cold War, organizations like Amnesty International became both fashionable and increasingly astute about publicity (Risse and Ropp 1999: 238). They worked to emphasize the relationship between individual citizens and the state and managed to get human rights issues on to international conference agendas, including the global UN-sponsored human rights conference in Vienna in 1992 and the conference on women's rights, held in Beijing in September 1995.

In sum, in the 1990s four external factors combined to encourage demands for better human rights observance in developing countries:

1 *The collapse of authoritarian governments in Central and Eastern Europe.* During the Cold War, Western governments tended to turn a blind eye to allies' poor human rights records in the name of fighting communism. However, once communism was "defeated," pressure on such governments in the developing world increased. This was both exemplified and symbolized by the failure of the Soviet Union and its regional communist allies to maintain their political and economic systems. Their spectacular – and sudden – failure generally encouraged many people in the developing world living under authoritarian regimes to demand better human rights.

2 *Pressure from transnational civil society.* Pressure from human rights-orientated transnational civil society groups, such as Amnesty International and Human Rights Watch, encouraged governments to reform by adopting – and implementing – international human rights norms.

3 *Global economic integration.* Moves towards a global economy not only facilitated the movement of capital, labor, and goods across national boundaries but also increased international economic competition. This led to the growing dominance of market forces: while sometimes producing greater economic efficiency, this also often had the effect of diminishing the already weak economic position of the poor. This led to growing demands for more global economic justice, notably expressed in the anti-World Trade Organization demonstrations witnessed in Seattle and elsewhere from the late 1990s.

4 *Transformation of production systems and labor markets.* Globalization of the world economy weakened the power of organized labor to pressurize governments to enforce labor standards, such as mini-

mum wage legislation. Adoption of structural adjustment programs in many developing countries led to widespread failure to fund adequate welfare programs.

Taken together, these four international developments encouraged many people in the developing world to demand more and better human rights.

Domestic factors

International developments interacted with domestic factors. For years, millions of people in developing countries lived under unelected governments, often characterized by brutal and wholesale violations of human rights "justified" in the name of national security and the collective good. Democratic and economic struggles, discussed in chapters 3 and 4, not only encouraged the growth of stronger civil societies but also provided a focus for demands for wider change, including better human rights. Processes of modernization were also of importance, although hard to measure in relation to events in individual countries. However, the spread of television and radio and Western-style education is seen as important in helping inform people about their human rights (Risse 2000).

Are there universal human rights?

The discussion so far has begged an important question: to what extent are there universal human rights? Some governments of developing countries claim that there is no such thing; beyond a bare minimum, very few rights can logically have *universal* application. For example, while (nearly) everyone would agree that it is wrong to kill people without justification or let them starve willfully, should states *guarantee* citizens a place to live, paid holidays, and potable water? They are, of course, highly desirable, but are they "rights"? Probably not, when we bear in mind that the great majority of developing countries may not have the financial means to provide them to *all* citizens. In short, it might be argued that individual cultures have culturally rooted rights, but there are few universal rights. Accused of violating human rights, governments of developing countries often claim that they should not be judged by "inappropriate" Western, individualistic conceptions but by the standards and concerns of their own cultures and societies. Does this defense hold water?

The issue is problematic as it involves the issue of cultural relativity. Cultural relativity is the idea that because different cultures have differing cultural reference points, it is not appropriate to judge all societies according to one universal standard. That is, individual cultures have their own norms and rules of social and individual behavior; consequently, which human rights are observed is a function of a society's own cultural characteristics and history. Therefore, it is not for those from other cultural milieux to pronounce judgment because their different worldviews preclude them from objective assessment of another culture and its human rights norms. However, if the logic of the applicability of *universal* rights is denied, then governments claiming to be rooted in *specific* cultures have carte blanche to rule as they see fit – provided they do not violate their society's cultural norms, which of course the government itself is instrumental in identifying and defining! This raises an important question to which we turn next: is the claim that there are *universal* human rights any more than an example of the West trying to impose its values on non-Western societies?

To examine this issue we need to look at the development of human rights in historical context. We have already noted that international law recognizes powers, constraints, rights, and duties that transcend the claims of sovereign states. While they may not be backed by institutions with coercive powers of enforcement, they nonetheless have far-reaching consequences. In this respect, international law has evolved over time. In the nineteenth century, international law was conceived as law between states; that is, states were its subjects, individuals its objects. Later, exclusion of the individual from the provisions of international law was challenged and undermined, especially in the aftermath of World War II. Together, the Universal Declaration of Human Rights (UDHR, 1948) and the Covenants on Rights (1966) served to enshrine recognition of individuals' rights and obligations over and above those formulated by individual countries' judicial and authority systems. For example, by recognizing conscientious objection some states conceded that individuals might legitimately refuse to serve in national armies. Many states also came to accept that there are occasions when individuals have a moral obligation – beyond that of his or her obligation as a citizen of a state – to disobey morally unacceptable orders, for example from a military officer to murder someone in cold blood. In short, over time a gap opened up between, on the one hand, rights and duties bestowed by citizenship and, on the other, the creation, via international law, of new forms of liberties and obligations.

After World War II the development was exemplified by the results of the International Tribunal at Nuremberg (and the parallel Tribunal in Tokyo). The tribunal laid down, for the first time in history, that when *international rules* protecting basic humanitarian values are in conflict with *state laws*, individuals *must* transgress state laws (except when there is no room for "moral choice"). The legal framework of the Nuremberg Tribunal marked a highly significant change in the legal direction of the modern state: the new rules challenged the principle of military discipline and subverted national sovereignty at one of its most sensitive points: the military and its characteristically hierarchical relations. Since then, international law has generally endorsed the position taken by the tribunal, by affirming a rejection of the defense of obedience to superior orders in matters of responsibility for crimes against peace and humanity.

Of all the international declarations of rights made in the postwar years, the European Convention for the Protection of Human Rights and Fundamental Freedoms (1950) is especially noteworthy. In marked contrast to the UDHR and the subsequent Covenant of Rights, the European Convention aimed for a *collective enforcement* of certain of the rights stated in the Universal Declaration. The European initiative was committed to a remarkable and radical legal innovation: individuals could initiate proceedings against their own states. European Union member countries now accept an (optional) clause of the convention that permits citizens to petition directly to the European Commission on Human Rights. The latter can take such cases to the Committee of Ministers of the Council of Europe and (given a two-thirds majority on the Council) on to the European Court of Human Rights. This development, taken with other legal changes introduced by the European Union, no longer leaves member states free to treat their citizens as they see fit. Moreover, the Treaty of European Union (the Maastricht Treaty) makes provision, in principle, for the establishment of a European Union citizenship and an ombudsman to whom citizens can directly appeal.

The relevant point for our concerns is that Europe's leadership in terms of development of individual human rights, as against those of states, had an impact upon other regions. This came about partly via the recent innovation of political conditionality and partly in response to UN encouragement that human rights should be entrenched in institutions at regional levels. Notable developments in this regard occurred in both the Americas and Africa. Regarding the former, the American Convention on Human Rights came into force in 1978 and has validity in both North and South (Latin) America. The regime is strengthened by the existence of both a Commission and a Court, although so far they have been less well used than their European counterparts. Regarding Africa, the Organization of African Unity adopted the African Charter of Human and People's Rights (sometimes known as the Banjul Charter, as it was signed in Banjul, capital of the Gambia) in 1981. Like its American parallel, it too has a commission concerned to promote human rights. However, while citizens in many African countries have established organizations to seek compliance with the Banjul agreement, many of its leading provisions so far remain substantially unenforced.

These regional charters exemplify a gradual shift from the historic core principle of international relations: the belief that state sovereignty must be safeguarded in all circumstances, apparently irrespective of consequences for individuals, groups, and organizations. Over time, especially after World War II, respect for the autonomy of the subject, and for an extensive range of human rights in relation to individuals, created a new set of ordering principles in political affairs. The latter, where effectively entrenched as in Europe, can and does serve to delimit and curtail the older principle of the supremacy of state sovereignty.

There are two polarized views regarding the impact of human rights laws and norms on state sovereignty. Let's call them the "skeptical" and the "less skeptical" schools. Clark (1997) is an example of the former. Focusing on the alleged pervasiveness and universalism of the post-Cold War human rights regime, Clark argues that, in relation to the conflicts in former Yugoslavia, the wish to punish war criminals proved stronger than the international community's ability to do so. However, the arrest in mid-2001 of Yugoslavia's former leader, Slobodan Milosevic, suggested that the international community's determination was still present.

A second issue that Clark examines is perhaps of greater centrality to our concerns in this book: human rights and cultural relativity. Since the end of the Cold War there is not much to suggest that divisions between culturally orientated conceptions of human rights are narrowing. Instead, contending conceptions became part of the substance of international relations, a continuation of political dialogue by other means. The World Conference on Human Rights in Vienna (1992) was notable for the resistance to a generalized human rights regime by an alliance of Muslim and East Asian countries. They joined together to launch a confident counter-attack against a universalist assumption of human rights rooted in the primacy of individual over collective interpretations.

Held (1994) is an example of the "less skeptical" viewpoint. He argues that there is clear progress being made towards better human rights observance around the world, especially regarding the introduction of democracy. For him, this signals the beginnings of a new approach to the concept of legitimate political power in international law. This is because there are distinct indications that contemporary international law no longer regards a state as legitimate simply by virtue of the effectiveness of its claim to public power. Instead, according to Held, there is a tendency to reject a principle of legitimacy that is indifferent to the nature, form, and operation of political power.

The collective impact of international and domestic developments in the 1990s was to put human rights issues firmly on political and developmental agendas throughout the developing world. Governments failing adequately to address human rights concerns were not only likely to be ousted at the ballot box but also to be ignored or ostracized by international donors, often the only realistic sources of crucial foreign aid. Western aid donors tied the granting of aid to recipient governments' human rights credentials, especially those relating to democracy and to the treatment of minority groups. But to what extent is there now a universal human rights regime? To assess the situation we move next to an examination of individualist and collective conceptions of human rights in the developing world.

Collectivist and Individualist Conceptions of Human Rights

We noted earlier that the notion of universal human rights was placed on the international agenda in 1948 when the UN General Assembly adopted the Universal Declaration of Human Rights (UDHR). Over the next two decades, following decolonization, emerging developing countries, including India and more than 20 African states, adopted constitutions expressly referring to the 1948 Declaration.

By reference to the UDHR the claim that there *are* universal human rights, appropriate to *all* cultures, can be illustrated in three ways. First, many non-Western governments subsequently signed the 1948 Declaration. Second, when newly postcolonial Asian and African countries joined the UN they demanded changes to the UDHR, which were finally accepted in 1966. Three were particularly important: (1) rejection of the right to property and to full compensation in the event of nationalization; (2) toning down of the individualistic basis of the 1948 Declaration; and (3) acceptance of the principle that, on occasion, it might be necessary to set aside individual rights in the national interest – for example, at times of war. In short, negotiations about the content of the

UDHR led to a final version with much greater applicability than initially. Third, since the promulgation of the UDHR people have constantly appealed to its principles in their struggles against authoritarian governments. The latter have sought to *deny* the existence of unacceptable practices rather than shelter behind relativism and cultural autonomy. The point is that, in their own different ways, both peoples and governments have tacitly or openly accepted principles enshrined in the UDHR as the basis of good, that is acceptable, government.

The consequence is that, as the UDHR had aimed, these principles are increasingly becoming a common standard of achievement for all peoples and nations. They provide a valuable basis for freely negotiated and constantly evolving consensus on *universally valid* principles of what is often called good government. This means that, logically, governments cannot claim a "right" to ignore human rights they happen not to like. On the other hand, although the *concept* of human rights has became internationalized, a serious problem remains: the assumption that there is but *one*, simple to detail, objective set of human rights standards of *universal* applicability to all cultures. In this section we examine this issue in relation to the debate involving "Asian" and Islamic conceptions of human rights.

We should note that the position of the developing countries on the issue of human rights is marked by significant regional variations. For example, the overall position of Latin American nations contrasts sharply with that of East and Southeast Asian countries. Among the latter group there exist clear differences between, for example, Taiwan and China. On the other hand, there are a number of general areas in which the views of many developing governments seem to come together. Not least is the view that the issue of human rights must be linked to each nation's individual historical, political, and cultural circumstances. In addition, the developing countries have generally emphasized that economic rights, especially the right to development, should be given precedence over purely political ones in the global human rights agenda. Let us look at this issue next, in relation both to East and Southeast Asia and Muslim countries.

Human rights: the East and Southeast Asian view

Practices that are legal or acceptable in one society may be seen in others as an abuse of human rights. This idea, known as cultural relativism, has been upheld by the governments of come countries – such as

Singapore, Malaysia, and Egypt – to criticize the interference of the West in local practices. For the governments of such countries, economic development is always given priority over liberal democracy; as "economic rights are more important than political and civil rights, and individual rights are subordinated to the presumed collective good" (Johnson 1999: 161).

East and Southeast Asian countries have different political cultures and systems and dynamics of political and economic transitions, as well as varying levels of economic development and religio-ethnic diversity. However, in all these countries there is a common understanding of the importance of collective over individual rights. Regional polities include Singapore, Malaysia, Burma, Vietnam, China, Indonesia, and South and North Korea. Singapore has both a wealthy economy and a sociopolitical system characterized by high degrees of social control. Parliament has passed extensive legislation on individual and group political behavior, while the judicial system has played its part in reinforcing tight state control. In Malaysia, Prime Minister Muhammad Mahathir has long referred to what is known as the "Asian Values" thesis, while simultaneously seeking to limit political opposition. Both Vietnam and Burma also have tightly controlled governing regimes. Burma is an egregious example of a country that has never experienced democracy in over 50 years of independence, now ruled by the State Peace and Development Council. It is a government with a very poor record in relation to civil liberties and political rights: it has systematically abused citizens' human rights, with forced labor, torture of dissidents, and conflict with ethnic minorities, including the Karens (see chapter 5).

Vietnam is a one-party regime which, although politically repressive, is nevertheless committed to an economic liberalization program. China also has a program of economic liberalization under the auspices of the ruling Communist Party. This has coincided with a crime and corruption explosion, dealt with by large numbers of controversial executions, and new social and religious groupings, such as Falun Gong, which has been repressed by the state. Indonesia also has a poor human rights record, informed by separatist politics, forced migration, and serious state-level corruption. Despite international intervention, rebellious provinces such as Aceh and newly independent East Timor remain problem areas vis-à-vis human rights. The regional "success story" in human rights terms is sometime said to be South Korea which, since the mid-1980s, underwent notable democratization. Nevertheless, the country still has an oppressive National Security Law, used to silence pro-North Korea political activists.

East and Southeast Asian governments have stated their "cultural relativist" position. This amounts to rejecting the West's individualist conception of human rights and arguing for what is known as a "communitarian" perspective, an emphasis prioritizing the collectivity over the self. Malaysia's prime minister, Muhammad Mahathir, has regularly articulated this view. He sees the West's post-Cold War human rights campaign as a device to perpetuate the condition of dependency of the developing on the developed countries. Citing the example of the former communist countries of Eastern Europe, Mahathir contends that the campaign of human rights and democracy is a prescription for disruption and chaos in weaker countries, a campaign which makes the target ever more dependent on Western donor nations.

Other regional critics accuse the West of hypocrisy and selectivity in applying its human rights standards. Singapore's government suggests that this is not new but instead that concern for human rights in and by the West has always been balanced against other national interests. To support this claim, Singapore points to the contrast between the USA's continued, if increasingly tacit, support for absolutist regimes in the oil-rich Arabian Peninsula. In addition, there is the West's response to the crisis in Algeria, whereby Western governments acquiesced in the military coup that canceled the electoral process after the first round of voting in December 1991 looked set to produce an Islamic fundamentalist government.

Critics of the "Asian Values" view argue that authoritarianism is the key feature of human rights regimes in many East and Southeast Asian countries and is central to their political cultures. This makes it very difficult to develop Western-style *liberal* democracy and associated individualistic freedoms and rights. Several commentators, including Diamond (1999), Zakaria (1997), and Engberg and Ersson (2001), have examined regional governments and their human rights regimes. Zakaria contends that many regional regimes are what he calls "illiberal democracies." This implies a mix of characteristics: "democracy, liberalism, capitalism, oligarchy and corruption" coexisting much as they did in "Western governments circa 1900" (Zakaria 1997: 28). The point is that regional regimes may well have political systems with periodic, relatively free and fair elections – and some meaningful rules and regulations to determine their conduct and content – while lacking a "full" array of individualistic, liberal freedoms. Such rulers wield power with little reference to other political institutions, ordinary citizens enjoy only a relatively narrow range of civil liberties and, other than at election times, there are notably low levels of popular political participation.

Christie and Roy (2001) focus on the politics of human rights in East and Southeast Asia. The authors address the debate over whether human rights are universal or bound up with Western historical development and political traditions. They also discuss whether the political traditions and culture of regional societies produce a different practice of rights and duties than in their Western counterparts. Critics such as Engberg and Ersson (2001) have attacked traditional models of values and order and their use by regional elites, charging that they are no more than a cloak for continuing authoritarianism and the narrow political interest of the rulers.

Whatever the merits of the "Western" versus "Asian Values" debate, there are regional groups seeking Western-style, individualistic human rights, often encouraged by the region's economic downturn in 1997–8. For many years, authoritarian government and suppression of political opposition were justified by regional governments such as Malaysia and Indonesia as a necessary price to pay for impressive economic growth. That legitimation took a major knock when regional economies experienced problems following the collapse of the Thai currency in 1997. As we saw in chapter 2, this event triggered a regional domino effect of collapsing currencies and economic problems subsequently affecting the region. The economic malaise not only made it plain that authoritarian development models were fallible, but also encouraged demands for a new focus on improving human rights (Jetshke 1999). Some regional leaders, such as Mahathir, suggest that local human rights groups act at the behest of foreign actors. However, Hewison claims that "demands for the opening of political space, with calls for increased democracy in Southeast Asia, are not originating in the West or among Western-influenced actors, but have domestic causes" (Hewison 1999: 231).

In conclusion, perhaps the core dynamic in relation to human rights in East and Southeast Asia lies not in differing cultural approaches but in the processes of social change and economic development, which create new political dynamics and tensions. In other words, the most important tension seems to be not between "Western" and "Asian values" but between modernization and tradition (Christie and Roy 2001: 6). In this vein there is speculation that economic growth and globalization will create the space for groups and political movements to build a new human rights culture. We have also seen that regional diversity can only be poorly treated with a macro-approach based on a dichotomy between "Asian values" and "Western values." That is, the important dynamic is not necessarily between, on the one hand, "Western" and, on the other, "Asian values." Rather, as most regional governments view opposition groups with great suspicion or worse, they may be tempted to commit human rights violations in the name of national stability and security.

Human rights: the Islamic view

There are two key Western complaints in relation to human rights observation in the Arab Muslim countries of the Middle East: (1) generally poor human rights regimes; and (2) serious democratic shortfalls. Both shortcomings are said to be linked to the strong regional influence of Islam (Huntington 1991; Fukuyama 1992; Diamond 1999). Speaking at the 10th Non-Aligned Summit Conference held in Jakarta, Indonesia, in 1992, Egypt's foreign minister warned the West against interference in his nation's internal affairs on the pretext of defending human rights. Was this simply a pretext, a desire by the Egyptian government to deflect Western attacks on their poor human rights record by playing the "cultural relativity" card?

The social importance of Islam cannot be denied: every country in the region, with the exception of Israel, has a population that is at least 89 percent Muslim (Beeley 1992: 296–7). What impact does Islam have on regional human rights observances? The first point is that Islam is both premised and rooted in the emphatic importance of collective over individual rights; in other words, there is a high regard for social solidarity within Muslim countries. The Muslim community – the *umma* – is a "compact wall whose bricks support each other." The role of the individual "is not merely to act so as to ensure [the community's] preservation, but also to recognize that it is the community that provides for the integration of human personality realized through self-abnegation and action for the good of the collectivity" (Vincent 1986: 42). As far as girls and women are concerned, as we shall see in chapter 7, if they do not wish to court social opprobrium they must act within norms of behavior sanctioned by Muslim conventions.

Second, in Islam the "language of duty seems more natural than that of [individual] rights" (ibid). That is, because of the primary importance attached to obedience to God, in Islam rights are seen as secondary to duties. Rules of conduct were laid down by God fourteen centuries ago through his mouthpiece, the Prophet Muhammad. Since then,

Muslims have sought to serve God by thorough obedience to divine rules. As Vincent notes, if rights are thought of as "freedoms" then in Islam "true freedom consists in surrendering to the Divine will rather than in some artificial separation from the community of God . . . rights remain subordinate to and determined by duties" (ibid).

Governments of Muslim countries typically claim divine sanction for their existence and for what they do. That is, their rule is God's will and their policies are, implicitly, sanctioned by God. This is, of course, a potential justification for harsh or arbitrary rule, which has been used to justify denials of democracy and freedom of speech, and harsh treatment of women (Owen 1992). There is, however, an emergent trend among some educated Muslims and revisionist ulama (theological teachers) questioning the poor position of women and of non-Muslim minorities in some Muslim countries; these are areas, it is claimed, that have seemed for a long time to be outside the Islamic critical gaze. Islamic revisionists feel that "many Muslims confuse some inherited traditional cultural values with Islamic values" (Saif 1994: 63).

Despite current concern with the position of females and minorities, there are several reasons why it is unlikely that individual rights will soon take precedence over collective rights in the Arab Middle East. First, regional societies are conservative. Second, incumbent political elites do their best to ensure the continuity of the status quo. Since independence, political elites in the Middle East, often in alliance with the military, have striven to modernize their political systems while retaining a tight grip on power. The avowed aim in, for example, Syria and Tunisia has been to build nation-states along Western lines. As a result, the status of Islam was at least temporarily downplayed and religious professionals were either incorporated into the state elite or their power was neutralized. The result was a modernist superstructure balanced uncomfortably upon a substructure deeply rooted in traditional beliefs, with Islam the cement holding the social system together. Elsewhere, in the region's more socially and religiously traditional countries, such as Saudi Arabia, the United Arab Emirates, and Morocco, governments sought to deepen their Islamic credentials and limit the spread of Western ideas.

Our brief survey of the Muslim view of human rights in the Arab Middle East leads to similar conclusions to those drawn above in relation to East and Southeast Asia. The core dynamic in relation to human rights in the Arab Middle East lies not in differing cultural approaches but in the processes of social change and economic development, which create new political dynamics and tensions. The most important tension seems to be not between "Western" and "Islamic values" but between modernization and tradition. There is some, albeit limited evidence that in the Middle East, like in East and Southeast Asia, economic growth and globalization create added space for groups and political movements to seek a new human rights culture. However, Middle Eastern regional diversity also squares poorly with a macro-approach based on a dichotomy between "Islamic values" and "Western values." As in East and Southeast Asia, the important dynamic is not necessarily between "Western" and "Islamic values." Most regional governments view opposition groups with suspicion or worse and, even under their own laws, regional regimes are prone to commit human rights violations.

Regional Analysis: Political Rights, Civil Liberties, and Human Development in the Developing World

The conception of "good government" does not necessarily imply that polities must have Western-style, liberal democratic regimes to be just, representative, or respectful of citizens' human rights. However, in recent years in practice this has often become the case. Still, it might be argued that countries with different political cultures should be free to determine nationally appropriate forms of government – as long as the form is acceptable to citizens; the latter *may* choose liberal democracy or they may not. The "bottom line" is that for a government to exhibit the fundamentals of good government then it must have concern for the public good uppermost. In sum, the notion of good government – that is, effective, "user-friendly" rule, respectful of citizens' human rights, with state–society relations informed by political relationships of reciprocity and authority, trust and accountability – is at the core both of the exercise of power and of a desirable human rights regime. Such regimes have three important qualities. They are:

- politically accountable to their citizens via the ballot box;
- purposive and development oriented;
- seeking with vigor to improve the mass of people's quality of life

At least roughly, the "amount" of good government in a country can be gauged by reference to the level of political rights and civil liberties, and human development. We look at these concerns next, in relation to regional situations in the developing world.

In chapter 4 we examined the state of democracy in developing countries with the help of a scale devised by the US organization, Freedom House (FH). Using a rigorous, if somewhat controversial, methodology FH annually calculates political rights and civil liberties (PR/CL) within all countries. With comparable data now available for a 29-year period (1972–2000), the FH index is the most useful available comparative measure to compare countries in terms of their political and civil rights and freedoms (the methodology of FH is presented in Appendix 2).

A second measurable element of good government is how far do states ensure that the mass of people enjoys an acceptable level of socioeconomic development? Many states attempt to increase the general level of affluence in their country, perhaps by supporting a welfare state or by seeking to introduce a progressive taxation regime. "Gross domestic product" (GDP) is a standard indicator that measures a country's overall economic output. However, GDP says nothing about the "quality of life" or "the level of human development," measures which allow us to assess a country's degree of socioeconomic fairness. The United Nations Development Program's "human development index" (HDI) was devised in 1990 to measure countries' levels of human development and is updated each year. The HDI is a composite indicator of "quality of life" which measures the following:

- life expectancy at birth;
- adult literacy rate;
- combined primary, secondary, and tertiary education gross enrollment ratio (%);
- GDP per capita.

Combining these indicators in individual countries allows us to gauge the "quality of life" and assess the degree to which governments achieve the goals of *human development*. There are three categories: "high human development" (0.8 or better); "medium human development" (0.5–0.799); "low human development" (up to 0.499).

Next, I present data on developing countries' political rights/civil liberties (PR/CL) and "human development index" (HDI) positions, measured, on the one hand, by a country's PR/CL rating according to Freedom House and, on the other, by its location in the HDI. For reasons of space, we focus upon the most populous developing countries – those with over 10 million inhabitants, except for Caribbean island nations, which have relatively low populations and where the criterion for inclusion is a population of at least 1 million people. The aim is threefold: first, to examine the veracity of Mitchell and McCormick's (1988) contention that countries that enjoy higher levels of economic well-being have better human rights records than those that do not. Another way of putting this is the claim that "for a given level of income, improvements in social indicators are associated with freedom and liberty" (World Bank 1991: 134).

If these hypotheses are correct then we should note a strong correlation between the position of countries' PR/CL and their HDI. Table 6.1 shows the average scores of PR/CL and HDI for each of the five developing country regions. There are a number of correlations between HDI and PR/CL to note. For example, Latin America and the Caribbean do best on both indicators. East and Southeast Asia does well in terms of HDI but performs less well than Latin America and the Caribbean in relation to PR/CL. Turning to the Middle East, the region does reasonably well in terms of HDI but is worst of all five regions vis-à-vis PR/CL. The South Asia region performs relatively well in terms of PR/CL, but is the second worst region where HDI is concerned. Finally, Africa's position is variable: it performs third best of the five developing regions in relation to PR/CL but is bottom of the pile when it comes to HDI.

Data presented in this table do not provide a definitive answer to the second area of concern: is democratic or authoritarian rule most conducive to sustained economic growth and human development? There can be no clear answer because in the following section we can see examples of both democratic and undemocratic governments presiding over relatively good HDI positions. For example, during the 1970s and 1980s authoritarian governments in Chile and South Korea, and in the 1980s and 1990s Malaysia and Singapore, managed to preside over impressive, sustained economic growth. More generally, however, it is impossible to establish a durable connection between authoritarian rule and protracted economic growth, as there are too many examples of authoritarian governments with appalling records in this respect. This is underlined by the fact that, in the 1990s, both Taiwan and South Korea had democratically elected governments and good growth records.

While the link between freedom and development is not really in dispute, it is problematic trying to decide whether good political rights and civil liberties leads to enhanced human development or vice versa. Sometimes sustained economic development leads to increasing demands for democracy and human rights, as in Taiwan and South Korea. On the other hand, the opposite can also be true: Indonesia and

Table 6.1 Average HDI and PR/CL scores in developing regions, 2000

Region	No. of countries	Average HDI (0–1)	Average PR/CL (2–7)
Latin America and Caribbean	14	0.747	3.29
East and Southeast Asia	8	0.718	4.63
Middle East	9	0.642	5.72
South Asia	5	0.551	3.8
Africa	20	0.438	4.5
All	56	0.619	0.439

East and Southeast Asia does not include Taiwan and South Korea, for which data are unavailable. HDI: the nearer 1 the better. PR/CL: the nearer 2 the better.
Source: Human Development Index 2000 (http://www.undp.org/hdro/); Freedom House Annual Survey of Freedom Country ratings 1972–3 to 1999–2000 (http://www.freedomhouse.org/survey00/method/); World Bank (2001: 274–5, table 1)

South Africa experienced serious economic downturns that helped stimulate demands for democracy. And, in the Middle East, some oil producing states managed to preside over relatively good human development positions, yet with a relatively poor human rights position and without democratizing (Bill and Springborg 1994: 295–6). This leads us to the third issue in focus in the remainder of the chapter: to what extent do cultural factors affect a society's "quality of life" and freedom?

Africa

African countries featured in table 6.2 score worst of all developing countries in terms of HDI, with an average of 0.438. But they do better in relation to PR/CL than their counterparts in both the Middle East and East and Southeast Asia. We should however note wide variations in this regard: in particular, South Africa, but also Ghana, Madagascar, Malawi, and Mali, all do well in terms of PR/CL, while some others, such as Zimbabwe, Sudan, the Democratic Republic of Congo, Cameroon, and Angola, do poorly. Each scores between 6–7, indicating that they are "not free."

Judging from these data, in African countries there is not a strong correlation between HDI and PR/CL. Only South Africa is clearly within the "medium human development" category, while others achieving that position – Cameroon, Ghana, Kenya, and Zimbabwe – are at or near the lower margin of the category. All other African countries represented in table 6.2 have a "low human development" rating. Overall, the situation in Africa does not confirm the hypotheses relating to economic development and democracy; there is no apparent correlation between democratic performance and the delivery of "human development." On the other hand, nearly all improvements in PR/CL are recent – since the early 1990s – and may not last.

There are many different cultures, traditions, and religions in Africa, making it impossible to talk meaningfully about a unitary "African" culture (Haynes 1991, 1996). However, despite this diversity, Africans, it is sometimes claimed, have traditionally been more prepared to accept authoritarian governments and are less concerned with political freedoms than many people elsewhere (Howard 1986). Like the East and Southeast Asian and Islamic conceptions of human rights, the "African" notion vis-à-vis human rights is said to be characterized by societal concern with collective over individual rights. According to Bayart, individualistic conceptions of "democracy and of human rights [in Africa] are the products of Western history" (Bayart 1986: 109–10). Individualistic values are said not to have been widely respected by Africa's precolonial societies but introduced into the region following the instigation of colonial rule in the late nineteenth and early twentieth centuries. At the same time, however, Africans are said not to be "traditionally more tolerant of arbitrary power" (ibid: 110). Events over the last few years –when many African countries democratized – cast serious doubts on the assumption that Africans are more tolerant of authoritarian government than people elsewhere. In fact, the generally poor performance of authoritarian African governments in relation to both human development and democracy over time was said to be instrumental in stimulating challenges to non-democratic rule (Haynes 2001a).

South Asia

South Asia is an anomaly as far as the link between political and civil freedoms and human development is concerned. In terms of PR/CL, regional states achieve the second-best average position – 3.8 – behind Latin America and the Caribbean. The position of regional countries in terms of PR/CL and HDI is presented in table 6.3. However, regarding

Table 6.2 Africa human rights indicators, 1998–2000

Country	Population (millions, 1999)	Life expectancy at birth (1998)	Combined primary, secondary, and tertiary gross enrollment ratio (%) 1998	Adult literacy rate (1998)	GDP per capita (PPP US$) 1998	HDI (20000)	Global HDI ranking (2000)	Average of PL/CR (1999–2000)
South Africa	42	53.2	95	84.6	8488	0.697	103	1.5
Ghana	19	60.4	43	69.1	1735	0.556	129	3
Madagascar	16	57.9	40	64.9	756	0.483	141	3
Malawi	11	39.5	75	58.2	523	0.385	163	3
Mali	11	53.7	26	38.2	661	0.38	165	3
Nigeria	124	50.1	43	61.1	795	0.439	151	3.5
Mozambique	17	43.8	25	42.3	782	0.341	168	3.5
Tanzania	33	47.9	33	73.6	480	0.415	156	4
Burkina Faso	11	44.7	22	22.2	870	0.303	172	4
Zambia	10	40.5	49	76.3	719	0.42	153	4.5

Côte d'Ivoire	15	46.9	41	44.5	1598	0.42	154	5
Uganda	21	40.7	41	65	1074	0.409	158	5
Ethiopia	63	43.4	26	36.3	574	0.309	171	5
Niger	10	48.9	15	14.7	739	0.293	173	5
Zimbabwe	12	43.5	68	87.2	2669	0.555	130	5.5
Kenya	29	51.3	50	80.5	980	0.508	138	5.5
Angola	12	47	25	42	1821	0.405	160	6
Cameroon	15	54.5	48	73.6	1474	0.528	134	6.5
Congo (DR)	50	51.2	33	58.9	822	0.43	152	6.5
Sudan	29	55.4	34	55.7	1394	0.477	143	7

Source: Human Development Index 2000 (http://www.undp.org/hdro/); Freedom House Annual Survey of Freedom Country ratings 1972–3 to 1999–2000 (http://www.freedomhouse.org/survey00/method/); World Bank (2001: 274–5, table 1)

HDI, the region is the second-worst performer, with 0.551. Within the region there are notable variations in HDI. For example, there is an apparent development gulf between, at the top end, Sri Lanka (0.733, corresponding to "medium human development") and, at the bottom end, Bangladesh (0.461, that is, "low human development"). However, regional countries, with the exception of Pakistan, achieve fairly similar rankings in terms of PR/CL (the range is 2.5–3.5). It is worth noting, however, that democracy was only recently reintroduced in Bangladesh and Nepal and may not endure. Nevertheless, Sri Lanka's good HDI performance and reasonably satisfactory democracy rating, despite the two-decade civil war between the Sinhalese and Tamils, offers support for the following hypothesis: developing human resources and increasing per capita incomes is a better basis for developing democratic political systems than their absence.

Both Bangladesh and Pakistan have large Muslim majorities, while Sri Lanka has a majority Buddhist population. As we saw above in relation to Islam, religion and culture may impart certain characteristics to societies which affect how they perceive and relate to human rights. In relation to cultural factors in South Asia, the region is noteworthy because of the influence of Hinduism. An estimated 82 percent of India's billion-plus people and 90 percent of Nepal's population of 23 million are Hindus; in sum, over 60 percent of people in the South Asia region follow the Hindu religion. Many Indian Hindu traditionalists argue that their country's secular constitution runs counter to their core values. Kane maintains that "the [Indian] constitution engenders a feeling among common people that they have rights and no obligations whatsoever" (Kane quoted in Chiriyankandath 1993: 247). Traditionalists claim that the values of Hinduism are "essentially derived from the social duties and status hierarchies based on *varna* (the classic all-India caste categories) and *jati* (the multiplicity of locally relevant castes" (Chiriyankandath 1993: 247). As a result, the rights and duties of Hindus are said to be determined by their position within an essentially hierarchical system of relationships that constitute an "all-embracing cosmology." Such a view might imply the "duty of any Hindu [state] ruler to recognize and [seek to] maintain the caste system . . . and consequently reject the primacy accorded to individual rights and the idea of human equality," foundations of both the Universal Declaration of Human Rights, of which India is a signatory, and of the Indian Constitution (ibid).

The fact is, however, that encounters with the West helped to encourage non-hierarchical currents within Hinduism. An agnostic,

Table 6.3 South Asia human rights indicators, 1998–2000

Country	Population (millions, 1999)	Life expectancy at birth (1998)	Combined primary, secondary, and tertiary gross enrollment ratio (%) 1998	Adult literacy rate (1998)	GDP percapita (PPP US$) 1998	HDI (20000)	Global HDI ranking (2000)	Average of PL/CR (1999–2000)
India	998	62.9	54	55.7	2077	0.563	128	2.5
Sri Lanka	19	73.3	66	91.1	2979	0.733	84	3.5
Nepal	23	57.8	61	39.2	1157	0.474	144	3.5
Bangladesh	128	58.6	36	40.1	1361	0.461	146	3.5
Pakistan	135	64.4	43	44	1715	0.522	135	6

Source: Human Development Index 2000 (http://www.undp.org/hdro/); Freedom House Annual Survey of Freedom Country ratings 1972–3 to 1999–2000 (http://www.freedomhouse.org/survey00/method/); World Bank (2001: 274–5, table 1)

Jawaharlal Nehru, was India's first prime minister (1947–64), the chief drafter of the Constitution. He was a modernizer who sought to reduce the influence in the postcolonial state of "inappropriate" Hindu traditionalism. He was also concerned to try to update traditional cultural norms to take account both of domestic change as well as to embed India more thoroughly in the emerging global consensus in relation to the appropriateness of universal human rights. However, in India, as in the rest of South Asia and the developing world more generally, the controversy over human rights has been implicated not only with problems of culture and religion, economic development, and social change, but also with the concern of how to build a nation-state from diverse peoples.

East and Southeast Asia

As table 6.4 shows, of states in the East and Southeast Asia region with populations greater than 10 million, only South Korea (and almost certainly Taiwan) are "high human development" countries. All other regional nations – with the exception of Burma – are "medium human development" countries.

FH classifies four countries – South Korea, Taiwan, Thailand, and the Philippines – as "free states." Indonesia and Malaysia are judged to be "partly free," and the remainder – China, Vietnam, Burma, and North Korea – are "not free." In relation to the HDI, all countries in table 6.4 – with the exception of North Korea for which data are unavailable – are classified as enjoying either "medium human development" or, as in the case of South Korea (and almost certainly Taiwan), "high human development." In relation to the hypothesis about the correlation between freedom and economic development, the data are once again inconclusive.

Whereas the average PR/CL score for Latin American and Caribbean countries in table 6.5 is 3.29, that for the countries of East and Southeast Asia (detailed in table 6.4) is 4.63. In other words, the former region does better than the latter when it comes to political rights and civil liberties. Turning to the HDI, East and Southeast Asian countries in table 6.4 achieved an average HDI of 0.718, compared to that of the Latin American and Caribbean average of 0.747. Thus, in both HDI and PR/CL terms, Latin America and the Caribbean out-performs East and Southeast Asia.

Relatively poor PR/CL ratings in some of the region's states led to

Table 6.4 East and Southeast Asia human rights indicators, 1998–2000

Country	Population (millions, 1999)	Life expectancy at birth (1998)	Combined primary, secondary, and tertiary gross enrollment ratio (%) 1998	Adult literacy rate (1998)	GDP per capita (PPP US$) 1998	HDI (20000)	Global HDI ranking (2000)	Average of PL/CR (1999–2000)
South Korea	47	72.5	90	97.5	13478	0.854	31	2
Taiwan	20				13235 (1999)			2
Thailand	62	68.9	61	95	5456	0.745	76	2.5
The Philippines	77	68.6	83	94.8	3555	0.744	77	2.5
Indonesia	207	65.6	65	85.7	2651	0.67	109	4
Malaysia	23	72.2	65	86.4	8137	0.772	61	5
China	1250	70.1	72	82.8	3105	0.706	99	7
Vietnam	78	67.8	63	92.9	1689	0.671	108	7
Burma	45	60.6	56	84.1	1199	0.585	125	7
North Korea								

Recent data for Taiwan and North Korea are not available.
Source: Human Development Index 2000 (http://www.undp.org/hdro/); Freedom House Annual Survey of Freedom Country ratings 1972–3 to 1999–2000 (http://www.freedomhouse.org/survey00/method/); World Bank (2001: 274–5, table 1)

Western criticism of the region's human rights record. Speaking anonymously, a "senior diplomat" claimed in 1995 that there was growing concern about American intrusiveness in the region: "They want us to swallow an American culture of CNN and Hollywood, insist we welcome their rude and intrusive media, while they lecture us on human rights. The cultural arrogance of a country with such problems of race and crime is breathtaking to people on our side of the Pacific" (quoted in Walker 1995). Inoguchi claims that many people in the East and Southeast Asian region regard American attacks on human rights as politically or racially motivated. The aim, it is believed, is to try to undermine political and social stability, an essential element in the region's economic success that threatens the international economic position of the USA and the West more generally (Inoguchi 1995: 131).

In conclusion, leaders of the region's economically successful countries have won domestic support by attacking "foreign interventionists" while delivering economic growth that is fairly equitably spread (Thompson 1993: 481). In other words, Asian authoritarians have often argued from a position of economic success. On the other hand, the region's countries are vulnerable to charges of violating human rights when viewed from a Western perspective. As we have seen, many East and Southeast Asian states put the collective interest foremost, and individual well-being seems subordinate.

Latin America and the Caribbean

Table 6.5 shows that Latin American and Caribbean countries perform better overall in relation both to political rights and civil liberties and to human development than any other developing region. Table 6.2 shows a breakdown of PR/CL and HDI indicators in selected states in the region. Apart from Haiti, the poorest country in the Western hemisphere, none of the region's countries scores less than a "medium human development" rating in the HDI. In terms of PR/CL, Cuba scores very poorly (7) and Haiti also does relatively badly (5).

Chile, Trinidad & Tobago, and Costa Rica do very well in terms of both HDI and PR/CL. Each country scores more than 0.79 on the former and is regarded by Freedom House as a "free state"; that is, each has a clearly democratic political system. Jamaica, the Dominican Republic, Argentina, and Ecuador do reasonably well in respect both of PR/CL and HDI. The rest – with the exception of Cuba and Haiti – perform acceptably in relation both to the HDI and PR/CL. Haiti is the worst

Table 6.5 Latin America human rights indicators, 1998–2000

Region	Country	Population (millions, 1999)	Life expectancy at birth (1998)	Combined primary, secondary, and tertiary gross enrollment ratio (%) 1998	Adult literacy rate (1998)	GDP per capita (PPP US$) 1998	HDI (20000)	Global HDI ranking (2000)	Average of PL/CR (1999–2000)
Latin America	Chile	15	75.1	78	95.4	8787	0.826	38	2
	Argentina	37	73.1	80	96.7	12013	0.837	35	2.5
	Ecuador	12	69.7	75	90.6	3003	0.722	91	2.5
	Brazil	168	67	84	84.5	6625	0.747	74	3.5
	Mexico	97	72.3	70	94	7704	0.784	55	3.5
	Colombia	42	70.7	71	91.2	6006	0.764	68	4
	Venezuela	24	72.6	67	92	5808	0.77	65	4
	Peru	25	68.6	79	89.2	4282	0.737	80	4.5
Caribbean	Trinidad & Tobago	1.3	74	66	93.4	7485	0.793	50	1.5
	Costa Rica	4	76.2	66	95.3	5987	0.797	48	1.5
	Jamaica	3	75	63	86	3389	0.735	83	2
	Dominican Republic	8	70.9	70	82.8	4598	0.729	87	2.5
	Haiti	8	54	24	47.8	1383	0.44	150	5
	Cuba	11	75.8	73	96.4	3967	0.783	56	7

Source: Human Development Index 2000 (http://www.undp.org/hdro/); Freedom House Annual Survey of Freedom Country ratings 1972–3 to 1999–2000 (http://www.freedomhouse.org/survey00/method/); World Bank (2001: 274–5, table 1)

regional performer in terms of HDI and is second worst, behind Cuba, in relation to PR/CL. Cuba has a PR/CL score of 7, the lowest achievable, yet one of the best in terms of HDI: 0.793. This puts Cuba near the top of the "medium human development" category. Cuba is of course the Western hemisphere's only communist country; it performs badly in PR/CL not only because of the absence of genuinely competitive elections but also because of the propensity of the regime to deny liberty to people it judges to be unhelpful critics (Pinkney 1993: 149).

In relation to another issue of concern in this section of the chapter – the link between culture and human rights – Christian countries are sometimes said to be more likely to be democracies than non-Christian countries. "It seems plausible," Huntington avers, "to hypothesize that the expansion of Christianity encourages democratic development" (Huntington 1991: 73). Witte (1993: 11) notes that of the 32 new democracies that emerged between 1973 and 1993, 24 were Christian countries, mostly in Latin America. Many, including Argentina, Brazil, and Chile, were, like the Philippines, South Korea, Poland, Hungary, and Lithuania, countries which received a great deal of diplomatic and sometimes material support from the United States for (re)democratization. Several African Christian countries, on the other hand, such as the Democratic Republic of Congo, Togo, and Rwanda that are not democracies, were not objects of the United States' strategic interest in the same way; neither did they experience prolonged American pressure for democratization. In sum, Christianity may well be a feature in democratization and human rights observance in Latin America, but equally so was strong US encouragement.

The Middle East

None of the ten regional countries represented in table 6.6 gains either a "high human development" rating or is rated by FH as a "free state," implying a high level of political and civil freedoms for ordinary citizens. The average HDI for the region is 0.642, that for PR/CL, 5.72. FH rates Turkey, Morocco, Algeria, and Egypt as "partly free states," while the remaining countries in table 6.6 are "not free." On average, in relation to both HDI and PR/CL, the region's states do worse than Latin American and Caribbean countries and East and Southeast Asian nations. This is the case despite the considerable asset of oil wealth; however, governments of the region's most populous countries have managed to secure for their citizens only a medium level of human

Table 6.6 Middle East human rights indicators, 1998–2000

Country	Population (millions, 1999)	Life expectancy at birth (1998)	Combined primary, secondary, and tertiary gross enrollment ratio (%) 1998	Adult literacy rate (1998)	GDP per capita (PPP US$) 1998	HDI (20000)	Global HDI ranking (2000)	Average of PL/CR (1999–2000)
Turkey	64	69.3	61	84	6422	0.732	85	4.5
Morocco	28	67	50	47.1	3305	0.589	124	4.5
Algeria	30	6.9.2	69	65.5	4792	0.683	107	5
Egypt	62	66.7	74	53.7	3041	0.623	119	5
Yemen	17	58.5	49	44.1	719	0.448	148	5.5
Iran	63	69.5	69	74.6	5121	0.709	97	6
Saudi Arabia	21	71.7	57	75.2	10158	0.747	75	7
Syria	16	69.2	59	72.7	2892	0.66	111	7
Afghanistan								
Iraq	23	63.8	50	53.7	3197	0.583	126	7

Source: Human Development Index 2000 (http://www.undp.org/hdro/); Freedom House Annual Survey of Freedom Country ratings 1972–3 to 1999–2000 (http://www.freedomhouse.org/survey00/method/); World Bank (2001: 274–5, table 1)

development and only a few have managed to develop even a moderate level of political freedoms.

Overall, regional evidence offers little support for the claim that freedom and economic development go together. Two of the three best performers in terms of HDI – Saudi Arabia and Syria – are in the "not free" category of political rights and civil liberties. Three of the four countries – Morocco, Algeria, and Egypt – which score best in relation to PR/CL are near the bottom when it comes to HDI.

It is sometimes argued that the relatively rare incidence of regional democratic regimes is due in part to the influence of Islam (Huntington 1991; Fukuyama 1992). Human rights in the Arab Middle East were discussed earlier in this chapter, so I will not spend long on the issue again here. It will suffice to restate a few points. Certainly, as we saw earlier, the social importance of Islam in the Middle East region cannot be denied. We noted that Islam does have an impact on human rights perceptions in regional countries, as the faith is premised and rooted in the importance of collective over individual rights, with a corresponding high regard for social solidarity.

Conclusion

This chapter has addressed several questions in relation to human rights in the developing world. First, we considered whether there could be a universal concept of human rights and, if so, on what basis. Briefly delving into the literature, it seemed there could be such a concept, but only minimally stated.

The main problem was the second issue we examined: the relative positions of individual versus collective rights. We saw that individual rights are at the core of Western conceptions of liberal democracy, while concern with collective rights has traditionally been paramount not only in the socialist countries but also in several developing regions, including East and Southeast Asia, the Arab Middle East, and Africa. Like other issues we have looked at in this book, it was events associated both with the end of the Cold War and more generally with globalization that had an impact on human rights in the developing world. At its root was the old dispute: which system – liberal democracy or socialism – was best poised to deliver human rights? In other words, was socialism – built on the premise of providing collective benefits to all citizens who accept the legitimacy of the sociopolitical system – better at delivering human rights than individualistic liberal democracy? While

Western individualistic conceptions of human rights focus on the freedom of the individual not to be controlled by the state, the socialist formulation was more concerned with a variety of socioeconomic, rather than political, rights, including the right to employment and adequate housing and healthcare for all.

Third, we explored human rights in the five regions of the developing world by focusing on human development and political rights and civil liberties. We examined Mitchell and McCormick's (1988) contention that "countries that enjoyed higher levels of economic well-being have . . . better human rights records than those that do not." The conclusion was that in two regions – Latin America and the Caribbean, and East and Southeast Asia – there was some evidence for the veracity of the hypothesis, but in the other three regions – Africa, the Middle East, and South Asia – there was not. We need to bear in mind that advances in political rights and civil liberties (PR/CL) in many developing countries are mostly recent and, consequently, unlikely already to be entrenched. The implication is that anti-democratic reversals are quite possible and perhaps likely, especially in economically depressed regions such as Africa and South Asia. In these regions many countries continue to experience poor positions in relation to human development.

Regarding cultural factors and human rights, we examined Huntington's (1991) contention that Christianity is especially conducive to democracy. We saw that Latin America and the Caribbean – whose regional countries scored an average of 3.29 in PR/CL terms – is a strongly Christian region. On the other hand, the region that did second best in terms of PR/CL – South Asia, with an average PR/CL of 3.8 – is filled with Hindus, Sikhs, Muslims, and Buddhists, and relatively few Christians. The region with probably a slim majority of Christians over Muslims – Africa – achieved an average PR/CL score of 4.5, much better than the strongly Muslim Middle East with 5.72. Muslim and Hindu countries, Fukuyama (1992) maintains, are very likely to be nondemocratic and poor respecters of human rights. Yet some Muslim countries are "partly free" countries, while India and Nepal – both predominantly Hindu countries – also have democratically elected governments. The conclusion must be that cultural factors cannot be taken in isolation from others. It seems reasonably clear that, whatever a country's dominant culture, when it has a reasonably good HDI and has been a democracy for a longish period then it is likely to have a comparatively good human rights record.

One important indicator of the extent to which human rights have become a legitimate concern for both individual states and international society is the support which the former give to the various human rights conventions to which they have signed up. In particular, nearly all states assert their commitment to freedom from racial discrimination and slavery, refugees' rights, and the sociopolitical and economic rights of women. However, as we noted in chapter 5, despite the existence of international conventions it is not necessarily the case that national minorities are in reality treated equitably by governments in relation to majority peoples. Additionally, it has been observed that in some countries the rights of women begin and end with the right to vote. In this chapter we have seen that there are cultural issues linked to human rights observances in many developing countries. In chapter 7 we move on to the sociopolitical and economic position of women and assess to what extent this issue is bound up with issues of culture, religion, traditionalism, and modernization.

7

Women and Gender

The main aim of the this chapter is to describe and assess a range of women's groups in developing countries in terms of what they do and how they do it. Overall, the main sociopolitical significance of such women's groups is not that they threaten the stability of the state; rather, it is that, in some male-dominated societies, albeit imperfectly and partially, such organizations can enable women to improve their social, economic, and political positions.

The first section of the chapter examines the rise of the international women's movement and the formation of thousands of women's groups in the developing world. The second section looks at two kinds of women's empowerment groups: "feminist" and "feminine." The third section explores the generally poor socioeconomic position of females in the developing world. In this context we investigate the better position of women in the Indian state of Kerala and, briefly, in the Caribbean island of Cuba. This is not to claim, incidentally, that the position of the latter is anything but bad. Because economic malaise has widely served to reduce – still further – the already inferior position of many poor women, we examine, in section four, the impact of globalization and structural adjustment on women. In the final section of the chapter, we examine an array of women's groups in the regions of the developing world.

Gender Discrimination and Poverty in the Developing World

Starting in the early 1960s, the creation and gradual rise of the international women's movement has helped to change Western perspectives about the political, social, and economic position of women. Such concerns were recently put under the global spotlight, notably in a series of United Nations-sponsored global conferences: human rights (Vienna, 1992), the natural environment (Rio, 1992), population (Cairo, 1994), human development (Copenhagen, 1995), women and gender (Beijing, 1995), and social development (Geneva, 2000). Their cumulative effect was to help move international and domestic agendas "from the relatively safe area of 'women's issues' to focus debate on mainstream political, economic, social, environmental, and military issues" (Brittain 1995). The 1980s and 1990s also saw the birth not only of numerous domestic women's groups in the developing world, but also the creation of many transnational groups which "took advantage of the series of United Nations conferences to form a thick weave of interconnections" (Florini and Simmons 2000: 10).

Some idea of the numbers of women's groups may be gauged from the fact that the New York-based International Women's Tribune Center (IWTC) is the contact and referral office for over 6,000 women's groups from over 160 countries, an average of nearly 40 from each. In addition, there are probably additionally tens of thousands of women's groups in developing countries *not* registered with the IWTC (Fisher 1993: 40). For example, Durning reports that during the 1980s in rural Brazil the growth of women's groups was "explosive." However, virtually none of these organizations would be registered with the IWTC (Durning 1989: 28). Another example comes from Zimbabwe. Sylvester declares that women's organizations in the country have managed to "flourish in a climate in which all the main political forces in the country have, at some point in their histories, been masculinized" (Sylvester 1995: 409).

Why are women's groups necessary? Gender-based prejudice seems to be prevalent throughout much of the developing world, with millions of women discriminated against and living in poverty. This is despite legal and other measures to overcome inequalities. Such actions, the World Bank believes, "must be accompanied by efforts to raise awareness about culturally based attitudes . . . towards women." This is not only because "values, norms, and social institutions may reinforce persistent inequalities between groups in society," but also because "social divisions can become the basis of severe deprivation and conflict" (World Bank 2001: 117).

To redress gender inequality requires increasing female "empowerment" to enable women to assume their rightful place in society in relation to men. The term "empowerment" refers to the acquisition of the awareness and skills necessary to take charge of, and to make the most of, one's own life chances. It is also about facilitating the ability of individuals (and groups) to make decisions by and for themselves, in order, as far as possible, to shape their own destinies. Notwithstanding cultural distinctions, to achieve more power women must, as a starting point, be able to participate in decision-making at local, national, and international levels. And to achieve better empowerment it seems to be helpful to live in a democratizing, or already democratic, society. This is because such environments have more of the crucial social and political "space" within which to pursue goals than do authoritarian polities.

However, this no doubt oversimplifies things. A book edited by Shirin M. Rai (2000) has two main themes. The first is the difficulty of securing a public role for women in societies where they have long been consigned to the private, domestic sphere. In such circumstances it would be fanciful to assume that the introduction of formal democracy on its own would be sufficient to empower women. It is also necessary to do something harder: fundamentally to change the attitudes of many men and women. The first step might be quotas for women's representation in the political sphere. As the World Bank notes, "efforts are underway in at least 32 countries to increase women's political representation by reserving seats for them in local and national assemblies" (World Bank 2001: 120). For example, in India one third of local council seats are now reserved for women. In Argentina women must legally comprise at least a third of candidates on national election lists. In Pakistan the military government has decreed that women must fill 6 of the 21 seats on new local councils (McCarthy 2001). Finally, in South Africa women of the ruling African National Congress have achieved considerable success arguing for institutionalizing women's participation in the country's post-apartheid political organizations (Marais 1998: 170).

The second central theme of Rai's book is how important an activist role for women can be in achieving empowerment. This is not only in the opposition movements that, prior to democratization, played a critical role in undermining authoritarianism, but also in the civil society networks, both within and between countries, that proliferated during democratization. For example, during recent democratization in Guatemala, the political work of the country's women's organizations was effective in bolstering the notion that civil and political rights are human rights. The latter underwrite, safeguard, and ensure citizenship. Nevertheless, in many developing countries there are entrenched gendered imbalances and silences. These include the right of husbands to restrict the kind of employment that their wives can undertake outside the home (World Bank 2001: 118).

The main point is that although women's groups are to be found throughout the developing world, what they manage to achieve – socially, politically, and economically – is closely linked to prevailing sociocultural conditions. While women's empowerment is essential to facilitate wider female access to decision-making and resources, outcomes are dependent on various factors. Consequently, as we shall see below, there are encouraging signs of progress in parts of Latin America and South Asia, notably India. However, in some parts of the developing world, for example in many African countries, women's organizations tend to fall prey to what has been called the "civil society gap" or "trap." This occurs when there is a market-oriented decline in state services, for example during structural adjustment. This is partially compensated for by the unpaid (and largely unacknowledged) caring labor of women. Some women's groups, for example Kenya's predominantly women's *harambee* groups and Ghana's 31 December Women's Organization, are very concerned with improving members' developmental position and highlight the declining position of women during structural adjustment.

Women's Empowerment: "Feminist" and "Feminine" Groups

There are two broad kinds of women's empowerment groups found in developing countries. First, there are Western-style *feminist* groups, with memberships made up primarily of "Westernized, middle-class, university-educated women who . . . defy the classification of passive, voiceless and tradition-bound" women (Marchand 1995: 61). While intermittently influential, feminist groups tend to be regarded as rather elitist by less educated women. Second, and by far the most common, are *feminine* groups, concerned with an array of mostly material concerns: from consumption issues to questions of sociopolitical status. In sum, feminist groups pursue what are known as "strategic" objectives, while feminine groups aspire to more "practical" goals (Molyneux 1985; Jaquette 1989; Alvarez 1990; Safa 1990). According to Alvarez,

> feminist organizations [in Latin America] focus on issues *specific* to the female condition (i.e., reproductive rights), [and] feminine groups mobilize women around gender-related issues and concerns. The cost of liv-

ing, for example, is one such issue . . . Women . . . may organize to protest the rising cost of living because inflation undermines their ability to
adequately feed, clothe, and house their families. (Alvarez 1990: 25)

The point is that the "unitary category of 'woman' undifferentiated
by class, race or nationality" is not at all helpful intellectually when
seeking to analyze the sociopolitical impact of women's groups in the
developing world (Waylen 1993). One way of seeking to deal with the
problem is to divide women's groups into two categories. First, there
are those that conceptualize their chief concerns around "practical"
gender interests – for example, economic survival. Second, some groups
involve themselves with what are known as "strategic" gender interests, associated with more "feminist" objectives. It is important to note,
however, that such a dichotomized categorization is mostly for analytical convenience; in practice, there is much blurring between categories. Nevertheless, there are fairly clearly defined social divisions
between the practical concerns of the feminine organizations and the
concerns of the more "educated" feminist groups. On the other hand,
many urban working-class women's organizations not only address
"bread and butter" survival issues, but also concern themselves with
issues like domestic violence and reproductive rights. These are interests they share with the feminist groups (ibid: 574).

However, the feminine–feminist dichotomy is not only a heuristic
device. It is actually employed by women themselves in order to de-
note the class position of the activists. For example, middle-class, more
educated women tend to classify themselves as feminists, while poorer,
less-educated women often reject the "feminist" label (Alvarez 1990;
Marchand 1995). Yet, as Safa (1990) points out, an initial involvement
in the "practical" interests of the feminine organizations often leads
later to a consideration of more "strategic" concerns. Consequently, the
"distinction between feminist and [feminine] organizations is beginning to blur in some countries, as middle- and lower-class women define their common interests" (Fisher 1993: 103). Perhaps the best
analytical way forward is not to try to dichotomize the types of wom-
en's groups extant in the developing world, but to see them on a continuum with a large middle area where women's concerns overlap: both
practical and strategic (Marchand 1995: 64). The obvious analytical benefit of concentrating on the middle ground is that it allows us to overcome the private/public dichotomy whereby "practical" concerns are
relegated to the private sphere and "strategic" issues to the public realm
of politics.

Before looking at regional examples of women's groups, we examine the overall socioeconomic position of females in the developing world.

The Socioeconomic Position of Females in the Developing World

Females, around 50 percent of the world's population, do an estimated two-thirds of the world's work, yet they earn only 10 percent of global income and own less than 1 percent of the world's property. This implies that much of their work is unpaid, often connected with familial duties, such as bearing and rearing children, cleaning and maintaining households, caring for the aged and the sick, tending animals, and fetching water and fuel for domestic use. In addition to such domestic chores, many women also undertake – often poorly paid – work outside the home (Ekins 1992: 73; World Bank 2001: 117–22). Of the 1 billion illiterates in the world, two-thirds are female, and more than 60 percent of children deprived of primary education – 81 million out of 130 million people – are girls. In sum, as James Grant, the then Executive Director of Unicef, explained: "Employment rights, social security rights, legal rights, property rights, and even civil and political liberties are all likely to depend on the one, cruel chromosome distinguishing human male from female" (quoted in Brittain 1994).

The position of girls and women is reflected in an array of statistics. In most developing countries, girls and women score unsatisfactorily compared to males in most conventional measures of development: literacy, school enrollment, clinic attendance, rates of pay, access to land, availability of credit, and political office-holding at local, intermediate, and national levels (UNDP 1996: 138-43; World Bank 2001: 117–22). In short, in nearly all developing countries indices of modernization that promote self-perpetuating change in society favor men over women, including the spread of modern education, increases in literacy, urbanization, and prolonged economic growth. However, it would be incorrect to claim that there is nowhere in the developing world where the position of women is less bleak. Let's look at the situation in Cuba and the Indian state of Kerala, where the position of females is qualitatively better than in many other developing countries.

Women and development in Cuba and Kerala

Kerala provides a model of incremental yet comprehensive poverty alleviation under democratic and decentralized rule, while Cuba exhibits the success of long-term measures to improve the status of women. In Cuba since the inception of the communist regime in 1959, the state has worked assiduously to improve the socioeconomic position of women. This is reflected in a variety of comparative developmental statistics: in Cuba, infant mortality per 1,000 live births is just 14, compared with some of Cuba's neighbors at higher levels of development: Trinidad & Tobago, 20; Argentina, 30; Brazil, 59; Mexico, 37; Venezuela, 34. The same picture of sustained effort to improve women's well-being is shown in Cuba's literacy statistics: 93 percent of Cuba's women can read, compared to 80 percent in Brazil, 21 percent in Peru, 53 percent in Guatemala, and 29 percent in Honduras (Thomas 1994: 74–5).

While Cuba is a relatively well-known women's "success story," that of Kerala is less often highlighted; as a result, I shall focus on Kerala in the rest of this section. Kerala's governments have for decades been putting the poor – including women – first. This is not necessarily because the state's politicians and bureaucrats care more about the plight of the underprivileged than their counterparts elsewhere in India or, for that matter, in many other developing countries. Rather, it is because politicians have been compelled by popular opinion – expressed via the ballot box – to distribute resources according to where society believes they are most needed. This has been possible because, within the context of India's federal structure, Kerala is a highly democratic and literate state and many people there are keenly aware of the divisiveness caused by disparities of wealth and power in society.

Kerala is located in the southwest of India. It has a population of more than 30 million people who inhabit an area the size of Switzerland (41,000 square kilometers), a country with a much smaller population of 7 million people (World Bank 1995: 162–3; World Bank 2001: 275). Because state policy in Kerala has consistently been directed towards general poverty alleviation, the position of the poor – including poor women – has improved greatly since the early 1960s. Kerala has an adult literacy rate of more than 90 percent, much better than India's overall rate (56 percent). Its people live on average to the age of 72, compared to India's national rate of 61 years. In addition, Kerala's birth rate is more than 30 percent lower than India's generally, while the death rate of infants – 27 per 1,000 – is one third of the Indian average (World Bank 1995: 162-3; http://www.undp.org/hdro/ (UNDP website)). Moreover, nearly all of Kerala's villages have access to basic health, education, and transportation services at a level unknown elsewhere in India. The state has schools and clinics spread throughout its territory, while ubiquitous "fair price shops" sell basic goods at low prices. Durning (1989: 63) reports that Kerala ranks first in provision of basic services among India's states in three quarters (15/20) of categories. Safe water supplies and family planning services are available to a large majority of the population, while comprehensive and successfully implemented land reform programs has redistributed land to more than 1.5 million formerly landless people, including women. Overall, the result is that in Kerala inequalities between the "sexes are less pronounced than in any other [Indian] state" (ibid: 64).

These outcomes were achieved in part because the poor, including impoverished women, are both well organized and vocal. Successive governments, concerned for their own longevity, are of necessity committed to help them. Over time, a political culture has developed in Kerala geared towards the improvement of the position of have-nots, including poor females. It is important to understand that the position of women in Kerala is not typical of that of India more generally. Calvert and Calvert report that in India "since 1911 there has been a steady decline in the ratio of women to men ... There are now 929 women to every 1,000 men" (Calvert and Calvert 2001: 242). This is not due to some mysterious biological cause, but the result of the murder of thousands of baby girls each year. This practice, perhaps more than anything else, emphasizes the lowly position of females in Indian society – Kerala excepted. Why kill baby girls? The main reason is the rising costs of dowries: girls are a very expensive liability for parents; to have one can – and often does – mean future financial ruin. Although dowries were made illegal by decree of the federal government more than 30 years ago, the custom still flourishes. In fact, the trend is towards larger and larger sums of money payable from the parents of the bride to that of the bridegroom on marriage. If the agreed price is not paid, the woman may well be returned to her parents. Sometimes such women are badly treated for not bringing in larger dowries; on extreme occasions, bride-burning is the outcome: the bride will be set on fire by paraffin or kerosene to simulate an accidental fire in the cooking area. According to official figures, 2,500 women were killed in this way in 1991, although the figure may be much higher (ibid: 243). While such deliberate cruelty is unusual, more common is the impact of cultural norms promoting inequality. It is primarily this sense of traditional cultural normality which India's women's empowerment groups seek to change.

Kerala's overall developmental record shows what can be achieved through mobilization and organization and provides others in India with a ready-made model to emulate. In relation to females, Kerala's achievements are summarized as follows:

- *Increased literacy.* This facilitates wider access to written sources of information which for women can lead both to improved health and smaller families.
- *Secure land rights.* This allows the impoverished – including women – to increase income and hence economic security.
- *Improved local control over common resources.* This helps to break the cycle of economic–ecological degradation.
- *Better access to credit.* This enables poor people – both women and men – to buy essential livestock and tools.
- *Clean drinking water and community-based health care.* This serves to protect adult lives from debilitating diseases and also saves many babies and children from early deaths.
- *Cheap, efficient family planning.* This offers women the chance to control their own fertility effectively, enabling them to space births at healthy intervals, in turn improving their own health. Many couples have smaller families in Kerala than elsewhere in India.

Women's empowerment in both Cuba and Kerala underlines the crucial importance to have both a responsive government as well as a relatively educated and concerned electorate. In Kerala especially, this has meant that citizens have been willing over time to vote for politicians who would sincerely work towards improving the poor development positions of women and other disadvantaged people. Because of the overall success of state governments in Kerala in achieving poverty reduction and developmental goals there was less need than in many other places for single-issue action groups to pursue the aspirations of subordinated women.

The Impact of Structural Adjustment and Globalization on Poor Females

Structural adjustment programs (SAPs)

The combined effects of SAPs, economic crisis, poverty, and globalization served to propel millions of women in dozens of developing countries into even greater poverty than before. Critics asserted that, as a result, there was a "feminization of poverty," with females suffering disproportionately compared to males. The numerous ways in which women absorbed the fallout from generalized economic instability or crisis amounted to what feminist economists called the "gender-related costs of invisible adjustment." The impact was twofold: (1) the world of work and (2) declining health and welfare programs (Marchand 1995).

IMF-sponsored SAPs in developing countries were primarily designed to correct balance of payments imbalances. Had the kinds of measures adopted in Kerala been incorporated into SAPs then they might well have fundamentally improved the lot of the poor, including impoverished women. They might also have enabled larger numbers of poor people to generate more income for themselves – in turn aiding the project of national development. Or, alternatively, SAPs might have focused on removing economic distortions and inefficiencies primarily benefiting the better off. But because SAPs were generally drawn up quickly in response to crises, their architects adopted what seem to have been the most immediately effective solutions to budgetary imbalances, such as removing subsidies on basic foodstuffs to the poor. But rarely, if ever, did SAPs focus on invisible subsidies to the rich, such as protection of industrial subsidies. The outcome was that SAPs nearly always had deleterious outcomes for the poor. And, given that women are very often the poorest of the poor, it is not surprising that poor women were often among the hardest hit.

SAPs also affected health and welfare programs in many developing countries, with females losing out. *Paying for Health*, a 1994 Oxfam report, states that Zimbabwe's SAP led directly to steep increases in user fees for medical services and, between 1989 and 1991, led to a 250 percent increase in maternal deaths. Overall, death rates in the capital, Harare, doubled among women in 1991–2 as a consequence of SAP-induced cuts in spending (Oxfam report quoted in Brittain 1994: 12).

Structural adjustment had an impact on women's access to welfare programs as well. Not only were women likely to suffer from cuts in public services as health services deteriorated, but in addition many were called upon to look after sick relatives; and when education cuts reduced school hours, they had to spend more time supervising children than before (UNRISD 1995: 147). When social safety-net programs were introduced to provide employment opportunities to those worst affected by structural adjustment, women typically received far fewer work chances than did men. For example, in Bolivia, only 1 percent of those employed in social programs were women. India had a better record: 16 percent of such workers were females, and in Honduras "only" three-quarters of "social jobs" were held by men (ibid: 53).

There were three further outcomes linked to the declining position of poor females as a result of SAPs. First, poor women were likely to spend more time than before shopping for small quantities of cheaper items if they could not, like most women in the developing world, afford a refrigerator. Second, they may also have been forced by economic pressures to try to grow more of their own food. Sparr's (1994) study of poor women on the Indonesian island of Java found that economic downturns led to many women spending more time growing vegetables on privately owned plots for family consumption and in some cases for outside sale. Third, poor women in Ecuador were compelled to pass increased female work burdens on to their daughters. This is because, when mothers worked outside the home, daughters were encouraged, frequently at the expense of their education, to spend more time on domestic work (ibid: 26).

In sum, SAPs led to increased poverty for the poor, including women, in numerous developing countries in the 1980s and 1990s. This was manifested in three main ways. Many poor women: (1) had to work harder than before, both in the home and outside to try to maintain income levels; (2) experienced declining levels of healthcare and welfare; (3) received fewer benefits than men from job-creation schemes.

Poor women in the developing world: the impact of globalization

Because millions of poorly paid workers' saw their incomes seriously squeezed, critics argued that globalization amounted not only to increased global movement of capital but also "increased exploitation of labor" (Ackerley and Okin 1999: 134; ILO 1994: 108). And women, already receiving proportionately lower wages than men in virtually all developing countries, found their wages hard hit (UNRISD 1995: 28). However, empirical evidence shows that one of the impacts of economic globalization, trade reform, actually had "differential effects on men and women" (McKay, Winters, and Kedir 2000: 4). There are examples where trade liberalization and other aspects of globalization actually favored the participation of women in paid employment, in both services and manufacturing. This is because in the developing world women are more likely than men to be employed in export-oriented activities. But this is not to suggest that all women benefited from the changing regime: many unskilled women, for example, are no better off. In addition, both "women and children may also lose from other consequences of trade reform, such as outmigration of males or increased pressure on their time" (ibid)·

What of women working either in the services or export sector? It is sometimes assumed that because women are increasingly represented in industrial work forces in some developing countries then it must mean that their socioeconomic position generally is improving. Kamrava, for example, asserts that in many developing countries "through industrialization . . . traditional values, such as the importance of motherhood, the inadmissibility of women earning money, and other primordial core symbols" are being eroded. As a result, the general social and economic position of women is "somewhat ameliorated " (Kamrava 1993: 115). However, others claim that, on the whole, females' socioeconomic levels are actually declining *despite* increasing numbers of job opportunities linked to globalization. This is because, as Okin points out, "women's access to paid work is constrained both by discrimination and sex segregation in the workplace and by the assumption that women are 'naturally' responsible for all or most of the unpaid work of the household" (Okin 1994: 13)

However, it should be noted that the participation of women in the paid work force is higher in some developing regions than others. As table 7.1 shows, in 1999 females amounted to 45 percent of the work force in East and Southeast Asia (a figure comparable to that of many European countries), 42 percent in Africa, 35 percent in Latin America, a third in South Asia, and 27 percent in the Middle East (World Bank 2001: 279). Table 7.1 also indicates that, with the exception of Latin America and the Caribbean, the proportion of females in labor forces in developing regions has remained relatively static since 1980.

Does the increased involvement of women in paid employment have negative or positive effects on their well-being and that of their families? There is no simple answer. Like the debate about world trade dis-

Table 7.1   Women as a percentage of the labor force in the developing world

Region	Females as % of labor force in 1980	Females as % of labor force in 1999
East Asia and Pacific	43	45
Latin America and Caribbean	28	35
Middle East	24	27
South Asia	34	33
Africa	42	42

Source: World Bank (2001: 279, table 3)

cussed in chapter 2, arguments about the benefits to women of paid employment in the developing world are polarized. On the one hand, there are the "globaphiles" – for example, the IMF, the World Bank, and Western governments – contending that increased exports are always good for the poverty stricken, including poor women. In the opposite corner are the "globaphobes." Their argument is that trade is innately exploitative for the poor; liberation can only come from less trade and more self-reliance (Watkins 2001).

There is another dimension to the argument, involving cultural and social issues. Over half of the East and Southeast Asian women in the labor force are factory workers; the highest of any developing region. Many work in the export sector. Does joining the paid labor force liberate such women? It has been suggested that female involvement in the labor force does not necessarily mean that women become more active participants in public life than before. Why? Cammack, Pool, and Tordoff (1993) argue that such females are rarely free agents within the labor market, but instead are "resources mobilized by the family" for perhaps 15 years, that is, the period between leaving primary school and marriage. They also claim that, despite a high level of involvement in the labor force, females in East and Southeast Asia do not loudly demand changes in either family or gender relations (ibid: 221). The World Bank puts it like this: "While women in [South] Korea have become educated and participate actively in the labor force, their unequal status serves to maximize their economic contribution while minimizing advances in gender equity" (World Bank 2001: 118).

Focusing on the export processing zone of Ashulia, Bangladesh, both "globaphile" and "globaphobe" views seem wide of the mark. Watkins

(2001) reports on the case of Shawaz Begum, an 18-year-old Bangladeshi woman who works in a South Korean-owned factory in Ashulia on the outskirts of the capital, Dhaka. She spends 10 hours a day sewing garments for Western brands, including Tesco, Pierre Cardin, Harrods, Nike, and Levi's. Does Shawaz Begum benefit or not from her employment? On the negative side, she and the other half a million female Bangladeshis employed in the export garment industry have very poor working conditions. Demonstrations to demand improved working conditions in late 1991 resulted in thousands of female Bangladeshi garment workers locked out from their jobs. Twenty-five, mostly female workers were injured. In addition, women garment workers in Bangladesh are sometimes forced to work for no pay, and "many" have been sexually assaulted at work. According to a July 1992 report in the Toronto Star newspaper, one tenth of all female garment workers have been beaten or tortured by their employer. Some are compelled to "stand on their heads for extended periods as punishment for flaws in their work" (Human Rights Internet 1993: 16). On the positive side, for many Bangladeshi women a relatively well-paid job in the export sector means the difference between struggling to survive and the ability to have a little spare cash. Shawaz Begum earns US$1.70 a day – a very poor wage by Western standards, but double what she could earn in the informal sector. This money is sufficient both to provide food for her widowed mother and to keep a sister in school.

A second example, also from Ashulia, is provided by the story of Mosammat Aleya, a female garment worker. Because her husband's wage from his job in another garment factory was inadequate to support their family, Mrs Aleya began paid work in 1985. While she faced criticism from her extended family for working outside the home, her wages, like those of Shawaz Begum, are crucial for the family's well-being. However, some relief from economic pressures for Mrs Aleya is partially counterbalanced by her having to work an extremely long day. She must get up at 4 a.m. to do housework and prepare breakfast for her children and large extended family. After taking the children to school she walks a few miles to work, beginning at 8 a.m. She arrives home after the children get home from school. But she has been able to buy them a stereo and a television to offset her absence at work when they get home (Braid 1995).

The overall point of these two stories is that work might be exploitative but without the wages it provides, Mosammat Aleya and Shawaz Begum – and numerous other Bangladeshi women – would find their material conditions even worse. Neither of the polarized stances on globalization completely reflects the reality of such people's socioeconomic positions. On the one hand, the "globaphobes" do not seem to understand that access to developed markets furnishes millions of people in Bangladesh and elsewhere with opportunities to construct, albeit slowly, a better life. The "globaphiles," on the other hand, do not appear to grasp that unless globalization does much more for the poor than it currently does then the credibility of the international trading system will continue to be undermined.

Regional Analysis: A Woman's Place

In the case studies that follow we see how women in various countries – including Argentina, Brazil, and India – have pursued their interests. Overall, these case studies suggest that attempts to improve women's socioeconomic and political positions usually start from a concern with so-called "women's projects," such as enhancing housekeeping skills, handicraft production, and micro-enterprise development. Eventually, however, many women come to the realization that a general amelioration of their position depends on changing society's prevailing power structure to improve, *inter alia*, infant mortality rates and environmental protection. What is needed are initiatives to educate women to defend and then to improve their overall societal position. Overall, the case studies show that much can be done to improve women's voice and access to resources via increases in

- political representation;
- legal rights;
- command over physical, financial, and human capital.

Africa

Because Africa is a huge region of around 50 countries, we might expect the position of women to vary from country to country. Tordoff notes that "in precolonial African societies, great variations existed in the social and economic positions of women" (Cammack, Pool, and Tordoff 1993: 211). It is pertinent to note, however, that during the first half of the twentieth century, Africa underwent a period of quite unprecedented modernization, almost revolutionary in its medium- and long-term effects. Urbanization was an important effect of this process, leading to mass migrations and patchy, slow industrialization. Preexisting towns expanded and new urban centers grew following the formal establishment of colonial rule. Arriving in the late nineteenth and early twentieth centuries, European colonial rulers brought with them their own conceptions of gender relations and responsibilities which, in Britain, were the result of the established mores and morals of Victorian society. Colonial rulers assumed that men's domination of women was universal, a God-given fact. The Europeans often accepted Western gender stereotypes that assigned women to the domestic domain, leaving economic and political matters to men. As a result of these factors – modernization, Western conceptions of women's role and position in society, and improvements in men's social standing – the status of women in Africa is said to have worsened during the colonial era. In short, for many African women, the colonial period was characterized by significant losses in both power and authority (Parpart 1988: 210).

During the 1950s and 1960s, the key period of African agitation against European rule, many men welcomed women's political participation. At this time, women were promised economic and political benefits from independence. But these promises, for the most part, failed to materialize. Following independence some limited attempts were made to involve women in state-linked activities. However, as a group females were systematically neglected and underrepresented in African countries' central institutions. In other words, the postcolonial state in Africa is a male preserve. The comments of a (male) Tanzanian MP may not be atypical of men's attitudes towards women. He proclaimed that women "were meant to serve men and they can never be equal to men" (quoted in Parpart 1988: 216). In addition, as Geisler notes, in certain southern African countries, including Botswana, Lesotho, Namibia, and Swaziland, women lack the ability to make their mark on politics primarily because of men's discrimination (Geisler 1995: 46).

Discrimination against females also extends to the world of work. Generally, African females are prevented from developing their full potential by restricted employment opportunities. For example, fewer than 10 percent of lawyers, engineers, and medical doctors in Kenya are female, while in Nigeria only about 6 percent of academic staff are women. Generally, "opportunities for wage labor are few"; even when they do arise women are usually paid less and are promoted slower than their male counterparts (Parpart 1988: 217). Informal economic activities are however widely open to women. Many make a resounding success of trading, yet even then it is men who usually own the larger, more profitable shops. In an attempt to get round the often small

scale of their trading activities and the fact that banks are rarely willing
to extend credit, women in Nigeria, Kenya, and Ghana, for example,
have established their own credit organizations (Fisher 1993: 40;
Aryeetey 2000). In addition, many African women have found a niche
in the NGO sector, where "women's groups and funding from international donors abound" (Geisler 1995: 46).

To summarize, in the postcolonial era the position of women in Africa has not clearly improved. Most African women are restrained from
developing their full potential, not only by men's resistance but also by
social and cultural mores. Unlike in Latin America or India, the political marginalization of women in Africa has not led to attempts to build
solidarity, in part because of often pronounced class, ethnic, and/or
religious divisions. Nevertheless, *some* women have done well out of
the existing arrangements, by exploiting their commercial skills or by
finding a niche in the NGO sector.

South Asia

We saw that in Latin America their supposedly conservative Catholic
backgrounds and traditions did not inhibit many poor women from
organizing their own groups. The same could be said of India, with a
cultural background of Hinduism, where millions of women have organized themselves into thousands of different groups to pursue economic, social, and political goals. On the other hand, women in two of
the region's predominantly Muslim countries, Bangladesh and Pakistan, have not organized themselves to anything like the same extent.
This disparity is sometimes explained by the influence of Islam. Many
Muslim men are said to be innately conservative. This is thought to
dovetail with religious tenets that are widely interpreted as viewing
women as subservient.

The relatively advanced position of women in India is linked to the
fact that the country has been a democracy for more than 50 years. While
for much of this period the political scene was dominated by the Congress (I) Party, there is a national tradition of women's political activism, especially at the grassroots level. This may reflect the fact that many
females are skeptical about the efficacy of the party system to allow
them a meaningful political voice. For example, the Congress (I) Party
failed to allow women an adequate voice in party decision-making, as
did a rival party, the Communist Party of India (Marxist) (CPI (M)).
The CPI (M) was predicated on an organizational democratic centralism.

This meant that its women's wing got very little autonomous space within which to function (Omvedt 1994: 37). Women responded by forming a range of non-party women's organizations, such as *Sangathana*. However, while this enabled such groups to be free from the constraints of electoral politics, it helped lead to a political marginalization. In other words, ideological "purity" was maintained at the cost of not participating in, and thus potentially influencing, the institutionalized political system (Rai 1994: 534). The point is that Indian women faced similar choices to their counterparts in Latin America: "liberty or association"; each path, it appears, could lead to political marginalization.

Until the third wave of democracy, India was an exception among Asian countries in that it had – except for the 1975–7 "Emergency" period – "opted for and maintained a parliamentary system since independence" (Shah 1988: 262). Yet, while formally democratic, successive governments have not been very good at enhancing the material position of females, half the population. This may be one of the reasons why the country has thousands of women's empowerment groups with sociopolitical, as well as economic, goals. Many emerged in the 1970s and 1980s, a time of "crisis of [the] political–economic system and [of] ideologies," choosing direct action as the best way of expressing popular aspirations and grievances (Omvedt 1994: 35).

The position of women in Bangladesh, more than 80 percent Muslim, has become an issue for discussion since 1971, when the country gained its independence from Pakistan. Bangladesh is one of the poorest and most densely populated countries in the world; women suffer disproportionately more than men from poverty. "Microcredit programs in Bangladesh find that giving income-generating loans to women improves the nutritional status of their children, a result that does not hold for men" (World Bank 2001: 119). However, violence and discrimination against women remain common features of Bangladeshi society, even though the 1972 Constitution established equal rights for men and women in all spheres of the state and public life. Many Bangladeshi women live in a state of dependency on men as a result of poverty and a lack of education, employment, and training opportunities (Khan 1988: 1). Unsurprisingly, the political position of women is relatively underdeveloped.

In accordance with the traditional Muslim practice of purdah – the seclusion or veiling of adult females – women are expected to stay within the *bari* (home) and discouraged from contact with anyone outside their close family. This practice limits the social and educational development of millions of Bangladeshi women, while restricting access to employment opportunities. Although the institution of seclusion is being challenged – as we saw earlier in the chapter, poverty is forcing increasing numbers to seek paid employment outside the home – the ideals of purdah – modesty, humility, domesticity, and non-involvement in public life – are still strong. Despite good intentions, international aid programs often tend to reinforce rather than diminish such disparities because they usually work within established distribution systems, placing the "target population . . . in the passive position of recipients rather than participants" (Tomasevski 1988: 5).

Thus, in India a large number of women's organizations have formed for the purpose of raising public awareness about female issues and to lobby government to improve their social, economic, and legal position. In Bangladesh, on the other hand, women appear to be politically marginalized, unable to find a collective voice. To see why this is the case we next examine briefly two of India's numerous women's groups: (1) the Self-Employed Women's Association (SEWA) of Ahmedabad and (2) the Working Women's Forum (WWF). These organizations are engaged in similar areas of endeavor: coordinating women working in the informal sector into trade unions and credit organizations in order to enhance their positions.

The Self-Employed Women's Association (SEWA)

Until we became organized as a SEWA cooperative, the middlemen could cheat us. But now I can negotiate with them as the representative of our cooperative and as an elected member of our local council. One day near the bus stop, I heard a couple of men saying, "There's the woman who is giving us trouble. Shall we beat her up?" I said to them, "Go ahead and just try it. I have 40,000 women behind me." (SEWA leader, speaking at World Summit for Social Development and Beyond, Geneva 2000, quoted in World Bank 2001: 117)

SEWA is a large women-run non-governmental organization (NGO) which promotes its members' well-being and economic development. Based in Ahmedabad, Gujarat, SEWA was established in 1972 as a women-only trade union and credit organization for females working in the informal sector. Before SEWA existed such women would typically have to borrow 50 rupees (US$1.50) every morning from a money lender. With the money they would buy produce – fruit, vegetables, or grain – and then sell it. At the end of the day they would have to repay the 50 rupees – plus 10 percent interest. From their meager profits they would often have to find bribes to pay the local police to overlook their selling without a license. At the end of the working day they might show a net profit of 7 rupees (US$0.21), quite insufficient to buy the essential items they and their families needed. To combat such poverty, SEWA established its own "bank," providing loans at a very low annual rate of interest (12 percent). SEWA soon saw its membership grow as working women flocked to join and, by the late 1990s, it had more than 40,000 members. To get over the problem of bribes, SEWA successfully lobbied to the Supreme Court in Delhi to persuade the authorities to set up a municipal market for its members (Clark 1997: 109–10). SEWA also lobbied the government to finance a maternity program. SEWA works at the grassroots and its success can be measured by the fact that the "surrounding society and government came to have a greater understanding of the lives and needs of self-employed women workers" (Ackerley and Okin 1999: 144).

The Working Women's Forum (WWF)

Ms Jaya Arunachalam founded the WWF in 1978 in Madras. Ms Arunachalam was a social worker and formerly a prominent member of the Congress (I) Party, who resigned from the party because she felt that it was quite ineffective in reaching out to poor women (Fisher 1993: 203). The WWF began as a grassroots union of poor women workers in the informal sector with 800 members. Its growth was swift and by the early 1990s it was a national movement with tens of thousands of members focused in four states: Tamil Nadu, Karnataka, Andhra Pradesh, and Uttar Pradesh. It now has more than 150,000 members across India. "The most astonishing aspect of all this has been the ability of illiterate and extremely poor women to pass on the word and extend their movement to other districts, towns, and states in India" (Lecomte 1986: 118). Local WWF leaders set up groups to raise funds, build up savings, negotiate bank loans, and help provide for members' welfare needs (Fisher 1993: 203).

Following abortive attempts to forge links with a government-administered loan scheme, the WWF set up its own Working Women's Cooperative Society to issue credit. The only people able to apply for loans were WWF members, women not only marginalized by informal – and hence insecure – working status, but also by gender and poverty. Such people are of course at or near the bottom of the social pile, illtreated and exploited by money lenders and, if in work, employers. As

Ekins notes, it is an "extraordinary achievement for such women to have organized themselves in large numbers effectively to combat this oppression and materially improve their quality of life" (Ekins 1992: 119).

The success of WWF springs from the way that, like SEWA, it embedded itself and drew inspiration from the inputs of its members. Both WWF and SEWA share similar organizing characteristics: (1) placing the priorities of poor women first, (2) promoting leadership from below, (3) using organizational clout to get poor women their rights, and (4) working exclusively with poor women. Overall, both WWF and SEWA have achieved provision of credit for the poor, increased consciousness for tens of thousands of working women, and raised members' awareness of social and economic injustice, while putting political pressure on government to deal with members' pressing concerns.

East and Southeast Asia

We have noted that in recent years millions of women in both Latin America and the Caribbean and South Asia have pursued political and socioeconomic goals of empowerment. In the former region, women played a vital role in bringing an end to military dictatorships in the 1980s. In many East and Southeast Asian countries, on the other hand, women's social, economic, and political position remains relatively lowly.

Shin (1999: 258–62) suggests that in some such countries, including South Korea, this situation is in part because of the influence of the Confucianism – a philosophy or religion with strong patriarchal traditions of family organization and control of females. Traditionally, both community and family decision-making are heavily male-orientated. Until marriage, females are normally under their father's control; after it – normally women move into their spouse's familial home – their husband is the boss. Regarding paid employment, girls may leave school as young as 11 years in some East and Southeast Asian countries and soon after enter paid employment. For example, in Taiwan a quarter of the work force is made up of females aged between 15 and 29 years, with a large proportion employed in manufacturing. Up to three-quarters of their earnings may be handed over to the family, often for boys' education. Females may work for a decade in a factory before they marry, as fathers are reluctant to lose their daughters' earning power.

The widespread entry of young women into factory work in many of the region's countries in recent years does not appear to have led to dramatic changes in the character and extent of their political activity. This is probably partly a consequence of the fact that in many states of the region political activity by any group was, until recently, discouraged, and partly a result of the close connections between "family structure, family employment strategies, and women's entry to paid employment" (Cammack, Pool, and Tordoff 1993: 220). The relationship between work experience and gender politics is influenced not only by patriarchal traditions, but also by the interaction of these traditions with national economic structures and social and political factors. Many regional governments and employers have long opposed the organization of workers – whether men or women – in vigorous trade unions, as part of a general strategy of maintenance of a low-wage economy (ibid: 222).

In conclusion, there are generally weak labor unions and a paucity of embedded democratic institutions in most East and Southeast Asian countries. As the region's economies have advanced over the last two decades, increasing numbers of women have joined the formal work force. This has not, however, been sufficient clearly to advance the general social and political position of women. Unlike in Latin America and the Caribbean and India, there are relatively few influential women's organizations in the region.

Latin America and the Caribbean

While women are relatively well represented in political life in a few Caribbean islands, notably Trinidad & Tobago, generally the situation follows a pattern common in most developing countries: underrepresentation, in part a legacy of the past. The region's islands have a shared history of colonialism, slavery, and racism, factors instrumental in shaping local societies, cultures, economies, and political systems. Enslaved Africans were first brought to Jamaica, Trinidad & Tobago, and other Caribbean islands by the British for the production of sugar. After slavery was abolished in the 1830s, sugar production relied heavily on importation of indentured labor from India. Indian women, both Hindu and Muslim, were among those recruited in Calcutta and Madras to work on the sugar plantations. The descendants of these Africans and East Indians now comprise the two dominant ethnic groups in the Caribbean.

Several Caribbean islands, including Trinidad & Tobago, have a tradition of women's organizations dating back to the 1930s. In the 1970s and 1980s, in the context of declining political and socioeconomic conditions, women in several Caribbean islands, including Jamaica, organized themselves to combat male brutality against females – including rape and domestic violence. Numerous grassroots organizations developed, providing among other things day care centers and hostels for young working women, efforts that complemented those of the government.

Like the Caribbean, Latin America's recent history is also informed by distinctive modes of modernization, including export-led development and limited industrialization. These developments had a marked effect on the status of women. Until the recent regional wave of democratization (discussed in chapter 4), women's lack of political participation reflected a traditional subordination, said to be influenced by traditional Catholic ideas of female subservience. Recently, however, three factors – social responses to deep economic crisis, successful challenges to dictatorial rule, and dissemination of feminist ideas – led to a pronounced shift in the nature and scope of women's political activity and, to an extent, socioeconomic position.

Numerous women's groups emerged in Latin American countries during the 1970s and 1980s, years of dictatorship. At this time, the political awareness of many women increased, partly the result of governmental bans on pluralist political activities. One result of the ban on conventional party politics was to improve the availability of political space for women, by affording them greater visibility and prominence, with many enjoying leadership roles in human rights campaigns in the region. Waylen notes that "one effect of the suppression of organizations such as trade unions and political parties was to move the locus of much political activity . . . from institutional to community-based activities where women have greater opportunities to participate" (Waylen 1993: 576). A second consequence was that because many male activists were killed or imprisoned, it was often women that secretly kept parties going despite being officially banned. Third, military rule stimulated the emergence of feminist movements, galvanized in part by a realization that authoritarian power relations were not only present in the public sphere but also in the household and family. In sum, developments during military rule – including growth in female participation in community-based activities, women's involvement in political parties, and feminist ideas – served to encourage millions of women to pursue self-interested political, economic, and social goals.

Regional women's groups emerged in response to social, political, and economic conditions, linked to rule by military dictatorship. But once pluralist politics revived in the 1980s and 1990s, few managed to convert their mobilization into institutional representation (Safa 1990). Once normal party politics was reestablished, women's groups were confronted with a difficult choice: "liberty" or "association." Should they continue to operate outside the party political arena? If they did they risked political marginalization and loss of influence. But if they chose to link up with the male-dominated parties how were they to prevent cooptation and subsequent loss of autonomy? In the event, most women's groups opted for "liberty," that this, they opted to remain outside the confines of party politics in order to retain their independence (Waylen 1993). Consequently, Latin America's redemocratization in the 1980s and 1990s did not destroy the networks of women's groups. Instead, two parallel systems of political activity developed: (1) male-dominated legislatures and political parties; and (2) thousands of women's groups with political, economic, and social concerns. The latter represent an innovative form of politics, recasting political agendas and forms of political action (Slater 1985; Jelin 1990; Redclift 1988).

Human rights issues were a key stimulus for many regional women's groups during the 1970s and 1980s. In Latin America thousands of men "disappeared" during military rule and, not surprisingly, their women tried to extract information from reticent authorities about the fate of their loved ones. When adequate information was not forthcoming, women became crucial to human rights protests throughout Latin America, which eventually helped to hasten the end of military rule throughout the region. The most famous of women's human rights groups was Argentina's Las Madres of the Plaza de Mayo (the Mothers of the Plaza de Mayo). Others included the Mutual Support Group in Guatemala, the Group of Relatives of the Detained–Disappeared in Chile, and the Mothers and Relatives of Those Tried by Military Justice in Uruguay (Radcliffe and Westwood 1993: 16–17). What these groups had in common was a concern with human rights and justice. To illustrate these concerns, we examine Argentina's Las Madres. This will highlight how members' initial requests for information concerning their missing loved ones later developed into a wider demand for greater sociopolitical justice for women.

Las Madres of the Plaza de Mayo (Argentina)

Formed in April 1977 by the wife of a diplomat and the spouse of a factory worker, Las Madres was a response to the policy of abduction and killing of individuals during the military dictatorship that began in 1976 (Feijoo and Gogna 1990: 87). Inaugurated by the military regime, the euphemistically named "Process of National Reorganization" (*proceso*) led to an intense repression during which an estimated 9,000 people died at the hands of the state's security services. Many victims were young: nearly 70 percent were aged between 16 and 30 years (Elshtain 1995: 548–9).

Initially, Las Madres comprised just 14 women aged between 40 and 60 years, parents of some of the individuals who had disappeared. Gaining no information from the authorities regarding their children's whereabouts, they began to demonstrate regularly in the Plaza de Mayo, Buenos Aires, in front of the main government building. By July 1977 the group had grown in size to about 150 women. In October of that year Las Madres presented to the authorities a petition signed by 24,000 people. It demanded an investigation into the disappearances of their children and the freeing of the thousands of prisoners detained without trial. However, the police dispersed those trying to deliver the petition, using tear gas and firing live rounds into the air. During the fracas, about 300 women were briefly detained and their identity papers checked (Feijoo and Gogna 1990: 87).

For Las Madres, the treatment of its members at the hands of the state – simply for asking for information regarding the whereabouts of their sons and husbands – "gave political form and shape to their protest, linking them to an international network of associations and watchdog societies," including Amnesty International and Americas Watch (Elshtain 1995: 551). During the first half of the 1980s Las Madres maintained their demands to release their menfolk. Eventually, in 1986, after the restoration of democracy, an amnesty law was passed which not only effectively absolved the military of responsibility in relation to the "disappeared," but also required that prosecution for acts of repression should take place within 60 days of the alleged disappearance. This meant in effect that the military remained above the law; and there were very few – if any – prosecutions for human rights violations in Argentina in relation to the "disappeared."

In conclusion, the case of Las Madres is important because it illustrates that what began as a women's demand for information about disappeared loved ones developed over time into a wider search both for an enhanced sociopolitical role for women and a fundamental questioning of the female role in society. Las Madres' experience also presents a very interesting case from two different perspectives which converge: one is that of people concerned with the creation of a political scenario to legitimize the process of democratization and of new ways of conducting politics; the other stresses the gender of the political agents.

Working women's organizations in Brazil: São Paulo's Shantytown and Unemployed Movements

Like in Argentina, during Brazil's period of military rule (1964–85) ordinary people were excluded from institutional politics. As a result, non-institutional politics, in the form of popular movements, became an important arena for citizens' opposition to government by the armed forces; and women played a significant role (Brydon and Chant 1989). Thousands of women took part in popular protests at the lack of employment opportunities and the failure of the authorities to provide basic services to the slums.

Favela (shantytown) organizations in São Paulo and other large Brazilian cities are good examples of women-dominated groups that developed both political consciousness and group solidarity among working females. The movements I have selected for examination are the Shantytown Movement (O Movimento de Favela) and the Unemployed Movement (O Movimento dos Desempregados). They are significant because working women were strongly represented among their leaders and activists. Thousands of poor Brazilian women were encouraged through their membership of such groups to agitate for "recognition of their roles and rights as workers, residents, and citizens" (Corcoran-Nantes 1993: 138).

The number and types of social movements in Brazil grew in the 1980s in line with the rise in popular protest against continued military rule. Some had overtly welfare-orientated goals, demanding that both state administrations and the federal government took action to ameliorate deteriorating socioeconomic conditions among the poor. In São Paulo there was strong growth in the numbers of activist groups, stimulated in part both by increasing social polarization – the result of a structural adjustment program – and a more general economic decline. Many among the poor experienced an often acute sense of exclusion, exacerbated in many cases by the fact that large numbers lived in the favelas, often situated alongside wealthy areas. Favelas expanded rapidly in the 1970s and 1980s, principally as the result of rural–urban migration. This placed enormous pressure on the already limited capacity of public services to provide clean water, electricity, sanitation, transport, housing, and healthcare (ibid: 141–2).

The Shantytown Movement was founded in 1976 with two main aims: (1) to secure land titles for favela dwellers and (2) to seek improvements in basic services and communication infrastructures. The Unemployed Movement was formed in 1983. Its goals included trying to deal with the problems of mass unemployment in São Paulo, by (1) seeking unemployment benefits for those without work. and (2) the formation of workers' cooperatives to build houses. Both movements began on a very small scale with meetings taking place in activists' homes, before expanding in size and aspirations. Together, the two organizations were representative of the popular movements which mushroomed in the urban periphery of São Paulo in the 1980s. Many of their leaders and activists were poor women. First, we examine the role of women in the Unemployed Movement, before turning to the Shantytown Movement.

Following its founding, the Unemployed Movement experienced swift growth, spreading from São Paulo to other urban areas in Brazil. Initially, there were separate women's groups within the movement, although men had overall organizational control. Male leaders wanted to remove what they regarded as "women's issues" from the movement's demands. However, the women's groups quickly became an important forum for the discussion of a wide range of issues of particular relevance to females, including women's political participation and sociopolitical and economic role, as well male domestic violence. As time went on, the women's groups expanded their activities, becoming mutual support collectives. Both cooperative work and mutualist schemes were useful in helping develop solidarity among the women (Mainwaring and Viola 1984). Women were centrally involved in cooperative money-making schemes, covering a wide range of petty commodity production, including bread and confectionery making, tailoring, and craft production. They were all eminently suitable for women's participation because production could be located in or near their homes, using flexible work rota systems and offering highly useful supplementary incomes. According to one source, many such cooperatives were organized along democratic lines, with group decisions made by the collective (Corcoran-Nantes 1993: 151). A second form of collective endeavor was a range of "mutualist" schemes, for example to provide services such as clean water, basic education, childminding crèches, house construction for the homeless, and community refuse collection. Such activities benefited all among the local community, not just those who individually participated in them as in cooperatives. There were also more overtly political goals. Female members of the

Unemployed Movement joined other women's organizations and feminist groups on demonstrations and political protests concerning issues such as abortion, violence against women, and family planning. Later, some of the women went on to become elected local and regional coordinators of Committees of the Unemployed (ibid: 147).

The overall point is that the initial impetus to form a group linked to unemployment helped convince many women that, via collective effort, they might actually achieve a range of wider social and political goals. Over time, women began to assume leadership positions within the Unemployed Movement. As a result, its focus shifted to a greater concern with "women's problems."

Like the Unemployed Movement, the Shantytown Movement also set up a variety of mutualist schemes in the 1980s, for the same reason: the difficulty in getting the authorities to install general services. For example, in 1983–5 the Shantytown Movement in Vila Sezamo, an area of São Paulo, organized a mutualist scheme both for the construction of its headquarters and for local rubbish collection. Volunteers, mostly women, did the necessary physical work, and others donated money, tools, and food to sustain the workers. The movement liaised with the local authorities, persuading them to supply a truck each week at a prearranged point at the edge of the favela. Local refuse collectors then collected rubbish and deposited it in the truck. The local council also provided placards aiming to prevent dumping as well as a number of large litter bins in various locations in the area. Members of the local Shantytown group also held consciousness-raising meetings about the importance of the scheme for local people's health. The scheme was a success, and encouraged São Paulo's umbrella Shantytown Commission to start other kinds of schemes, including cooperative work projects (ibid: 151).

In conclusion, the types of consciousness raising developed by poor women in São Paulo and other Brazilian cities helped to raise female awareness in relation to a number of socioeconomic and political issues, while stimulating the development of an array of alliances between women covering a number of issues. Over time, poor women acquired a greater sense of themselves and of gender inequality through their participation in the Unemployment and Shantytown Movements. The result was that their own organizations in the low-income areas emerged, developed, and grew in strength and numbers. Developing a political identity – as women of the working poor – such females were able to define their social, political, and economic relationships more clearly than before.

The Middle East

Like East and Southeast Asia there are important cultural and political factors in the Middle East that combine to inhibit women from organizing themselves in pursuit of self-interest. According to Freedom House data (see p. 93), no newly democratized country enjoys "free" status. Except for Israel, all countries of the region are predominantly Muslim. Is there a connection between these two aspects of regional life? The influence of Islam on the cultural norms of the region is said to be important as it helps constrain "female economic and political activities through purdah or ritual seclusion" (Parpart 1988: 209). In addition, women rarely hold public positions of authority and are prohibited from holding religious offices. The result is that in many Muslim societies in the Middle East, women constitute a "subordinated group" (Reveyrand-Coulon 1993: 97). Women are expected to remain at home to run domestic affairs, including childrearing, rather than seek a wider role in society. However, while commentators have suggested that Islam is an influential factor in explaining the typically lowly social and political position of women, any link between the inferior status of women and Islam is complex and varied. As Held notes, this is not only because "factors like regime ideology, power relations within the family, low literacy rates and employment opportunities . . . play a determining role," but also because the faith itself and interpretations of Islam vary from country to country (Held 1993: 23). It is the case, however, as table 7.2 shows, that 85 percent or more of women in a dozen regional countries do not have jobs outside the home.

The following examples will serve to illustrate the degree of women's social and political subordination in some regional countries. The first comes from Iraq where, in 1990, a proclamation by the ruling Revolutionary Command Council announced that: "any Iraqi (male) who kills *even with pre-meditation* his own mother, daughter, sister, niece, or cousin for adultery will not be brought to justice" (Ekins 1992: 76; emphasis added). A second example comes from Jordan, a Muslim kingdom torn between strict religious and ethnic traditions and swift modernization. There, at least a quarter of all premeditated murders in 1994 were so-called "honor killings"; that is, women were killed by male relatives for a variety of allegedly "immoral" types of behavior, from "flirting" to losing virginity before marriage (Sabbagh 1994). The third example is from Iran, where women's subordination is not "just" a question of inter-family issues and concerns; it is also an integral facet

Table 7.2 Women as a percentage of the labor force in the Middle East

Less than 10%	10–15%	16–20%	Over 20%
Algeria	Egypt	Iran	Turkey
Iraq	Jordan	Morocco	
Libya	Kuwait		
Oman	Syria		
Saudi Arabia	Tunisia		
United Arab Emirates	Yemen		

Source: UNDP (1994: 146–7)

of societal control. In 1994 an all-party British Parliamentary Human Rights Group reported a catalog of state-sanctioned crimes against women, including mutilation, execution, disfiguring women's faces with acid for not wearing the veil, and the rape of women detainees (Coles 1994).

In only one predominantly Muslim regional "country," the Palestine Authority, does the political position of women seem to have been enhanced, albeit temporarily, in recent years. As Serhan (1993: 165) suggests, a mix of political, economic, and social factors were central to the eruption of Palestinian anger. From 1967, when Israel took control of the Occupied Territories, Palestinians were denied the right to organize for socioeconomic and political goals. Because of the absence of "normal" political channels, numerous grassroots organizations grew – often clandestinely. By the early 1990s there were hundreds involved in a variety of tasks, including Islamic education, community kitchens, and urban farming (Fisher 1993: 25).

According to Bennis, the "visible leadership role of many Palestinian women" during the Intifada "directly challenged – although it did not entirely end – the legacy of women being kept at home and out of public life" (Bennis 2000: 183). Bennis quotes the leader of one of the women's organizations as follows:

> The role of women has changed a lot in the course of this uprising, and we have been very involved in all aspects of this uprising: from participating in demonstrations, throwing stones, to taking care of what we call now "being ready" for the civil disobedience stage. Taking care of the work at home, being ready in their houses with [stored] food, with supplies . . . And women's lives in general, have been hit badly by the Israe-

lis. They have been shot in the streets, they have been gassed, they have miscarried because of the tear gas, they have been imprisoned under administrative detention – so you can feel that there's a big change in the role of women during this uprising, in their day-to-day lives and in their role in the whole society and the Palestinian cause. (Ibid: 193–4)

However, despite high hopes, the democratic promise of the Intifada, not least in relation to the position of women, was not to endure. After a peace treaty was signed with Israel in 1993, things seemed to return to "normal" as far as the position of Palestinian women was concerned. The result has been that women are by and large marginalized politically and socially, having few avenues to express their concerns and great difficulty in pursuing goals of empowerment.

Conclusion

This chapter has illustrated how the socioeconomic and political position of poor women in developing countries is dependent on a number of factors. I described how the position of women in Kerala is better than in other areas of India. This was because the state government was forced to be responsive to an educated and sophisticated electorate which values equality. As our discussions of the position of poor women elsewhere in the developing world made clear, the Keralan position is, to say the least, unusual.

The case studies highlighted two factors necessary to improve the position of poor women. There must be (1) sufficient political and social space for women to organize, and (2) a strong desire among them to work collectively. We saw that Argentina's Las Madres began as a group with a narrow aim – to discover what had happened to their men after being picked up by the state's security services – which over time led to wider questioning of the social and political position of females in Argentina.

The case studies of Brazil's Shantytown and Unemployed Movements made clear that when government is unwilling to legislate to improve the position of poor women – and the poor more generally – then probably the only realistic choice such women have is to organize themselves. The stimulus for both groups was poverty and the absence of services supplied by the authorities. In addition, for India's WWF and SEWA, the lowly position of women workers was the key stimulus to organize. Women's solidarity was one of the most important factors in the groups' successes.

Two overall conclusions suggest themselves. First, vehicles of women's empowerment rarely if ever threaten the state's paramount position. However, they *do* alarm many men, who feel that their relatively privileged positions are thereby undermined. Second, women's empowerment seems more likely in a democratizing or democratic environment. The paucity of examples of women's empowerment groups in both the Middle East and Africa warns against being overly optimistic when assessing the chances of general improvements in the sociopolitical and economic position of poor women in the developing world. On the other hand, the success of several women's organizations in Latin America and India suggests that progress is being made in some countries.

8

Politics of the Natural Environment

Environmental problems emerged in the 1970s in many developing countries, quickly becoming in numerous cases an important focus of societal concerns. In this chapter we focus on the political, economic, and social dimensions of environmental issues in the developing world. The overall aim is to explain how and why environmental issues are often linked to wider demands for sociopolitical change and/or economic reform from groups lacking power. We examine (1) environmental groups within developing countries; (2) their interaction with transnational environmental organizations, such as Greenpeace International; and (3) case studies from a number of developing countries. The overall conclusion is that while environment groups do not always gain their objectives, they should not be written off as insignificant. Collectively, they comprise an important new element in emerging civil societies in many developing countries, helping challenge state power and thus increasing that of ordinary people. We start with some background information on global environmental issues.

From Stockholm to Kyoto: 25 Years of Growing International Environmental Awareness

The "first formal awareness of the international dimension" of environmental issues was the United Conference on the Human Environment held in Stockholm in 1972 (Vogler 2001: 192). The conference, attended by representatives from 113 countries, drew up 26 Principles calling upon governments to cooperate in protecting and improving the natural environment. During the 1980s Stockholm's message was reinforced by a series of developments, including the

1984 Bhopal (India) disaster, when an explosion at a factory producing toxic chemicals killed more than 4,000 people; a near-meltdown of the nuclear reactor at Chernobyl, Ukraine, in 1986; the destruction of forests in Europe due to acid rain; an expanding hole in the ozone layer and consequential skin cancers; pollution of the seas and overfishing; and global warming, threatening the existence of many low-lying countries and islands. The overall result was that the 1980s became known as the "decade of the discovery of the environment" (Hadjor 1993: 105).

Consequently, the relationship between people's social and economic demands and the natural environment began, for the first time, to be discussed in a serious and scientific way. The 1992 United Nations-sponsored "Earth Summit" held in Rio di Janeiro, Brazil, was a tangible sign of growing global concern. More than 100 heads of state and 30,000 bureaucrats and representatives of NGOs attended. They discussed 24 million pages of preparatory documents and sought to make wide-ranging decisions regarding the future of the global environment. The Earth Summit was called specifically to confront two pressing interlinked problems: environmental degradation, and poverty and underdevelopment. Coming just after the end of the Cold War, there was expectation that relaxation of international tensions would facilitate progress on these issues. The Earth Summit produced Agenda 21, trumpeted as "a plan of action to save the planet" and endorsed by representatives of all countries present. Agenda 21 was a compromise between, on the one hand, most Western states (promoters of environmental conservation) and, on the other, many developing countries (advocates of growth, often with scant apparent regard for environmental protection).

Many developing country governments seemed ambivalent about the very principle of environmental protection, perhaps irritated by Western attempts to prescribe universal environmental standards and goals. Many governments claimed that the West's industrial development was the long-term result of often thoughtless environmental exploitation, both at home and in colonial possessions. As the West's development was the result of thorough environmental exploitation, why should that of the developing world be different? The West stood charged with hypocrisy on two counts: (1) concern with environmental protection was seen by many developing countries as a blatant attempt to prevent them from catching up developmentally by adopting the West's own tactics; and (2) while the West professed to deplore environmentally harmful policies, it strongly urged dozens of developing countries to open up their economies to foreign investment and increase exports of agricultural products and timber, leading to more environmental damage (Miller 1995).

Agenda 21 reflected this polarization of views. Critics argued that it was no more than an inadequate, aspirational response to public concern, a document without enough teeth to ensure progress. However, despite failure to produce an agreement on tropical rain forest destruction (one of Rio's main concerns), the Earth Summit did give rise to a Framework Convention on Climate Change. This was significant because, as Vogler notes, it "marked the beginnings of a systematic international attempt to grapple with the problem of 'global warming'," one of the most significant threats with which the human race has had to deal (Vogler 2001: 193). At the end of 1997, measures were agreed to control emissions of the greenhouse gases held responsible for global warming. In July 2001, despite the withdrawal of the United States from the protocol, 185 countries agreed limited but concrete measures to try to deal with the problem (Brown 2001).

Environmental Crisis in the Developing World

In the developing world the 1980s and 1990s were decades of environmental crisis affecting millions of mainly poor people. Not only did global economic developments widen further the gulf between rich and poor, as prices for poor states' exports generally fell and international indebtedness grew, but also often swift population growth placed increasing pressure on natural environments. Next, we discuss four major environmental problems that affect many developing countries: (1) desertification and deforestation; (2) poverty and skewed land use patterns; (3) large-scale hydroelectric dams; and (4) the environmental impacts of structural adjustment.

Desertification and deforestation

"Desertification" refers either to invasion of arable land by sand or to irreversible damage to vegetative cover. The United Nations Environmental Program (UNEP) estimates that more than 1.2 billion hectares – about 10 percent of the earth's vegetated surface – have undergone moderate or severe soil degradation since 1945. UNEP calculates that an area the combined size of North and Latin America was imminently threatened by desertification. Large swathes of the Middle East, Africa, Asia, and Latin America, where rainfall is low, are at particular risk.

Two theories compete to explain desertification. The first blames so-called "primitive" farming measures – that is, smallholder agriculture and nomadic pastoralism – and population pressures which combine to produce both famine and hunger. However, evidence suggests that neither smallholder agriculture nor nomadic pastoralism leads to desertification *providing* there is sufficient land available for all. If so, land has sufficient time to recover before a resumption of farming (Harrison 1987). The second theory argues that the main problem is the farming practices of modern, capitalist enterprises: over-intensive mechanized agriculture and large-scale raising of cattle, sheep, and other animals. While the real reason for desertification probably lies in a combination of these two areas of concern, it seems clear that it is symptomatic of several social and economic factors, such as changing land use and landholding patterns, combining to deprive the poor of the use of adequate land.

"Deforestation" refers to massive and often irreversible destruction of forests. Globally, tropical moist forests ("rain" forests) are the "richest ecosystems in biomass and biodiversity on land" (Thomas 1994: 62). They cover an area of 1.5 billion hectares with about 65 percent found in Latin America, and the rest divided between Africa and East and Southeast Asia. During the 1990s, around 20 million hectares were destroyed *each year* and, at current rates of destruction, *no* rainforests will be left in 70 years' time.

Rainforest is destroyed for a variety of reasons, including farming and timber extraction. For example, more than 150 million cubic meters of rainforest were destroyed in Brazil each year in the 1980s and 1990s. Over 75 percent of forest loss was the consequence of slash and burn farming, undertaken by poor, landless people desperate for arable land. Less than 1 percent of the timber was exported. In Malaysia, on the other hand, the proportions of timber exported and burned for farming were the reverse: 80 percent of timber is exported. The Malaysian government argues that it has a perfect right to exploit and export timber because "economic growth is needed first, to generate the ability to clean up the environment later" (Eccleston 1996: 134).

Whether for farming, as in Brazil, or for export, as in Malaysia, deforestation leads to negative local, regional, and global consequences. Locally, it threatens or destroys lifestyles of forest-dwelling peoples; regionally, it leads to leaching and erosion of soils, flash floods, and desertification; globally, it results in reduced biomass stocks and species diversity, changing patterns of rainfall, and long-term climate change. During the 1980s and 1990s popular struggles took place against deforestation in several developing countries, including India, Kenya, Malaysia, Indonesia, and Brazil. These conflicts – in Brazil between rubber tappers, loggers, and farmers; in Sarawak, between loggers and the indigenous Penan people; and in India between the Chipko movement and tree fellers – reflect conflicting interests of forest dwellers and the state or business interests in managing and exploiting forest resources.

Poverty and land use patterns

It is suggested that the environmentally destructive effects of desertification and deforestation are exacerbated by development patterns and programs that take natural resources away from the poor, who tend to use them sustainably, and pass them to the less poor, who may exploit them less sustainably. Lack of secure control over resources, population growth, inequity, and misguided policies comprise the common context of poverty leading to environmental deterioration of both agricultural and non-agricultural land. Leonard (1989) has calculated that more than 350 million of the 800 million poorest people in the developing world live on marginal or fragile lands and consequently serious environmental degradation is virtually certain. However, whether poor people are displaced by influential individuals who use their land for cash-cropping, plantations, or ranches, or whether it occurs by state policy – for example, the Brazilian government's plan to populate the Amazon basin – results tend to be similar. When displaced people are forced to seek livelihoods on marginal or unsuitable land, struggles for survival will result in often serious environmental damage (Peluso 1993: 46–70).

Poverty drives environmental deterioration when desperate people over-exploit their resource base, sacrificing the future to try to salvage the present. Often the logic of short-term needs encourages poor landless families to burn sections of rainforest or farm hardly viable land, such as mountain slopes. Unsurprisingly, the most impoverished, most overcrowded regions suffer the worst ecological damage. For example, in parts of South Asia, including Nepal and Bangladesh, millions of poor people inhabit environmentally degraded regions such as crowded hill country on the margins of the Himalayas. In China many impoverished people live on the Loess Plateau, where soil is swiftly eroding. In the Philippines, northeast Thailand, Brazil's Amazon basin, and several West

African countries in the Congo basin, impoverished farmers try to eke out precarious livings on plots reclaimed from the forest. In parts of East and Southern Africa, on the other hand, poor people try to exist on already deforested land turning to desert (Durning 1989: 44–5).

Typically, the poor knowingly harm their environment to a serious degree only when under severe duress. Pushed to the brink of starvation, often evicted from familiar land by big commercial interests, such people will lack access to a sustainable livelihood with adequate land, water, and capital. Two common sequences, whereby poor people are involved in downward spirals of environmental degradation, are illustrated by the contrasting examples of Nepal and Costa Rica. In Nepal, swift population growth threatens environmental viability, while in Costs Rica large commercial interests have ousted numerous smallholders from their land for cattle ranching (Stiefel and Wolfe 1994). In both cases, the outcome is the same: large tracts of unsuitable land are used for farming and many among the rural poor are seriously disadvantaged.

Large dams for hydroelectric power and irrigation

In one environmental sense, large hydroelectric dams are desirable: they produce energy without atmospheric pollution. But they also have environmental costs. Apart from displacement of people, Timberlake (1995) notes that dams cause "salinisation of land, water-borne diseases, increasingly unequal distribution of wealth, disruptions to fisheries, loss of forests and wildlife, siltation due to erosion, excessive water losses due to evaporation and even an increase in earth tremors." By the end of the 1980s the world was using 40 percent of the estimated hydropower potential (Harrison 1993: 281). Yet because dams quickly silt up – on average by about 1 percent a year – large dams are only a short-term, unrepeatable makeshift solution to energy shortages. Within a century or so from now, most existing hydroelectric dams will evolve into dry valleys.

Until recently, large-scale dams, both for irrigation and hydroelectric power, were regarded in numerous developing countries both as a panacea for energy shortfalls and spectacular symbols and crucial components of economic development. In India, for example, the first post-independence prime minister, Jawaharlal Nehru, saw big dams as the new "temples" of modernizing India (Ekins 1992: 88). He and his successors believed that large dams were justifiable in terms both of the necessary huge capital investments and displacement of thousands of people forced to leave their homes and livelihoods as waters rise. Now, however, in India large dams are viewed with ambivalence, galvanizing resistance not only from affected local people but also from transnational organizations such as the International Rivers Network (Stiefel and Wolfe 1994; Khagram 2000).

Structural adjustment

A World Bank vice-president, Armeane Chokski, suggested in 1995 that no country has managed significantly to reduce poverty without sustained economic growth and "the way to growth is through market reform." Chokski added that too much attention is focused by "advocacy groups" on the negative effects of structural adjustment programs (SAPs), such as the removal of safety nets, user fees for basic services, and "necessary" environmental damage caused by economic growth (Black 1995). As there are multiple, complex linkages between economic policies, social forces, natural resource management practices, and environmental degradation, it is impossible to determine *direct* causal connections between SAPs and environmental damage distinguishable from that caused by "normal" economic growth.

However, critics believe that SAPs are connected to three deleterious environmental impacts. First, general damage to the natural environment. Governments of SAP-ped countries are desperate for more foreign exchange and may "tolerate uncontrolled exploitation of forests and mineral resources and ecologically dangerous practices of commercial agriculture" (Fisher 1993: 31). This can damage not only forests, but also wetlands, mangroves, and other natural resources, while some industries – such as mining – increase pollution. Second, states often fail to push through or enforce environmental laws. Adjusting countries are encouraged to reduce state expenditures. This leads to the removal or postponement of various measures, including, in some cases, introduction or enforcement of environmental laws. Third, there are often increased pressures on the natural environment from redundant government employees who take up farming in the absence of alternative employment opportunities. Such people often embark upon slash and burn agriculture which is very environmentally damaging, especially to forest areas or marginal lands like mountain slopes (Miller 1995: 31). In sum, the effects of SAPs on developing countries can be environmentally damaging in a number of ways.

Environmental Concerns and Politics in the Developing World: The Domestic Dimension

Power . . . is Brazilian rubber tappers struggling to preserve the forests upon which their livelihoods depend. Power is Indian peasants resisting hydroelectric projects that will flood their land . . . Around the world, ecology movements are demanding and creating the power to shape their own environments. (Breyman 1993: 129, 124)

The state's claim to defend threatened resources and its exclusive right to the legitimate use of violence combines to facilitate its apparatus-building and attempts at social control. State threats or use of violence in the name of resource control helps them to control people, especially unruly regional groups, marginal groups, or minority groups who challenge its authority. (Peluso 1993: 47)

These quotations indicate that in the developing world environmental and political issues are often linked. Breyman points out that environmental groups may see goals in relation to members' overall subordinate positions. Peluso notes that states may use violent means to gain or ensure control of valuable natural resources. However, the issue is not, simplistically, one of "goodies" versus "baddies," with local environmental groups striving to protect their local ecology and nasty outside state or business interests trying to destroy it for profit. In fact, not all subordinate people support or wish to join environmental groups. Some derive their incomes from working in polluting industries or are impelled by land hunger towards anti-ecological methods of farming

It is beyond dispute that globally, in the 30 years since the Stockholm environment conference, numbers of environmental groups have grown. There are now "tens of thousands" in the developing countries (Fisher 1993: 209). As table 8.1 indicates, many are located in Latin America, India, and East and Southeast Asia, relatively fewer in Africa, hardly any in the Middle East or Asian communist countries. Given the comparative development of civil societies in these regions (noted in chapter 4), this distribution is not unexpected.

Environmental groups in developing countries seem to attract many members of subordinate groups, such as young people and women, and often people who share a view that the status quo is inimicable to their interests (Fals Borda 1992: 311). Bayart points out that there is nothing inherently "natural" in such groups' subordination. Instead, political and societal circumstances dictate such inequality, linked to

Table 8.1 Environmental groups in the developing world

Objective	To protect local environment – land, water, air – from hostile outside interests
Organizational levels	Various: local, national, or transnational
Perceptions of the state	Either independently or with big business to take away or degrade local people's environment
Role in the political process	Variable
Membership profile	Usually people affected by environmental degradation or loss of land
Tactics to achieve goals	Direct action, lobbying, and campaigning
Where found	
Many	Latin America, India, East and Southeast Asia
Some	Africa
Few	Middle East, Asian communist countries

"relationships of economic production, legal relations and . . . cultural particularities" (Bayart 1993: 112). Fals Borda argues that some members of these "two oppressed, marginal groups" now strive to "bring about a new ethos, a better kind of society and social relations in which unity may coexist with diversity" (Fals Borda 1992: 311). As we saw in chapter 7, many women no longer submit passively to the powerful. In addition, in numerous countries, including Algeria, Egypt, and Brazil – all hard hit by debt burdens and the rigors of SAPs – numerous young people react militantly when they find themselves excluded from the possibility of gaining salaried employment (Haynes 1997). Subordinate groups may also be attracted to environmental issues not only because of concern with ecosystem decline, but also because environmental issues are often linked to wider concerns: human rights, employment, and development (Sethi 1993: 125–6). In other words, groups with overtly environmental concerns may also have broadly political goals. Escobar and Alvarez aver that they challenge "conventional culture and economic models of development to advance their politics. The creation of political facts by the environmental movement . . . takes place through the generation of spaces wherein new meanings are forged" (Escobar and Alvarez 1992: 15).

We saw in chapters 3 and 4 that state policies in developing countries are influenced by a variety of factors, especially the nature of domestic political structures and distributions of wealth and income. Typically, agricultural pricing policies, investment incentives, tax provisions, and credit and land concessions privilege elite interests. Elites will be wealthy people, often with commercial interests in environmentally damaging activities, such as commercial logging, mineral and oil exploitation, plantation cropping, and large-scale irrigated farming. We noted above that, for the benefit of elites, poor rural people suffer socioeconomically and environmentally, losing homes, farms, and fishing grounds, usually without compensation (Miller 1995: 42).

Protecting the natural environment is only likely to attract the commitment of state officials and policy-makers when they – or their allies – personally benefit. For example, the governments of both Kenya and Zambia only came to support a global ban on ivory trading when their own countries' elephant herds seriously declined. Ellis (1994: 62) notes that those benefiting most from the ivory trade were state personnel, such as senior politicians and superior military personnel. For such people, a primary purpose in seeking a ban on the global trade in ivory was to allow elephant stocks to recover, perhaps to facilitate a resumption of the trade later. But exploitation of elephants for ivory is but one example of elite domination with ramifications for environmental protection. Another is a highly significant revenue-generating strategy: extraction of valuable natural resources, officially undertaken for "society's greater good." What this usually amounts to is that those with power have the greatest interest in preserving or gaining jurisdiction over natural resources. Redistribution of resulting wealth comes low in their priorities. The powerful interpret the value of a natural resource in relation to three factors: (1) the world market price of a product: does the going rate make it worthwhile to trade in it? (2) by what strategies can it best be exploited?; and (3) for what purpose(s) can resulting monetary benefits be allocated? When the view of the powerful, relating to what is the correct procedure and weight of the distribution of the benefits, differs from that of local communities, there can be serious political conflict with local environmental groups which share some or all of the following characteristics:

- Most environmental groups are rurally based.
- Environmental protection groups mobilize local people to defend their land and neighborhood against outside attack, typically from the state or big business.
- Women and young people are often well-represented in their membership.
- While some environmental groups have a narrow conservation focus, most have wider socioeconomic and/or political concerns.
- Environmental groups are more likely to achieve their goals if they successfully exploit democratic and legal avenues.
- It helps to enlist foreign allies, such as Greenpeace International, but it does not ensure success.
- Environmental groups often do not win their struggles; failures outweigh successes.

The External Dimension of Environmental Protection: The IMF, the World Bank, and Greenpeace International

Transnational and international interactions have helped to promote a universalization of environmental concerns and globalization of ecological activism (Scholte 1993: 54). Rosenau identifies transnational forces as one of the sources of what he calls "turbulence in world politics" and to him the contemporary era reflects the reality of a multicentric world. This comprises not only states but also numerous non-state actors existing "in a non-hierarchical relationship with the state-centric system" (Rosenau 1993: 75). His claim is *not* that non-state actors, including International Non-Governmental Organizations (INGOs), are replacing states and international governmental organizations as the leading global actors. Rather, it is that in *some circumstances* INGOs have significant international clout. For example, some environmental INGOs – including Greenpeace International, Friends of the Earth, the Rain Forest Action Group, Global Witness, and the International Rivers Network – have considerable influence with governments and international governmental organizations such as the United Nations (Haynes 1999; Khagram 2000).

There are "said to be several hundred" environmentally orientated INGOs, about 85 percent of which have their headquarters in Western countries (Fisher 1993: 109). It would be fair to say that, in comparison to Western INGOs like Greenpeace International, Friends of the Earth, and the US-based Environmental Defense Fund, the global influence of most developing country environmental protection NGOs is very limited. On the other hand, some are beginning to acquire the necessary expertise and to learn the necessary strategies to influence both domestic policies and governmental inputs into international environmental policies (Princen 1994: 39). To help them grow in significance and focus their efforts, many environmental groups in developing countries are building links with transnational environmental organizations in developed countries. Environmental INGOs, acting transnationally, also manage to develop relations with environmental groups in the developing world. This not only encourages redefinition of relations between states and populations and those governing appropriate "human action towards nature," but also contributes "to changed policies and patterns of behavior" (Peterson 1992: 387).

Critics point to differences between, on the one hand, transnational environmental protection groups and, on the other, big business and Western IFIs. First, they argue that the latter prioritize economic growth far above environmental protection and conservation. On the other hand, Western environmental pressure groups such as Greenpeace International have as a central premise that "sustainable development" must be the chief global priority for environmental sustainability. Sustainable development was defined in the 1987 report of the UN World Commission on Environment and Development (often called the Brundtland Commission, as its leader was Mrs Brundtland, then Norway's prime minister) as "development which meets the needs of the present without compromising the ability of future generations to meet their own needs" (quoted in Thomas 1994: 62).

Second, Rich (1990) has argued that the World Bank and the IMF, while paying lip service to environmental protection and sustainable forms of development, privilege economic growth – seen as absolutely crucial for both global and domestic stability – far above environmental protection. Despite recent statements of concern with environmental protection, critics argue that the philosophy of both the World Bank and the IMF has been consistent for half a century: the chief objective is to ensure that there is no return to the economic anarchy of the 1930s which precipitated World War II; for this, sustained global economic growth is paramount. After World War II, under the General Agreement on Tariffs and Trade (replaced in January 1994 by the World Trade Organization), much effort was devoted to developing and sustaining a liberal trade order. Economic growth was prioritized over environmental protection to the extent that "national pollution controls [were] restricted on the grounds that they present[ed] non-tariff barriers to trade, both in industry and agriculture" (Miller 1995: 32). The philosophy of "growth first" became so ingrained in the thinking of Western governments and IFIs that even the 1987 report of the World Commission on Environment and Development, which helped to popularize the concept of "sustainable development," "proposed a fivefold increase in the gross world product through major influxes of capital, with no major revisions in the world's economic institutions" and with no recommendation for obligatory environmental safeguards to be built into SAPs.

What environmental awareness the IMF and World Bank do show is in no small part a result of the pressure from environmental NGOs and INGOs. Scholte argues that transnational environmental actors often serve as a "force of social transformation," helping local groups and communities to empower themselves, making them subversive to state practices because they have at least a degree of independence from both national and local conditions (Scholte 1993: 53). Although Greenpeace International has branches in dozens of countries, many INGOs have only a secondary regard for territoriality, preferring to operate by "affinity" rather than in relation to "vicinity" (Greenpeace USA 1990) Tactically, environmental INGOs often operate through a mixture of lobbying and more confrontational strategies.

To illustrate the activities of environmental INGOs we will focus on Greenpeace International (GI), perhaps the best known and most effective group of this kind. GI uses lobbying, direct action, and assiduous cultivation of public opinion to focus and help sustain global environmental attention on issues such as anti-nuclear testing, with which it has been engaged since the early 1970s. GI has sent small sailing boats into test areas in the South Pacific with the aim not merely to draw public attention to the tests, but to get them postponed or, better, cancelled. In 1973 one such intervention led to GI activists being beaten up by French troops. Twelve years later, in 1985, French secret agents blew up in Auckland harbor the GI flagship *Rainbow Warrior*, killing a Greenpeace photographer (McCormick 1989: 144–5). Later, in 1995–6, GI led an ultimately successful campaign to encourage the French government to abandon nuclear tests in French Polynesia. Eventually, the French government announced that it was reducing the number of tests from a scheduled eight to six.

GI has also been involved in other campaigns over the years, for example against whaling and the dumping of toxic waste. GI used public opinion to good effect in June 1995 when its campaign prevented the multinational oil company, Shell, from dumping an aged oil rig, the

Brent Spar, in the North Atlantic. Instead, Shell was compelled to seek a license from the British government to dispose of the rig on land, a much more expensive, although probably more environmentally satisfactory, option. A final example of GI campaigns is the one against serious oil pollution, allegedly perpetrated by the petroleum multinational Shell, in a small area of southeast Nigeria, the home of the Ogoni people. Some of these issues are examined in greater detail below.

Case Studies: Environmental Groups in the Developing World

We have already seen that large numbers of people in developing countries have become involved in campaigns against environmental degradation. For example, the fight against deforestation and accompanying loss of livelihood emerged as an important rallying point for popular organizations in several developing countries, including India (the Chipko movement), Kenya (the Green Belt Movement), and Brazil (the late Chico Mendes's National Council of Rubber Tappers (NCRT)) (Ekins 1992: 160–76). Such groups tend to emphasize the educational importance of links between environmental and sociopolitical concerns. For example, Projeto Seringueiro, the NCRT's main initiative, has sought to inform those working and living in Brazil's forests, particularly rubber tappers, that it is appropriate for them to identify closely with the forests and to defend them against excessive felling. Chico Mendes, a NCRT leader murdered in 1988 because of his pro-environment stance, maintained that "the strengthening of our movement has coincided with the development of the education program . . . all our advances, the fight against the destruction of the forest, the organizing of the cooperative and the strengthening of the union, were all possible thanks to the education program" (Mendes quoted in Breyman 1993: 129). Elsewhere in the developing world, other coordinating bodies have also realized the interconnectedness of environmental, human rights, and political issues. For example, since the mid-1980s the Coordinating Council for Human Rights in Bangladesh has provided legal aid to environmentally threatened local communities, and now coordinates a network of human rights and environmental organizations (Fisher 1993: 31, 105, 148). In addition, other environmental groups, such as the anti-nuclear testing campaign in French Polynesia and the Ogonis' fight against Shell and the Nigerian government, have also been involved in recent years in political battles with the authorities.

What these environmental groups have in common is that they have managed to acquire international repute and recognition, a result of their tenacity in striving to protect their local environments. They also reflect how growing awareness of the relatedness of socioeconomic and political issues led to environmental concerns serving as a focus for wider problems. Moreover, transnational links can help them to pursue their goals, not only to broaden the environmental groups' horizons, but also to help support their struggles by supplying welcome publicity. To illustrate these contentions we will examine various case studies on environmental groups and politics in India, Kenya, Indonesia, French Polynesia, and Nigeria.

Environmental groups and politics in India

The Chipko movement

India's forests cover about one-tenth of the land area and are an essential resource for millions of rural and indigenous peoples, providing food, fuel, and fodder (Sethi 1993: 124). The Chipko movement is a result of hundreds of decentralized and locally autonomous initiatives, often led by women. The movement's slogan – "ecology is permanent economy" – epitomized its chief concern: to save forest resources from commercial exploitation by outside interests. "In effect the Chipko people are working a socioeconomic revolution by winning control of their forest resources from the hands of a distant bureaucracy which is concerned with selling the forest for making urban-oriented products" (United Nations Environment Program, quoted in Ekins 1992: 144).

The Chipko movement is that rare thing among environmental groups in the developing world: a success. It was founded in 1973 in Uttar Pradesh to stop excessive tree-felling. By the late 1970s it had spread to many other districts of the Himalayas (Sethi 1993: 127). The movement's name comes from a local word meaning "embrace"; people – mostly women, the bedrock of the movement – stopped the felling of trees by standing between them and the loggers, literally embracing them. Chipko protests in Uttar Pradesh achieved a major victory in 1980 with a 15-year ban, since renewed, on green felling in the Himalayan forests of the state. In the 1980s the Chipko movement spread throughout much of India: to Himachal Pradesh in the north, Karnataka in the south, Rajasthan in the west, and Bihar in the east. Its successes included prevention of "clear felling in the Western Ghats and the Vindhyas and generated pressure for a natural resource policy more sensitive to people's needs and ecological requirements" (Ekins 1992: 143).

The Chipko movement is an example of how non-violent resistance and struggle by thousands of ordinary people, without the guidance and control of any centralized apparatus, recognized leadership, or full-time cadre, can succeed under certain circumstances.

Overall, Chipko helped to shift attention to the centrality of renewable resources – soil, air, water, and trees – at a time of swift industrialization in India. The movement was also a voice from the margins of Indian civil society which managed to demonstrate "that the crucial environmental conflicts are not just city-based [such as pollution] or related to the depletion of non-renewable resources useful for industry, but arise directly from the philosophical premises embedded in the modern Western and capitalist vision" (Sethi 1993: 127).

The Narmada Valley project

A second Indian example of an environmental campaign is the Narmada Valley project (NVP). The NVP is a huge hydroelectric dam and irrigation undertaking that potentially involves more than 3,000 major and minor dams. The Narmada is India's largest western-flowing river, the country's fifth largest overall, with a length of 1,312 kilometers. More than 20 million people – including numerous minority tribal peoples – live in its basins, and use the river as an important economic and ecological resource. However, the World Bank claims that the Narmada river "is one of [India's] least used – water use is currently about 4 percent and tons of water effectively are wasted every day when it could be put to use for the benefit of the region" (quoted in Ekins 1992: 89).

The NVP was judged to be the solution to the river's alleged underuse. It would comprise two very large dams – the Sardar Sarovar Project (SSP) and the Narmada Sagar Project (NSP) – and 28 small dams and 3,000 other water projects. Planned benefits included irrigation of 2.27 million hectares of land in the states of Madhya Pradesh, Gujarat, and Rajasthan, as well as pisciculture, drinking water, and electric power. The two main dams would also be designed to moderate floods. Initially, the World Bank agreed a US$450 million loan for SSP and was considering support for NSP until its backing for the project came to an abrupt end in 1994 (Tran 1994). The World Bank's decision to withdraw was linked to the unwelcome publicity generated by a vociferous grassroots anti-NVP campaign, which erupted when it became clear that the project would entail massive displacement of local people. The campaign originated, not as a fight against the dams *per se*, but as a movement to ensure both that the environment would be protected and that people displaced by the dams were properly financially compensated. Soon, however, separate groups joined together in common cause against the dams, forming what one source describes as "one of the most powerful social movements ever to emerge in post-independence India" (Ekins 1992: 90). Anti-dam activists – including about 1 million potential "oustees" from more than 150,000 families, voluntary social groups, and local and foreign environmentalist groups – were pitted against an opposing coalition made up of the state governments of Madhya Pradesh, Gujarat, and Rajasthan states, the World Bank, and big local landowners. The latter saw a potential in the scheme for a major boost to irrigation and supply of electrical power. Local building firms foresaw a construction bonanza and thus supported the project. In addition, many ordinary citizens believed that the benefits of the scheme would lead to an all-round growth in prosperity "through flood control, increased drinking-water supply, new jobs through a spurt in industry and allied activities" (Sethi 1993: 133).

But at several levels – grassroots, provincial, national, and global – the anti-NVP struggle soon focused not only on the pros and cons of the project itself but also, more generally, on the benefits and disbenefits of large "development" projects. The anti-NVP campaign gradually built into a powerful anti-dam coalition, with a coalition of local smallholders', women's, youth, environmental, and transnational groups, including Greenpeace International, Friends of the Earth, and the US-based Environmental Defense Fund. In 1994 the anti-dam campaign forced the World Bank – because of adverse publicity – to withdraw its funding. As a result, the project was temporarily suspended in the absence of alternative funding to that of the World Bank. As Lori Udall of the Washington-based International Rivers Network explained, the suspension "sent a strong signal to international donors that large dams are risky, expensive and destructive investments and that they should support smaller, more flexible projects" (Vidal 1995a).

While at the time of writing the Indian government remains determined to complete the NVP, there is no certainty that it will ever be finished. Despite the uncertain eventual outcome, it is clear that the anti-NVP campaign was a success, at least in terms of mobilizing popular opinion against the project to the extent that now large dams in India soon encounter "dwindling acceptance and militant resistance" (Stiefel and Wolfe 1994: 180). Environmentally, the overall importance of the Narmada issue was that it struck directly at one of the fundamental development tenets: big is beautiful. It also showed that ordinary people, when successfully organized, could slow down – perhaps ultimately defeat – such a massive state and business-led project.

Two conclusions emerge from the accounts of the Chipko movement and the anti-NVP campaign. The first is that it not only takes a high degree of popular organization and mobilization to achieve influence on outcomes, but also a responsive government prepared to react favorably to such efforts. Second, it helps to have influential external allies, although this in itself is no guarantee of success. When such conditions are absent it is very difficult for environmental action groups to achieve similar successes. In the next two case studies – those of environmental groups in Kenya and Indonesia – partial success was achieved in the latter because activists managed to build a powerful local coalition to exploit legal avenues to challenge the government. In Kenya, however, the clout of local environmental groups was undermined not only by their inability to amend government policy, but also in the failure to attract powerful external allies.

Politics and the environment in Kenya and Indonesia

Kenya

Emerging in the 1970s and initially devoted to tree planting, the Green Belt Movement was founded and led by Professor Wangari Maathai (Fisher 1993: 102–3). At first, the Kenyan government lauded it for its efforts in seeking to hold back desertification. But in 1989 Professor Maathai became prominent in opposition to the government's scheme to build a "world media center" in the country's capital, Nairobi. The scheduled building was planned to be the tallest construction in Africa, with a giant sculpture of Kenya's president in pride of place. Unfortunately, the building was to be in the middle of one of the few public parks in the capital, thus removing public access to one of the few green spaces in the city.

Maathai sought to mobilize both domestic and international opposition to the plan. As a result, "she was vilified and placed under virtual house arrest . . . In November 1990, [she] was prevented from returning to Kenya after a trip to the USA" (Ekins 1992: 151–2). The absence of the charismatic Maathai meant the collapse both of opposition to the world media center and, temporarily, the Green Belt Movement itself. In sum, the Maathai story is a good example of a connection between human rights abuses, "prestige project" development, and the unsustainability of environmentally destructive policies in the name of development.

The second example from Kenya indicates that it is not only urban land space that is under threat. In the late 1980s Kenya developed a robust policy of wildlife conservation and eco-tourism under the leadership of the archeologist-turned-politician, Richard Leakey (Leakey became a leading figure in an opposition political party, Sarafina, in the mid-1990s). Following a plane crash in 1994 when he lost both legs at the knee, Leakey stood down from his post as director of Kenya's Wildlife Service. He was successful in attracting US$300 million from foreign donors for his highly effective, yet controversial, conservation campaigns.

The parks and reserves Leakey managed were once the lands of nomads and hunters and gatherers, people such as the Masai, Turkana, and Ndorobo. The policy of displacing them from land they had used for centuries began during the colonial era. Kenya's colonial conservationists had claimed not only that African hunters were cruel and wasteful, but also that their livestock over-grazed the land, out-competing wild animals. However, many contemporary conservationists believe that over-grazing was the exception rather than the rule; people and wildlife normally lived in equanimity. The only way to protect the region's wildlife, the colonialists believed, was to keep it apart from people – in effect, to create animal-only theme parks where the natives were unwelcome. Consequently, the country's national parks were created and people were excluded. But the locations for the parks were not "empty" land. Instead, the homes of local people, unsurprisingly in the most fertile areas where wildlife also congregated, were unceremoniously razed.

Leakey sought, in effect, to revive colonial policy, arguing that successful animal conservation was only possible if humans were excluded. This dovetailed neatly with the ambitions of Kenya's political elite. The issue was largely to do with what foreign tourists wish to see on their holidays in "exotic" Kenya; if they do not see plenty of big game they will go to other places – such as Zimbabwe or South Africa – where they can. During the 1990s foreign tourists, mostly Europeans, spent annually "around US$50 million . . . to view the elephants and other wildlife" (Peluso 1993: 55). (Tourism brings in 20 percent of Kenya's annual foreign exchange earnings.) Leakey argued that tourists did not want to see people in the parks and, in any case, the natives wanted "development" (including better roads, piped water, and medical and educational facilities) that was incompatible with his conservation vision.

Whatever the rights and wrongs of Leakey's policy the fact is that local people were ousted from their ancestral lands without compensation and Kenya's political elites benefited financially from the policy. The Masai protested that they lost most of their dry season grazing to the parks and reserves and that "the misinformed expectations of tourists have become more important than the lives of local people" (ibid). Before resigning from his post in 1994, Leakey was the target of attempts by certain politicians – self-declared champions of the Masai and other tribal groups – to oust him in an effort to control the tourism industry themselves. But the issue was not "only" about the rights and wrongs of ousting local people from land traditionally in their control. There was a further human cost. In the two years following Leakey's appointment as director of Kenya's Wildlife Service in April 1989, more than 100 poachers were shot and killed. Many of them had "no chance for discussion or trial . . . The [wildlife] rangers are licensed, like military in a state of emergency, to shoot-to-kill" (ibid: 57).

It is not only that Leakey instituted the draconian policy at the behest of the government. The recent story of nature conservation in Kenya also involves an important role for foreign environmental organizations. The policy of shoot-to-kill poachers was actively encouraged by various foreign groups, including the Worldwide Fund for Nature (WWF), the African Wildlife Foundation, World Conservation International, the International Union for the Conservation of Nature, Conservation International, and the National Geographic Society. Declaring unequivocally that local tribal people were "poachers," the WWF argued that the Masai's "increasing population was a major threat to the survival of elephants and other wildlife," omitting to note that the Masai and other tribal people had lived in harmony with local wildlife for thousands of years (ibid).

In conclusion, the Kenyan government uses its power to protect and manage resources and to assert its authority where local people resist state controls. The political implications of this trend in conserving Kenyan wildlife are clear. Although equipment and funds are ostensibly allocated to protect nature – no doubt a laudable aim – they are also used by the state to serve its own political ends. In this way, the commitment to preservation of wildlife for tourism and research serves both the economic and political interests of the Kenyan government, while its effectiveness in doing so is questionable.

Indonesia

The Kenya outcome was a triumph for the state, as was the result of the next case study: Indonesia's forest reserves management policy. Organs of the state on the island of Java interact differently with international conservation interests than those in Kenya. While international conservation groups do not arm the Indonesian government in an effort to help protect tropical forest habitats as they do in Kenya, they nonetheless play a significant role in legitimating the state's use of violence to protect its claims to the nation's natural resources. By lobbying for sustainable forestry, for example, and defining sustainable forestry in the terms traditionally used by Western foresters or ecologists (who generally neither acknowledge nor consider the role of people in creating so-called natural environments), they emphasize the formal, scientific, planning aspects of forest management.

In Indonesia local environmental groups have only patchily challenged the state's nature conservation policies. In October 1994 local environmentalists began a court case against the government to spark a broad inquiry into the government's Reforestation Fund. The lawsuit was brought by the Indonesian Forum on the Environment, Wanana Lingkungan Hidap Indonesia (WALHI), an umbrella group with board members from local business and from multinationals such as IBM (Fisher 1993: 149). WALHI's lawsuit challenged the decision of the then national president, General Suharto, to funnel US$185 million from the Reforestation Fund into the coffers of the nation's aircraft industry. According to WALHI, the decision violated the government's conservationist commitment to refurbish Indonesia's vanishing rainforests (Cohen 1994: 44). The government's defense lawyers maintained that WALHI had no legal standing to bring the suit, as the "non-government organization does not represent the interests of the general public" and "the reforestation issue should be aired in parliament, not in the courts" (ibid).

A confidential Asian Development Bank report commissioned by the Ministry of Forestry reported in 1994 that just one-sixth (16 percent) of the reforestation funds had been spent in the four years prior to March 1993. It also noted that direct funding of natural forest rehabilitation and conservation activity amounted to only 3 percent of allocated funding. In other words, in the first half of the 1990s, less than half of 1 percent of funds allocated for reforestation in Indonesia was spent for that purpose! The report commented delicately that "there is evidence of considerable and increasing flexibility on how funds are spent," although no details were given. Moreover, "many plantations have been situated in logged-over forest, prompting the clear-cutting of remaining trees so as to create a homogeneous forest suitable for Indonesia's rapidly expanding pulp and paper industry" (Cohen 1994: 44).

Despite the damning report, it appeared that WALHI's conservation message had some chance of getting through to Indonesia's forestry minister, Djamaloedin Soeryohadikoesoemo. He announced in late 1994 that Indonesia would reduce its timber output by 30 percent between 1995 and 1999 in the interests of "sustainable development." Djamaloedin also expressed interest in pilot projects in community forestry, then in operation in Kalimantan and other areas, allowing villagers more responsibility in protecting resources. This may or may not be a sign of the emergence of a primary environmental care policy in Indonesia. A scheme for eco-labeling promised to add conservation safeguards to sell tropical timber in developed-country markets like Sweden, Australia, Canada, and the US .This scheme would obviously involve integrating environmental concerns more fully into economic decision-making and, several years later, there were indications that this was not being done (Morris 2001; Aglionby 2001b).

In sum, the account of environmental protection endeavors in Indonesia shows that success is dependent on political circumstances.

The final two case studies – from Nigeria and Tahiti in French Polynesia – illustrate this contention further. The first recounts the struggle of Tahitian environmental groups against French nuclear testing in the mid-1990s. Their objective was both environmental and political, intended not only to stop nuclear testing (ultimately successful) but also directed against the French colonial presence (not successful). However, the anti-France struggle helped focus attention of the main groups in Tahiti's emerging civil society – Hiti Tau (an environmental, development, women's, youth, and cultural umbrella group), the main pro-independence party, Tavini Huira-atira, and Atia I Mua, a labor union – on the link between French nuclear testing and the island's claim to independence (Rood, James, and Sakamati 1995: 17; Vidal 1995b).

The case study on the Ogoni of Nigeria examines the crushing of a local environmental campaign. The Ogoni were protesting at decades of oil exploitation on their land, from which they seem to have gained little. The Nigerian government was able to stifle the Ogoni campaign in the absence of a coordinated response from the weak local civil society, despite the Movement for the Survival of the Ogoni People (MOSOP) gaining support from foreign organizations, including Greenpeace International (Haynes 1999).

Nuclear testing at Mururoa Atoll and Ogoni oil

Nuclear testing at Mururoa Atoll, Tahiti

The decision by the French government to detonate eight – later reduced to six – nuclear explosions at Mururoa Atoll in late 1995 and early 1996 was followed by a wave of global condemnation (Ghazi 1995). On Bastille Day, July 14, 1995, French products were boycotted and the country's embassy compounds around the world stormed by Greenpeace protesters. Anti-nuclear protesters staged raids on the offices of French companies in Sydney, Australia, while in Adelaide a wrecked Renault car covered with 5,000 signatures was taken to the parliament building. In Suva, Fiji, 2,500 protesters marched on the French embassy and presented a 50,000-signature petition. In Cambodia Buddhist monks and nuns marked Bastille Day with a demonstration outside the French embassy. Green Party activists in Germany demonstrated outside the French embassy in Bonn. In Prague, capital of the Czech Republic, anti-nuclear demonstrators collected signatures against the nuclear tests; the petitions were signed by among others (French) troops guarding France's embassy (Zinn and Bowcott 1995). However, despite these protests, President Chirac's government stood firm: France detonated its first nuclear explosion at Mururoa in September 1995, and five others followed over the next few months. But the tests did not only stimulate global anger; they also encouraged Tahiti's independence movement, Tavini Huira-atira, to greater efforts. While global environmentalists saw the tests as contrary to the 1990s spirit of conservation, many Tahitians saw them as an example of French arrogance, further indication that the colonial power cared little for the views of its "subjects" in French Polynesia.

There is a long history of nuclear tests in French Polynesia. During the Cold War the islands of the South Pacific were linked directly to the grand strategies of some Western countries. The remoteness of some atolls and the strategic location of others made them attractive sites for nuclear weapons testing. British and American nuclear tests were conducted in the South Pacific in the 1950s. Following the Partial Test-Ban Treaty of 1963, France established a Centre d'Experiments du Pacifique, carrying out 41 atmospheric tests at Mururoa Atoll over the next decade before announcing a 20-year moratorium on further testing (Fry 1993: 228, 237).

Nuclear tests were disastrous for many local communities: the Chamoro people of Guam as well as the Tinian and Marshall Islanders were ejected from their homes; the Bikini Islanders suffered the effects of radioactivity and "all people in the region potentially suffer from the fallout of the 163 atmospheric tests conducted . . . before 1975" (ibid: 228). Despite such problems, the Cold War was used as justification by both the United States and France to continue testing, severely constraining islanders' efforts to achieve autonomy or independence. More generally for South Pacific societies, the Cold War was influential in two further ways: first, it molded the way in which regional security was conceptualized; second, it helped to foster a regional pan-nationalism. As Fry notes, while this originally affected "only relations among states, it increasingly affected social and political forces within them" (ibid: 234). In both American-controlled Palau and the French possession of New Caledonia, Cold War imperatives were used to justify opposition to moves for self-determination. Later, campaigns for greater autonomy and independence gained in strength, stimulated by perceptions that the end of the Cold War would lead to less bargaining power and a more stringent economic climate for the South Pacific as attention was focused elsewhere (Callick 1991). It was clear, however, that the traditional Cold War justification was not the only reason for France's involvement in the Pacific. French Polynesia retained its importance as a nuclear testing site, while the remaining colonial possessions, including Tahiti, gave the French reason for continued involvement in a region which contains important countries like Australia and New Zealand (Wollacott 1995).

France had long been successful in containing dissent by the assiduous use of money, spending close to US$2 billion dollars annually in the 1990s on its possessions in the South Pacific (*Economist* 1995b). At the time of the nuclear tests in 1995–6, French Polynesia was estimated by the World Bank to have a per capita GDP in the "high-income" category: over US$8,626 a year. This was four times that of independent Fiji (US$2,130), and many times greater than other independent island states in the region: Tonga (US$1,530), Vanuatu (US$1,230), Western Samoa (US$950), Solomon Islands (US$740) (World Bank 1995: 228). A report commissioned by the Tahitian government in 1995 on the economics of the island noted that while Tahiti "lives off a French military arsenal," its economy is "both prosperous and protected, without the worry of international competition" (*Economist* 1995a).

Despite withdrawal from the region by other erstwhile colonial powers (Britain, Germany, the Netherlands, and Portugal), France's Pacific policy has long been to try to retain its regional presence. This is because the French position is that its Pacific possessions are an integral part of France and that "[a] Tahitian has the same citizen's rights as a Parisian" (ibid). Over forty years ago the people of France's other Pacific possessions – French Caledonia, Wallis and Furtuna, and New Caledonia – were asked if they wanted independence, which would have meant a complete cessation of French aid. Referenda resulted in a wish by each territory to remain a part of the French "family." However, by the 1980s it was clear that the mood was changing. For example, in New Caledonia a vociferous pro-independence movement clashed with the governing administration. However, France was able to persuade native Kanaks to put off a decision about independence until 1998, promising in the interim to channel generous aid to the island (Fry 1993: 234)

A background of growing anti-French feeling underpinned riots in Tahiti in 1995. The island particularly benefited as a supply base for Mururoa Atoll, 1,400 kilometers to the southeast, with many Tahitians working at Mururoa, mostly in menial jobs, although many earned salaries in excess of US$40,000 dollars a year (*Economist* 1995a). Such jobs were of course highly valued in Tahiti itself, where unemployment was between 25 and 40 percent among young people (Vidal 1995b). Each year about 1,000 young people cannot find jobs when they leave school – disaffected individuals providing many recruits for the pro-independence movement. The shantytown of Faaa, 3 miles from the capital, Papeete, is a collection of "battered thatched huts and fetid beer halls clogged with jobless Polynesian youths" (Higson 1995). As George Pittman, pastor of a local evangelical church, commented: "[The youth] are aggressive, not like before . . . [t]hey are very angry and confused. I hear them shouting and screaming. This is the most dangerous bomb for us, not the atom bomb" (Higson 1995). Thus riots grew from an explosion of anger, especially by the youth, to become a broader-based demonstration of anti-French feeling. Vaihere Bordes, leader of a women's group, claimed that "everyone here is united against France and the nuclear testing [yet] local government does not listen" (Vidal 1995b).

After a two-decade hiatus, France's decision to resume nuclear testing at Mururoa Atoll was the catalyst for an eruption of anger against its colonial presence. For three days in September 1995, coinciding with the first nuclear test, demonstrators took to the streets destroying, burning, and looting. Tahiti's capital, Papeete, was badly damaged. Calls for social justice and an end to environmental destruction in French Polynesia were part of the same demand: key decisions affecting people's lives must be brought under their control, as exclusion from decision-making fueled popular resentment. As Bordes asserted, "France has said for years that if we allow the bombs then we can have work. It's political colonization, but its worse; it's colonialism of the mind" (ibid).

The overall point is that Tahitians felt divorced both from their culture and from the ability to decide their own futures. Denied self-determination, many Tahitians, especially the young and unemployed, were no longer prepared meekly to submit to the dictates of France. Having attempted to persuade the French for two months by peaceful demonstrations and petitions, it was perhaps understandable that protests would turn violent if the French disregarded both local and global calls for restraint. "The French have treated us as rubbish, as rats," declared Roti Make, a social worker, "and now you see what happens" (ibid).

The Tahitian outburst must also be seen against the background of global demonstrations against the decision to resume nuclear testing. Tahitians were well aware of this because with access to television and radio they were able to see the worldwide protests at first hand. As Bordes noted, "minds have changed. If you go back just 30 years our parents didn't realize what nuclear power meant. In 1966 we didn't have radio, TV or an airport. Now we're in contact with the world, and we see the catastrophe" (ibid). No doubt, Tahitians also perceived that local anti-French demonstrations would have the eye of the world and, as a result, the anti-colonial campaign would be encouraged.

In conclusion, the outburst of anti-French feeling in Tahiti united unemployed young people, women , labor activists, and the pro-independence movement behind the goal of autonomy or independence. Tahiti, in common with many other Polynesian islands, exhibits a dangerous demography, with an overly youthful population, and a clear division between "haves" and "have nots," overlapping with racial differences. It may well be that the decision to resume testing at Mururoa Atoll will in future be seen as a first step in two ways: (1) France's withdrawal from the Pacific and (2) rediscovery of French Polynesians' culture and pride.

Environmental activism in Ogoniland, Nigeria

Half a million Ogoni people – about 0.5 percent of Nigeria's population – live on the Niger delta in the province of Rivers State in the southeast of the country. The Ogoni are by tradition farmers and fishers, producing food for local people and for much of Rivers State. Large quantities of oil were discovered in Ogoniland in the late 1950s, the first major find in Nigeria. Since then, oil has come to dominate both the Nigerian economy and the Ogoni people's lives. Yet, despite repeated promises from the federal government, they have enjoyed very limited benefits. Naanen remarks that "patterns of power distribution between central government and the component units, on the one hand, and between the various ethnic groups, on the other, have politically emasculated the Ogoni people, causing them to lose control of their resources and their environment" (Naanen 1995: 46–7).

From an environmental point of view, perhaps most disastrous has been a succession of oil spills from ruptured pipelines driven – above ground – through farms and villages. Ogonis have had to live with the continuous noise and pollution of numerous burning gas flares. Ogoniland has two of Nigeria's four oil refineries, the country's only major fertilizer plant, a large petrochemical factory, and the fourth largest ocean port in the country – all located within a few kilometers of each other (Osaghae 1995: 330). The impact of industrialization and oil exploitation was especially serious because of the high population density: 500,000 Ogoni are crammed into 404 square miles (1,238 people per square mile). The vast majority depended on farming and fishing for their livelihoods. Both the Nigerian government and Shell were not over-anxious to publicize the Ogonis' plight: in the mid-1990s an attempt by an INGO, the Unrepresented Nations and Peoples Organization, to send a fact-finding mission to Ogoniland was frustrated by the Nigerian government, as was a pronounced visit by representatives of Britain's Body Shop company (Body Shop n/d).

Poor environmental conditions, lack of development, and the government's apparent unwillingness to listen to Ogoni demands drove the latter to rebel in the early 1990s. A trigger for the revolt came in October 1990 when villagers at Umuechen in Ogoniland attacked Shell production workers. Shell, active in the area since 1958, called in the Mobile Police (known locally as "kill-and-go"), who shot 80 villagers dead and burned down around 500 houses, some with the inhabitants trapped inside (*Africa Confidential* 1995). The uprising was led and coordinated by the Movement for the Survival of the Ogoni People (MOSOP). MOSOP was run by a steering committee drawn from various community groups. Its membership was made up of women, young people – organized in the National Youth Council of Ogoni People (NYCOP) – and representatives of professional groups.

Until his execution in November 1995, the writer Ken Saro-Wiwa led MOSOP. An international outcry was raised following the hanging of Saro-Wiwa and eight other Ogoni activists in November 1995 for the alleged crime of encouraging several MOSOP members to murder four pro-government Ogoni chiefs. Saro-Wiwa was the author of over twenty books, an Amnesty International Prisoner of Conscience, and a recipient of a prestigious environmental award and the "alternative Nobel prize," the Right Livelihood Award. His death was condemned by Western governments and INGOs, including International PEN, Amnesty International, Greenpeace International, Human Rights Watch, and UNPO. The British prime minister, John Major, called the treatment of Saro-Wiwa and his comrades "judicial murder." It was followed by the arrest of over twenty more Ogoni leaders and activists, including Ledum Mitee, MOSOP deputy president, who faced charges under the same "fatally flawed" judicial system (Ogoni Community Association UK 1995; Black, Bowcott, and Vidal 1995). A massive federal troop presence in Ogoniland continued and it was not until September 1998 that the government freed Mitee and the other detained Ogoni activists.

Not all Ogonis support MOSOP's aims. There is strong opposition from some traditional leaders whom MOSOP accuses of being state agents. Some MOSOP opponents among the Ogonis had their houses and other property destroyed by NYCOP members (Osaghae 1995: 334). An anti-MOSOP position was often stimulated by a belief that the organization sought to diminish the power of traditional leaders and encourage previously subordinate groups, including young people and women, to challenge established leaders. On the other hand, it seems clear that many, perhaps most, Ogonis were sympathetic to MOSOP: a banned march involving 300,000 black-wearing Ogoni took place in early 1996, and thereafter annually, both to commemorate "Ogoni Day" and to mourn the death of Saro-Wiwa and eight comrades killed at the same time. In 1996 federal soldiers killed six of the marchers (Duodu 1996).

Attempts to organize and mobilize the Ogoni people had begun in 1989, three years before Saro-Wiwa presented the Ogoni case before the United Nations Commission on Human Rights in Geneva. According to Naanen, this "marked an important turning point in bolstering people's confidence," and led directly to demonstrations in January 1993, involving 300,000 Ogoni, and to a subsequent appearance by an Ogoni delegation at the UN Human Rights Conference in Vienna later that year (Naanen 1995: 69). Later, in 1995, Saro-Wiwa received US$30,000 from the Goldman Foundation, an American organization, in recognition of his struggle for human and environmental justice. From around this time numerous environmental and human rights organizations, including UNPO, the World Rain Forest Action Group, Amnesty International, the Body Shop, and Greenpeace, sought to publicize the Ogonis' plight internationally. The British Parliamentary Human Rights Group also sought to pressurize both Shell and the Nigerian government to adopt different tactics in dealing with the Ogoni. The Nigerian government's response was mixed: entering into dialogue with MOSOP while jailing Saro-Wiwa and several other Ogoni leaders on probably trumped-up charges.

The Ogonis' struggle against the federal government and the oil companies is but the most recent manifestation of the their long-manifested desire for control over their own affairs. It took the British until 1908 to subdue them and during the colonial era the Ogoni, along with other Delta groups, demanded a separate administrative division. This was finally achieved after independence, with the creation of Rivers State in 1967 (ibid: 63). Following allegations of domination by the numerically larger Ijaw people, the Ogoni unsuccessfully petitioned in 1974 for the creation of a separate Port Harcourt state to be carved out of the Rivers State. In the quarter century since then, Ogoni demands for a separate state have dovetailed with economic decline, oil-based ecological degradation, and the undermining of traditional smallholder agriculture and fishing, long the mainstays of the local economy (Saro-Wiwa 1992). Ogoni discontent increased when oil resources were discovered under their land. By 1972 six oilfields produced 200,000 barrels a day. Despite the major contribution to Nigeria's economic development the Ogoni were denied desired material benefits, including piped water, electricity, medical facilities, and all-weather roads (Naanen 1995: 65). This led Naanen to describe the Ogoni–federal government relationship as a "modified version of 'internal colonialism' [helping] to illuminate the relationship between the central Nigerian state and the oil-producing periphery" (ibid: 49). Ethnic domination and peripheralization were furthered by multinational oil companies and state-owned enterprises, adding environmental degradation to the Ogoni list of woes. Oil-based environmental degradation undermined traditional farming and fishing in the oil-producing areas without producing a viable economic alternative. For decades oil wealth derived from Ogoni lands went to the central exchequer, with nothing coming to the Ogoni themselves. A former minister and the first president of MOSOP, Garrick B. Leton, claimed that the Ogoni were content to live in a federation. He claimed that they were not asking for the entire amount from rent and royalties, only an equitable portion: "If the land is ours, irrespective of the law put in place by the major ethnic groups, anything that comes out of the land should be ours" (quoted in Osaghae 1995: 327).

While the Ogoni demands were not successful in the short term there were a number of concrete achievements, especially the raising of national and international awareness about the Ogonis' predicament. Over the years their case has become an international *cause célèbre*. It is widely seen as an important test case regarding how the democratically elected Nigerian government will treat minority people's demands for control of their land and resources.

In summary, three main conclusions emerge from the Ogoni and Tahiti case studies. First, groups in both polities were fighting not only against perceived environmental injustices, but also for autonomy or independence from central control. In other words, the environmental objective was part of a wider political goal of empowerment. Second, among the leading figures in both campaigns were a large proportion of young men and women, subordinate groups with little to gain from the status quo. Third, both case studies illustrate once again that in the absence of a coordinated society-wide campaign against powerful state or foreign interests, environmental groups will find it very difficult to achieve their goals.

Conclusion

We have seen that bottom-up pressure from environmental groups on developing country governments has grown in recent years. Often it is an element in wider demands for greater socioeconomic justice and political reforms. Reflecting their lowly political position, environmental activists tend to come from subordinate strata, especially from among the poor, women, the young, and national minorities. The case studies from India, Kenya, Indonesia, Tahiti, and Nigeria are examples of why environment-oriented campaigns frequently form aspects of wider anti-government protests. We also saw that such campaigns only succeed under certain specific conditions. First, it is essential – although not necessarily sufficient – that there are democratic and legal avenues to pursue environmental goals. Second, it is crucial to build a relatively wide-ranging coalition of groups and organizations, large enough and representative enough to take on the state and its allies, such as large landowners, senior military figures, and important business interests. However, such struggles are only likely to be successful in democratic environments where strong civil societies have leverage vis-à-vis the state. Of the countries discussed in this chapter, only India falls into this category. The success of Chipko and the achievement of WALHI

Indonesia underlines that if environmental groups link together in a coalition, and are both well-organized and tenacious, then they may successfully challenge state policies with which they do not agree.

We also saw that numerous environmental groups challenge governmental and corporate practices in relation to sustainable development strategies, albeit with modest success. Underpinning the policies of the former is the belief that people at and near the bottom of the socioeconomic pile should have the unequivocal right and opportunity to participate in shaping their own destinies when it comes to the environment. But many local communities are not fully consulted on development projects that affect them. Instead, lacking both political and economic power, development policies and programs can be imposed on them, as we saw with the Narmada Valley project.

Finally, the struggles of the Ogonis and the Tahitians were examples of what happens when leaders of minority or marginal ethnic and social organizations, feeling dissatisfied with the structure of power sharing and resource allocation in their polities, seek to restructure the configuration of power. The failure so far of both campaigns to achieve the goals of independence or at least autonomy underlines how important it is for civil society to be powerful enough to take on the state in order to achieve its goals. While both the Ogonis and the Tahitians were successful in gaining foreign support they were incapable of putting together a domestic coalition of interest groups of sufficient strength to achieve their goals. The Ogonis found that neighboring ethnic groups – with some of which they had a history of tension – were encouraged by the state to attack them. In Tahiti the situation was complicated because France is an important employer paying salaries far above the local average. People may well have warmed to the notion of greater autonomy or even independence from colonial rule, yet such aspirations seemed to have been offset for many by concern at what would happen to their incomes if the French departed.

9

Conclusion

In this book I rejected the redundant concept of the "Third World," arguing that it is no longer useful analytically. I suggested that it is a label for a category of things confined increasingly to the past; that is, from during the Cold War, when the understanding of political outcomes in Africa, Asia, Latin America and the Caribbean, and the Middle East was primarily undertaken via modernization theory or dependency theory (or their variants). Instead, our focus was on what explains contemporary outcomes in developing countries, in terms of both internal and external factors, as well as the relative importance of structural and contingent factors. We examined a range of important issues – economic development, democratization and democracy, religious and ethnic conflict, human rights, gender issues, and the natural environment – in the chapters of this book.

In this, the final chapter, I discuss the general arguments and comparative implications of the material presented in earlier chapters. I also consider the implications for wider understanding of political, economic, and societal change, and, finally, make predictions for the future regarding the developing world. I structure the discussion by looking at domestic factors and international factors. We start with a brief summary of what we discovered in relation to democratization and democracy in the developing world. This will allow us to locate the other issues we examined in an appropriate and relevant political context.

I devoted chapter 4 to an explanation of patterns of democratization in the developing world over the last two decades, a period known as the "third wave of democracy." How best to characterize and understand the contemporary democratic position in the countries of the developing world? The short answer is that it is highly variable, with major differences between countries and regions. While the amount of democratically elected governments in these regions grew in the 1980s and 1990s, significant numbers of non-democratic regimes – including personalist dictatorships, single-party and communist states, and military regimes – remain. Of course, forms of authoritarian rule differ from regime to regime and from country to country. But what nearly all unelected governments have in common is that they deny their citizens both political rights and civil liberties. In addition, human rights are often downplayed or ignored, women's demands belittled, religious and ethnic minorities denied freedom of expression, and environmental safeguards bypassed or ignored.

How are things different in developing countries with democratically elected governments? There is no generally applicable answer because new democracies, like their authoritarian counterparts, may actually exhibit profound differences. On the other hand, elected governments usually have several common factors. First, and most obviously, all have some form of regular, relatively free and fair electoral competition. Often, however, as for example in Indonesia, Bangladesh, and Zambia, there are doubts whether this situation will endure. Second, democratically elected governments are – at least in theory – more accountable to their citizens than authoritarian regimes. Third, when democratically elected regimes are in place, a wide range of issues can – again theoretically – be contested. That is, they may appear on the political agenda and differing viewpoints may be freely expressed, debated, contested. In short, we saw that democratic progress *is* possible in the developing world: in 2000, Freedom House designated one in three new democracies in Latin America, Asia, and Africa as a "free state." On the other hand, it is clear that democratic consolidation – that is, the embedding and sustenance of democracy – does not *automatically* follow a transition from authoritarian rule; that is, it is not simply a matter of time. Rather, as Zakaria argues, "illiberal democracies" are common throughout the developing world.

> Far from being a temporary or transitional stage, it appears that many countries are settling into a form of government that mixes a substantial degree of democracy with a substantial degree of illiberalism. Just as nations across the world have become comfortable with many variations of capitalism, they could well adopt and sustain varied forms of democracy. Western liberal democracy might prove to be not the final destination on the democratic road, but just one of many possible exits. (Zakaria 1997: 24)

The political role of the armed forces is important in this context. It should be noted that the military has been an important political actor in numerous developing countries for long periods, and authoritarian political systems typically depend on the armed forces' support to stay in power. Given Latin America's propensity for military takeovers in the 1960s and 1970s, it would be hard to argue that Costa Rica's abolition of its armed forces in the late 1940s, followed by five decades of democracy, were not closely linked. And, as Pakistan's successful coup d'état of October 1999 highlighted, when senior or occasionally junior figures harbor political ambitions and act upon them, it is highly likely that democracy will suffer.

In the past, "waves" of military coups have swamped whole regions, for example West Africa in the 1960s and Latin America in the 1960s and 1970s. This suggests that military coups have sometimes seemed contagious, bringing on a "reverse wave" (in Huntington's (1991) terminology) away from democracy. Various countries, for example Ghana and Thailand, have seen periodic coups followed by the reinstatement of democracy, seemingly *ad infinitum*. And during the 1990s new military coups occurred – for example in Côte d'Ivoire and the Gambia – in countries that until then had managed to keep the military out of power. Elsewhere, for example in Turkey, military personnel have remained enthusiastic, if now less open, political actors. Often, the military's political involvement is linked to a desire to help defend members of the political and economic elite from demands for democracy.

The overall point is that political and economic outcomes in developing countries are not easily explicable by reference to general theories, such as modernization or dependency theory (discussed in chapter 1). Instead, we need to focus on an array of domestic and external factors to understand political, economic, and societal results in the developing world.

Domestic Factors: Political Participation, Civil Society, and Economic Development

Structured contingency

Political and economic outcomes in the developing world are linked to various interacting *structural* and *contingent* factors. In chapter 1 we conceptualized this as *structured contingency*. Structured contingency is a useful concept to help understand political and economic outcomes in the developing world. Structural legacies – they can be pro-democracy or anti-democracy – are important factors when political actors search for rules of political competition in post-authoritarian systems. In other words, there is no *tabula rasa*: no incoming regime, whatever its stated ideological proclivities or goals, democratically orientated or not, can erase historically produced societal behavior. Of what structures am I thinking? Although they vary from country to country, every nation has historically established structures, notably patterns of power, that involve regular, systematic interaction between power holders and the mass of ordinary people. This arrangement will be reflected in a country's established rules and institutions.

However, relevant structures do not only include *formal* fixed structures of public life, such as laws, organizations, offices, and so on. There are also important *informal* structures found in every polity; that is, "dynamics of interests and identities, domination and resistance, compromise and accommodation" (Bratton and Van de Walle 1997: 276). Significant political actors are well aware that (1) political competition and conflict are informed by both formal and informal structures and (2) they mold the range of realistic alternatives open to them. This predisposes political actors to select certain courses of action and not others.

While problems of representation can theoretically be addressed by developing strong, formal political institutions, we saw in chapter 4 that inherited structures of power – for example in South Africa and Indonesia – were actually of great significance in molding political outcomes. These examples indicated that consolidating democracy is a difficult and slow process, not least because traditional power holders are often against it or at least suspicious of what it might entail for their own privileged positions. However, as Shin remarks in relation to South Korea, democracy cannot logically "be run by the few as in oligarchies or autocracies; nor should it be guided by intelligence or professional expertise apart from the people" (Shin 1999: 137). In sum, consideration of institutional variations in new democracies needs to be complemented by an understanding of their *underlying political dynamics*: how, and with what results, individuals and groups gain access to political power and what they do with it

The problem, however, is that democratic *stability* depends to a considerable degree on integrating "the military and business elites into a stable framework of efficient democratic institutions *which do not threaten their interests*" (Merkel 1998: 56; emphasis added). But to create and then develop a democratic political system is likely to alienate traditional power holders and their allies (for example, senior military figures, big capital owners, large landowners). This is because such elites are likely to see a truly democratizing political system as an unacceptable attack on their own interests. Introducing regular tests of public opinion via periodic polls is normatively important – theoretically, an important step towards a more democratic political system. But if democratic rule it is to be more than a simple replication of the old order in a new guise then it must seek "to correct past inequalities or new hardships" (Leftwich 1993: 614).

Political elites may formally comply with the dictates of democratic politics yet still behave in unhelpful ways, by showing little or no regard for democratic principles and with little interest in developing public policy to benefit most citizens. The concern that elites have with not allowing ordinary people an important voice in political issues is neither a recent nor an exclusively third wave trait. Arblaster describes how in Britain elite interests were long instrumental in denying ordinary men and women the right to vote. Elite opposition in this regard was not finally overcome in Britain until the late 1920s, marked by the introduction of universal suffrage.

> Democracy has only become acceptable to the privileged classes because it has turned out to be less of a challenge to wealth and property than was feared, and also because democracy itself has been redefined in much narrower terms (as a method of choosing government) than it was given in the classical tradition reaching down from Pericles to John Stuart Mill and beyond. (Arblaster 1999: 33)

This is a way of saying that structures of power, whether in Britain or elsewhere, are often rooted in the interests of elites. What is an elite in this context? Pridham defines an elite as those "who are able, by virtue of their authoritative positions in powerful organizations and movements of whatever kind, to affect national political outcomes regularly and substantially" (Pridham 2000: 143). In developing countries the politically relevant elite can usefully be desegregated into, on the one hand, those people currently in power (or individuals close to figures in power) and, on the other hand, those who aspire to it. Among the latter will be figures that believe that electoral arrangements are rigged against them and the media's coverage is politically biased. The overall point, however, is that both elite groups – that is, the "ins" and the "outs" – are likely to have a vested interest in seeking to control the degree to which democracy empowers and emboldens ordinary people to seek real, as opposed to cosmetic, political changes.

Without considerable attention to important yet rather intangible indicators, interpretations of democratic failure or success are necessarily both judgmental and relativistic. Observers, including Huntington (1991), attach considerable responsibility to what elites do and the amount of respect they show for the democratic "rules of the game." Perhaps the gravest potential political threat to new democracies comes from among the elites – particularly from those who have accumulated and concentrated power in the executive branch and have weakened accountability of the rulers to the ruled. Fraudulent practices to retain and concentrate power have been common in several developing countries. They are a distinguishing feature not only in countries with underdeveloped democratic characteristics but also in many that have developed further in this regard. But making "political equality an unyielding requirement means that no country truly measures up . . . [especially] if democracy means social democracy." However, "striking the right balance between demands for reform from subordinate classes, and pressures to mitigate threat perceptions on the part of the economic elites, is obviously crucial to the successful installation of democracy" (Burnell 1998: 20–1).

But when leading political actors sincerely value democracy, that is, when the *idea* of democracy as a desirable political outcome serves as an important factor informing political decision making, then democracy can be built. This is the case in India, even though unpropitious conditions, such as a weak economy and ethnic and religious divisions, are present. Elsewhere, however, as in Indonesia – with a politically active military and serious ethnic divisions – such an outcome seems at present unlikely.

Overall, evidence from the chapters of this book highlights the importance to political outcomes of both structures *and* contingency. That is, a concern with structures does not mean that we should ignore the equally crucial role of contingency and one-off events in helping determine political outcomes in developing countries. For example, personal decisions taken by political leaders – such as South Africa's former president Nelson Mandela and Indonesia's long-time ruler General Suharto – were vital in determining political outcomes in their countries. Unplanned, serendipitous, one-off events can increase the chances of new political arrangements being built, while unplanned, baleful events can diminish them. For example, the desire of peripheral peoples – such as those of East Timor and Aceh – for freedom from central rule in Indonesia had a major impact on the country's democratic progress following the ousting of General Suharto in 1998. The point is that democracy can be put in place, but to become embedded – that is, consolidated – it requires leading political actors *and* the mass of ordinary people to "learn to love it. Until elites and citizens alike come to cherish rule by the people and exhibit a willingness to stand up for it . . . there will be no permanent defense against tyranny" (Bratton and Van de Walle 1997: 279). This can only be achieved by institutionalizing democracy; that is, when various organizations, norms, and procedures increasingly gain both value and stability among elites and the mass of ordinary people.

Both formal and informal institutions are significant in this regard because of the way they structure incentives and impose constraints. And inevitably they are instruments in the competitive struggle for power. Political actors will be cognizant of such factors, which not only limit the range of available – that is, realistic – alternatives open to them, but also predispose them to select certain courses of action over others. It is often argued that it is highly important for a government to make the "right" institutional choices. These should be (1) politically appropriate, (2) able to command society's respect, and (3) technically sound. The problem, however, is that failed attempts at engineering constitutional arrangements and electoral rules that turn out to be inappropriate can lead to serious problems. The parliamentary model is sometimes perceived as having more going for it than presidential models (characterized by separate and independent election of the executive and legislature and fixed terms of office). But there is no definitive evidence in this regard. However, in Latin America, Mainwaring and Shugart (1997) suggest that a combination of presidentialism and extensive multi-partyism – say, more than three effective parties at any one time – is highly conducive to political instability.

Because state power is always so valuable, those who have it go to very great lengths to retain it. It seems likely that, in the great majority of new democracies, public office at the apex of the political system is perceived as among the best – if not *the* best – way for individuals to achieve private profit. This is because the state is the locus of a process where "state rulers are defined by and obtain their power and resources on the basis of their office holding" (Forrest 1988: 439). Consequently, control of the state is nearly always too appealing to be easily abandoned by incumbent power holders. Free and fair elections on their own cannot ensure that power holders will strive to build the conditions necessary for democratic consolidation if it means that power would, as a result, move from their hands to those of others. Under such circumstances they will do all they can *not* to facilitate democratic consolidation. Pressure from civil and political society is of crucial importance in ensuring that they do.

Civil and political society

Democratic consolidation requires a shift from a situation where power is exercised by and for a numerically small elite to one where it is exercised for the good of the many. We have seen that the attainment of a democratic political environment is facilitated by *sustained* pressure on incumbent elites from civil and political society, especially opposition parties. But this is often hard to achieve, not least because once democracy is won then civil society tends to fragment, while opposition parties can become more interested in their individual quests to achieve power than to help extend democracy *per se*.

Such a situation plays into the hands of incumbent elites. Power monopolies at the apex long formed the political superstructure in most new democracies in Africa, Asia, and Latin America. Organski (1965) long ago identified such power monopolies, what he called the "syncratic alliance," as a non-democratic concord uniting traditional agrarian interests too strong to be destroyed with a modernizing urban-based elite. A bargain was struck between the two sets of interests: in exchange for obtaining the political support of agrarian interests, powerful urban-based actors agreed not to disturb significantly the often semi-feudal conditions of the countryside. The question is to what extent, when a democratically elected regime gains power, is there a shift in the power balance?

The momentum of political reform may not be maintained after the transition from authoritarian rule. As Arblaster notes, "transitions from dictatorship to democracy [in the third wave] were very often neither smooth, automatic, nor complete." Further, the "considerable obstacles to the wholesale adoption of the institutions of liberal democracy" and ability to "combine a quite minimal use of popular election with forms of strong, centralized government . . . amounted in some cases to presidential or prime ministerial dictatorship" (Arblaster 1999: 33). The failure of persistence led to "stalled," "flawed," or "incomplete" democracies. In other words, there is "transition from" authoritarianism but not "transition to" democracy; there is "stunted" rather than "full" democratic consolidation, meaning by the latter that all groups of significant political actors explicitly accept that democracy is, in the words of Linz and Stepan (1996), "the only game in town."

In Latin America and parts of Asia large landowners have traditionally represented the rural side of the power coalition. In India successive postcolonial governments, despite being legitimated through the ballot box for half a century (apart from the State of Emergency, 1975–7), have failed to break with powerful rural allies. Although rural-based powerful families were often formally shorn of traditional powers after independence in 1947, many still managed to maintain their long-standing position via a very successful alternative: the elected route to power. Although Organski's description may be less relevant to Africa, it seems clear that support from those with wealth and power was, and is, more crucial to political decision-makers than support from other classes. Clapham notes that personalist dictatorships have been in power for long periods in many African countries. This is a type of authority that "corresponds to the normal forms of social organization in [Africa's] precolonial societies" (Clapham 1988: 49). In short, while precise bases of power differ, and despite democratic transitions, elites have often managed to maintain control of the bases of economic wealth as well as the direction of political development.

Evidence suggests that such elite coalitions were an important means of maintaining upper-class power in several countries, including Thailand and the Philippines, even when there was a formally democratic system (Rueschemeyer, Stephens, and Stephens 1992: 174–5; Rocamora 1993). The crucial analytical point is that while many dictatorial regimes exited from power during the third wave of democracy and were replaced by elected alternatives, this was rarely sufficient to oust from positions of power and influence long-entrenched narrowly based elites and their supporters. In other words, while traditionally oligarchical political systems may officially be subsumed by new democratic procedures, long-established power monopolies have often remained politically and economically powerful.

This is where a strong civil society comes in, a crucial step toward realizing politically freer polities. It is very hard to imagine a participant political system that is capable of surviving for long without a vibrant civil society. But while the emergence of a dynamic and vigorous civil society is a necessary development, it is not on its own sufficient to consolidate democracy. When the first battle is won and the authoritarian *ancien régime* is gone, the struggle for democratic consolidation creates a new kind of political environment with novel challenges to both civil and political society. The rallying point of the common enemy is no longer there. Now, the challenge shifts from cooperating in the common goal of removing unwelcome rulers to institutionalizing democratic competition between the interests and aspirations of various groups, so that democracy truly does become the only game in town.

Demands put on the skills and commitments of leading actors to meet this challenge are different from those required during the transition phase itself. Karl emphasizes that political actors must show the "ability to differentiate political forces rather than draw them into a grand coalition, the capacity to define and channel competing political projects rather than seek to keep potentially divisive reforms off the agenda, and the willingness to tackle incremental reforms . . . rather than defer them to some later date" (Karl 1990: 17). Thus, while popular mobilization and organization undoubtedly improve democratic prospects, it is how popular power manifests itself *after* democratic transition that is crucial in consolidating democracy.

Much of the relevant literature contends that civil societies that struggled against one-party and military dictatorships had the potential to weaken the cultural foundations of authoritarianism – that is, to serve as a genuine base for democracy. What was needed, it was suggested, was the creation and embedding of a new democratic consensus that – while reducing political instability – must also erect and sustain robust electoral and institutional forms that enable democratic governments to work. If this were to happen, democratically elected regimes would not be at the mercy of self-interested elite politicians. But for this to come to pass, there has be a learning process, a development explicit to Linz and Stepan's (1996) conception of democratic consolidation: the destructive confrontations of the past must not be repeated by the new generation of politicians seeking power. Instead, they must seek to deepen and extend democracy to previously excluded classes and groups.

In this context the political importance of civil society is clear. While transitions to democracy are often explained by a focus on elites, it is important not to overlook upsurges in popular mobilization and organization which were nearly always a crucial factor in the genesis and initial development of democratization (Foweraker and Landman 1997). A strong civil society will improve the chances for democracy and make a return to authoritarian rule more difficult than it would be in its absence. This suggests the democratic importance of an array of civil society organizations. However, the democratic salience of such organizations is undermined when, as we saw in chapter 5, religio-ethnic groups are less interested in democracy *per se* than in their own particularistic aspirations. This is often because extreme self-interest, chauvinism, and animosity towards rival groups typically motivate religio-ethnic groups.

In the context of the development of civil society, we also examined the socioeconomic and political position of poor women in developing countries. We saw that it is dependent upon a number of factors. We saw how the position of women in Kerala is relatively better than in other areas of India because the state government was forced to be responsive to an educated and sophisticated electorate which values equality. However, as our discussions of the position of poor women elsewhere in the developing world made clear, the Keralan position is atypical.

Case studies in chapter 7 highlighted two factors necessary to improve the position of poor women: (1) sufficient political and social space for women to organize, and (2) a strong desire to work collectively. Two overall conclusions suggested themselves. First, vehicles of women's empowerment rarely if ever threaten the state's paramount position. However, they *do* succeed in alarming many men who feel that their relatively privileged positions are thereby undermined. Second, women's empowerment seems more likely in a democratizing or democratic environment. The paucity of examples of women's empowerment groups in both the Middle East and Africa warns against being overly optimistic when assessing the chances of general improvements in the sociopolitical and economic position of poor women in the developing world. On the other hand, the success of several women's organizations in Latin America and India suggests that progress is being made in some countries.

We turned to the natural environment in chapter 8. We saw that bottom-up pressure on many governments of developing countries has helped increase awareness that environmental issues are nearly always linked to political and economic issues. We also noted that such endeavors are linked to the growth of civil society. They are often an element in wider demands for greater socioeconomic justice and political reforms. Reflecting a typically lowly societal economic and political position, environmental activists frequently come from subordinate strata, such as the poor, women, the young, and national minorities. Case studies in chapter 8 – from India, Kenya, Indonesia, Tahiti, and Nigeria – illustrated why environmental campaigns are often elements in wider anti-government protests. However, we saw that such campaigns only succeed under certain specific conditions. First, democratic and legal avenues are essential – but not necessarily sufficient – successfully to pursue environmental goals. Second, there needs to be a relatively wide-ranging coalition of groups and organizations. Collectively, they should be sufficiently large and representative to take on the state and its allies, such as large landowners, senior military figures, or important business interests. On the other hand, we also saw that numerous environmental groups challenge governmental and corporate practices in relation to sustainable development strategies, but have little or no success.

Economic development and welfare

Chapter 3 was concerned with economic and welfare issues, issues of central importance to people throughout the developing world. What is the relationship between economic and political changes in the developing world? Everything else being equal, growing national wealth, relatively equitably distributed, and a governmental concern with extending welfare mechanisms to all citizens, should help reinforce political progress. Another issue too is important here: the distribution of material benefits and citizens' perceptions of the justice of the pattern of distribution. That is, do a privileged minority consume an inappropriate proportion of available resources? It seems plausible that popular support for an incumbent government is most likely to grow when it not only presides over sustained economic growth but also manages to convince the mass of people that it is not too unequally shared. Przeworski et al.'s (1996) comprehensive survey of evidence – covering 1950 to 1990 – suggests that democratically elected governments are more likely to survive when they manage to develop their country's economy in a sustained fashion and also reduce, gradually yet consistently, extant socioeconomic inequalities. On the other hand, some types of resource base, notably those conveying large sums by way of "rent" to numerically tiny elites – for example, oil revenues in several Middle Eastern countries – are often vulnerable to inequality, corruption, and a lack of democracy. This helps explain why only very few non-Western oil-exporting countries have managed to build democratic systems.

International Factors

Examples of international factors and actors that help determine political and economic outcomes in the developing world run through the pages of this book like the slogan in a stick of rock. For example, the pace of democratic progress, especially in poor countries in Central America and Africa, was often strongly "influenced, sometimes to a considerable degree, by various international . . . factors" (Leftwich 1997: 522). More generally, the concept of the "third wave of democracy" was premised on there being something happening at the global level to encourage democratization around the world. This not only included global events and developments (that is, "background factors" or the *Zeitgeist*), but also more specific, focused encouragement from bilateral and multilateral aid donors.

We saw that both democracy and economic development were important focuses of Western attention after the Cold War. Western governments and international financial institutions (IFIs) such as the World Bank and the IMF attached "political conditionalities" to aid and investment in the developing world. Governments of developing countries that sought to deny human and/or civil rights to their citizens could be denied funds from such sources. The reasoning behind political conditionality was partly economic. Western governments and IFIs argued that economic failures were very often linked to an absence of political accountability and human rights. Consequently, without significant political changes economic reforms would be unlikely to produce the desired results. However, in many cases, as we saw in chapter 3, attempts at economic reforms, expressed via structural adjustment programs, were often disappointing both in economic and societal outcomes.

Western governments, Gills, Rocamora, and Wilson (1993) argue, seek to control the pace and content of political and economic reforms in many developing countries. Such countries may even be controlled by Western allies, anxious to prevent "too much" democracy that would lead to political instability and perhaps their being thrown out of power. In other words, both local elites in many developing countries and Western governments are said to share a strong interest in limiting the extent of political changes. This theory, known as Low Intensity Democracy (LID), highlights the important role of Western actors in determining political (and economic) outcomes in the developing world. LID is said to satisfy Western governments' allegedly insincere concerns for deeper democratization. In sum, the LID argument is that external forces help deliver strictly limited processes of political change because this suits their own aims: (1) continued economic control of dependent countries, and (2) survival in power of indigenous allies.

There is little real evidence for the broad salience of the LID argument in the developing world. Critics contend that it seriously overestimates the extent of Western leverage on most developing countries. For example, despite major efforts, successive US governments were unable decisively to influence outcomes in several developing countries of great strategic influence, including Afghanistan, Iraq, Iran, Somalia, Nigeria, and Sudan. Overall, Western governments and supranational organizations such as the European Union have two, not necessarily congruous aims. They may well wish to see liberal democracy and economic liberalization in developing countries. At the same time, under some circumstances, they may also prefer powerful authoritarian governments, not least because they can be very effective in both suppressing and controlling popular dissent. For example, over the years successive US governments were ambivalent about the prospect of social democratic governments coming to power – even by the ballot box. Examples in this regard include Brazil and Chile in the 1960s and 1970s; both countries experienced successful military coups whose resulting governments were strongly supported by that of the USA (Arblaster 1999: 46–7). The main point is that Western governments often seem satisfied as long as governments in the developing world are politically and economically stable.

It is tempting to suppose that endorsement of Western-inspired economic growth strategies would go some way to compensate for the lack of "conventional" democracy in certain countries, such as Uganda (Haynes 2001b). And this would seem to be the case. During the 1990s, Uganda's president, Yoweri Museveni, made a successful diplomatic offensive to sell his "no-party" political system to the West. His success in convincing the West that his all-inclusive, party-less, "movement system" democracy worked satisfactorily surprised many observers. While neighboring countries such as Kenya were forced by Western backers to adopt a multi-party democratic system, Museveni managed to side-step this outcome by the use both of subtle diplomacy and innovative appointments, such as that of Vice-President Specioza Wandira Kazibwe, the highest-ranking female politician in Africa.

It is clear from the above that international demands can, in some cases, help explain outcomes in developing countries. Yet we should not see such pressure inevitably as one-way traffic. Forms can range from deliberate subversion to well-intentioned but unhelpful interventions. Structural adjustment programs, as Burnell notes, demanded "radical economic reforms that [often] prove socially damaging and politically destabilizing, or which encourage a greater executive concentration of power in order to make the unpalatable reforms enforceable" (Burnell 1998: 11). Withdrawal of peer pressure, external support, and encouragement – extended to political reforms by donor governments and international organizations like the Commonwealth following the Harare declaration of 1991 – were also important in keeping the pressure on recalcitrant regimes to allow more and better human rights. However, in general, such external pressure was applied rather unevenly.

In sum, international aspects are not as important as domestic factors in shaping political and economic outcomes in developing countries. On the other hand, an adverse external environment, such as a "global economic slump or international financial crisis" (ibid: 12), can be important, for example in East and Southeast Asia in 1997–8. Finally, international pressures on countries in the 1990s to adopt the neoliberal economic agenda may have helped persuade economically privileged elites that democratic transition would not seriously harm their interests, and thus helped to limit their opposition. But "by further entrenching such groups in the economy, these same international forces are possibly dimming the longer-term prospects for greater social and political equality" (ibid: 23).

Conclusion: The Future

I have argued in this book that successes and failures in the developing world in relation to attempts to consolidate democracy, develop successful economies, protect natural environments, and pay more attention to human and women's rights are explicable primarily by the impact of various domestic factors. I suggested that unhelpful structural factors can be overcome by the determination of individual political leaders, encouraged by political and civil society. This helps explain why, when there are apparently similar forces at work in different countries, there may be contrasting political, economic, and societal results. However, identifying and explaining a theoretically significant pattern can only take place after detailed empirical research in a large number of developing countries; so far, this has not been done. What does seem clear, however, is that we should not assume that all societies are destined to arrive sooner or later at similar political, economic, and societal destinations, or, indeed, that they should be expected to do so.

No doubt, multifaceted change will follow a variety of paths in Asia, Africa, Latin America and the Caribbean, and the Middle East. In some cases, people will be led in circles, only later to find themselves essentially back where they began. However, it is equally sure that the pressures to open up political systems will almost certainly not abate – and if civil and political society develop in ways conducive to democratization and democracy then issues of accountability and performance will be of growing importance. Despite democratization, many developing countries are unfortunately still characterized by regular encroachments upon the dignity of individuals and by often egregious denials of civil, political, and human rights. However, an optimist might agree that this book provides some evidence that, in some new democracies, there is a growing, if still gradual, focus on the rights of the individual. This is not only in respect of the right to be free of arbitrary abuse at the hands of the state, but also to enjoy an array of political rights, civil liberties, and economic benefits. A pessimist, on the other hand, might claim that such evidence is not only slight but also, ultimately, irrelevant. The time has not yet arrived, he or she might remark, when governments of developing countries must take seriously popular demands for greater human, civil, and political rights, or be concerned about economic justice. What do you think?

Appendix 1

Useful Websites

For further information readers can consult these useful websites, all of which are linked to issues examined in this book.

Economic development

www.imf.org/	International Monetary Fund
www.worldbank.org	World Bank
www.whirledbank.org	Anti-World Bank Organization
www.undp.org/	United Nations Development Program
www.usaid.gov/	US Aid Agency
www.adb.org/	Asian Development Bank
www.undp.org/hdro/	United Nations Development Program
www.undp.org/hdr2001/	Human Development Report, 2001
www.nccbuscc.org/cchd/	Catholic Campaign for Human Development
www.globalisation.gov.uk/	UK Government's Second White Paper on International Development
www.wto.org	World Trade Organization

Human rights

www.amnesty.org/	Amnesty International
www.freedomhouse.org/	Freedom House
www.pbs.org/globalization/home.html	Globalization and Human Rights

Natural environment

www.foei.org/	Friends of the Earth International
www.unep.org	United Nations Environment Program
www.wri.org	World Resources Institute
www.iisd.ca	Earth Negotiations Bulletin

International organizations

europa.eu.int/	European Union
www.un.org/	United Nations
www.oecd.org/	Organization for Economic Cooperation and Development

Globalization

www.worldexploitation.com/	Globalization News
www.warwick.ac.uk/fac/soc/CSGR/	Report on Globalization, Growth and (In)Equality
www.ifg.org/	International Forum on Globalization
www.sjc.uq.edu.au/global/	Range of materials related to globalization
www.globalisationguide.org/	Guide to globalization
www.nottingham.ac.uk/economics/leverhulme/	Leverhulme Centre for Research on Globalization

www.corpwatch.org/trac/   Corporate Watch's Globalization
    globalization/   and Corporate Rule index

Migration and refugees

www.unhcr.ch   UNHCR website
www.iom.ch   International Organization for
                                     Migration

Nationalism and religio-ethnic conflict

www.bsos.umd.edu/cidem.mar/   Minorities at Risk
www.incore.ulst.ac.uk   Websites related to religio-ethnic
                                     conflict

Appendix 2

Freedom House Survey Methodology

Since its inception in the 1970s, Freedom House's Freedom in the World survey has provided an annual evaluation of political rights and civil liberties throughout the world. The Survey attempts to judge all countries and territories by a single standard and to emphasize the importance of democracy and freedom. At a minimum, a democracy is a political system in which the people choose their authoritative leaders freely from among competing groups and individuals who were not designated by the government. Freedom represents the opportunity to act spontaneously in a variety of fields outside the control of the government and other centers of potential domination.

The Survey rates countries and territories based on real world situations caused by state and non-governmental factors, rather than on governmental intentions or legislation alone. Freedom House does not rate governments *per se*, but rather the rights and freedoms enjoyed by individuals in each country or territory. The Survey does not base its judgment solely on the political conditions in a country or territory (i.e., war, terrorism, etc.), but by the effect which these conditions have on freedom.

Freedom House does not maintain a culture-bound view of democracy. The Survey demonstrates that, in addition to countries in Europe and the Americas, there are free states with varying forms of democracy functioning among people of all races and religions in Africa, the Pacific, and Asia. In some Pacific islands, free countries can have political systems based on competing family groups and personalities rather than on European- or American-style political parties. In recent years, there has been a proliferation of democracies in developing countries, and the Survey reflects their growing numbers. To reach its conclusions, the Survey team employs a broad range of international sources of information, including both foreign and domestic news reports, NGO publications, think tank and academic analyses, and individual professional contacts.

Definitions and Categories of the Survey

The Survey's understanding of freedom encompasses two general sets of characteristics grouped under political rights and civil liberties. Political rights enable people to participate freely in the political process, which is the system by which the polity chooses authoritative policymakers and attempts to make binding decisions affecting the national, regional, or local community. In a free society, this represents the right of all adults to vote and compete for public office, and for elected representatives to have a decisive vote on public policies. Civil liberties include the freedoms to develop views, institutions, and personal autonomy apart from the state.

The Survey employs two series of checklists, one for questions regarding political rights and one for civil liberties, and assigns each country or territory considered a numerical rating for each category. The political rights and civil liberties ratings are then averaged and used to assign each country and territory to an overall status of "Free," "Partly Free," or "Not Free." (See the section below, "Rating System for Political Rights and Civil Liberties," for a detailed description of the Survey's methodology.) Freedom House rates both independent countries and their territories. For the purposes of the Survey, countries are defined as internationally recognized independent states whose governments are resident within their officially claimed borders. In the case of Cyprus, two sets of ratings are provided, as there are two governments on that divided island. In no way does this imply that Freedom House endorses Cypriot division. We note only that neither the predominantly Greek Republic of Cyprus, nor the Turkish-occupied, predominantly Turkish territory of the Republic of Northern Cyprus, is the de facto government for the entire island.

This year, Freedom House has divided the previously single related territory category into two parts: related territories and disputed territories. Related territories consist mostly of colonies, protectorates, and island dependencies of sovereign states which are in some relation of dependency to that state and whose relationship is not currently in serious legal or political dispute. Puerto Rico, Hong Kong, and French Guiana are three examples of related territories. Since most related territories have a broad range of civil liberties and some form of self-government, a higher proportion of them have the "Free" designation than do independent countries. Disputed territories represent areas within internationally recognized sovereign states which are usually dominated by a minority ethnic group and whose status is in serious political or violent dispute. This group also includes territories whose incorporation into nation-states is not universally recognized. In some cases, the issue of dispute is the desire of the majority of the population of that territory to secede from the sovereign state and either form an independent country or become part of a neighboring state. Tibet, East Timor, and Abkhazia are examples falling within this category. Freedom House added Chechnya to its Survey this year as a disputed territory of Russia, reflecting the decline of effective Russian central authority over this secessionist region.

Freedom House assigns only designations of "Free," "Partly Free," and "Not Free" for the eight related territories with populations under 5,000, designated as "microterritories," without corresponding category numbers. However, the same methodology is used to determine the status of these territories as for larger territories and independent states. The microterritories in the Survey are Cocos (Keeling) Islands, Rapanui (Easter Island), Falkland Islands, Niue, Norfolk Island, Pitcairn Islands, Svalbard, and Tokelau. The Survey excludes from its consideration uninhabited territories and such entities as the US-owned Johnston Atoll, which has only a transient military population and no native inhabitants.

Political Rights Checklist

1   Is the head of state and/or head of government or other chief authority elected through free and fair elections?
2   Are the legislative representatives elected through free and fair elections?
3   Are there fair electoral laws, equal campaigning opportunities, fair polling, and honest tabulation of ballots?
4   Are the voters able to endow their freely elected representatives with real power?
5   Do the people have the right to organize in different political parties or other competitive political groupings of their choice, and is the system open to the rise and fall of these competing parties or groupings?
6   Is there a significant opposition vote, de facto opposition power,

and a realistic possibility for the opposition to increase its support or gain power through elections?

7 Are the people free from domination by the military, foreign powers, totalitarian parties, religious hierarchies, economic oligarchies, or any other powerful group?

8 Do cultural, ethnic, religious, and other minority groups have reasonable self-determination, self-government, autonomy, or participation through informal consensus in the decision-making process?

Additional Discretionary Political Rights Questions

(a) For traditional monarchies that have no parties or electoral process, does the system provide for consultation with the people, encourage discussion of policy, and allow the right to petition the ruler?

(b) Is the government or occupying power deliberately changing the ethnic composition of a country or territory so as to destroy a culture or tip the political balance in favor of another group?

To answer the political rights questions, Freedom House considers the extent to which the system offers the voter the chance to make a free choice among candidates, and to what extent the candidates are chosen independently of the state. Freedom House recognizes that formal electoral procedures are not the only factors that determine the real distribution of power. In many Latin American countries, for example, the military retains a significant political role, and in Morocco the king maintains considerable power over the elected politicians. The more that people suffer under such domination by unelected forces, the less chance the country has of receiving credit for self-determination in our Survey.

The Civil Liberties Checklist

(A) Freedom of expression and belief

1 Are there free and independent media and other forms of cultural expression? (Note: in cases where the media are state-controlled but offer pluralistic points of view, the Survey gives the system credit.)

2 Are there free religious institutions and is there free private and public religious expression?

(B) Association and organizational rights

1   Is there freedom of assembly, demonstration, and open public discussion?
2   Is there freedom of political or quasi-political organization? (Note: this includes political parties, civic organizations, ad hoc issue groups, etc.)
3   Are there free trade unions and peasant organizations or equivalents, and is there effective collective bargaining? Are there free professional and other private organizations?

(C) Rule of law and human rights

1   Is there an independent judiciary?
2   Does the rule of law prevail in civil and criminal matters? Is the population treated equally under the law? Are police under direct civilian control?
3   Is there protection from political terror, unjustified imprisonment, exile, or torture, whether by groups that support or oppose the system? Is there freedom from war and insurgencies? (Note: freedom from war and insurgencies enhances the liberties in a free society, but the absence of wars and insurgencies does not in and of itself make a not-free society free.)
4   Is there freedom from extreme government indifference and corruption?

(D) Personal autonomy and economic rights

1   Is there open and free private discussion?
2   Is there personal autonomy? Does the state control travel, choice of residence, or choice of employment? Is there freedom from indoctrination and excessive dependency on the state?
3   Are property rights secure? Do citizens have the right to establish private businesses? Is private business activity unduly influenced by government officials, the security forces, or organized crime?
4   Are there personal social freedoms, including gender equality, choice of marriage partners, and size of family?
5   Is there equality of opportunity, including freedom from exploita-

tion by or dependency on landlords, employers, union leaders, bureaucrats, or other types of obstacles to a share of legitimate economic gains?

When analyzing the civil liberties checklist, Freedom House does not mistake constitutional guarantees of human rights for those rights in practice. For states and territories with small populations, particularly tiny island nations, the absence of trade unions and other types of association is not necessarily viewed as a negative situation unless the government or other centers of domination are deliberately blocking their formation or operation. In some cases, the small size of these countries and territories may result in a lack of sufficient institutional complexity to make them fully comparable to larger countries. The question of equality of opportunity also implies a free choice of employment and education. Extreme inequality of opportunity prevents disadvantaged individuals from enjoying full exercise of civil liberties. Typically, very poor countries and territories lack both opportunities for economic advancement and other liberties on this checklist. The question on extreme government indifference and corruption is included because when governments do not care about the social and economic welfare of large sectors of the population, the human rights of those people suffer. Government corruption can pervert the political process and hamper the development of a free economy.

For this year's Survey, Freedom House reorganized the existing questions in the civil liberties checklist into four subsets. A new question on personal autonomy was added under section (D), resulting in an increase in the total number of possible points that could be awarded in the civil liberties category.

Rating System for Political Rights and Civil Liberties

The Survey rates political rights and civil liberties separately on a seven-category scale, 1 representing the most free and 7 the least free. A country is assigned to a particular numerical category based on responses to the checklist and the judgments of the Survey team at Freedom House. According to the methodology, the team assigns initial ratings to countries by awarding from 0 to 4 raw points per checklist item, depending on the comparative rights or liberties present. (In the Surveys completed from 1989–90 through 1992–3, the methodology allowed for a less nuanced range of 0 to 2 raw points per question.) The only exception to the addition of 0 to 4 raw points per checklist item is additional discretionary question (B) in the political rights checklist, for which 1 to 4 raw points are subtracted depending on the severity of the situation. The highest possible score for political rights is 32 points, based on up to 4 points for each of eight questions. The highest possible score for civil liberties is 56 points, based on up to 4 points for each of fourteen questions.

After placing countries in initial categories based on checklist points, the Survey team makes minor adjustments to account for factors such as extreme violence, whose intensity may not be reflected in answering the checklist questions. These exceptions aside, in the overwhelming number of cases, the results of the checklist system reflect the real world situation and are adequate for placing countries and territories into the proper comparative categories.

At its discretion, Freedom House assigns up or down trend arrows to countries and territories to indicate general positive or negative trends that may not be apparent from the ratings. Such trends may or may not be reflected in raw points, depending on the circumstances in each country or territory. Only countries or territories without ratings changes since the previous year warrant trend arrows. Distinct from the trend arrows, the triangles located next to the political rights and civil liberties ratings (see accompanying tables of comparative measures of freedom for countries and related and disputed territories) indicate changes in those ratings caused by real world events since the last Survey.

Without a well-developed civil society, it is difficult, if not impossible, to have an atmosphere supportive of democracy. A society that does not have free individual and group expressions in non-political matters is not likely to make an exception for political ones. There is no country in the Survey with a rating of 6 or 7 for civil liberties and, at the same time, a rating of 1 or 2 for political rights. Almost without exception in the Survey, countries and territories have ratings in political rights and civil liberties that are within two ratings numbers of each other.

Political rights

Category number	Raw points
1	28–32
2	23–27
3	19–22

4	14–18
5	10–13
6	5–9
7	0–4

Civil liberties

Category number	Raw points
1	50–56
2	42–49
3	34–41
4	26–33
5	17–25
6	9–16
7	0–8

Explanation of Political Rights and Civil Liberties Ratings

Political rights

Countries and territories which receive a rating of 1 for political rights come closest to the ideals suggested by the checklist questions, beginning with free and fair elections. Those who are elected rule, there are competitive parties or other political groupings, and the opposition plays an important role and has actual power. Citizens enjoy self-determination or an extremely high degree of autonomy (in the case of territories), and minority groups have reasonable self-government or can participate in the government through informal consensus. With the exception of such entities as tiny island states, these countries and territories have decentralized political power and free subnational elections.

Countries and territories rated 2 in political rights are less free than those rated 1. Such factors as gross political corruption, violence, political discrimination against minorities, and foreign or military influence on politics may be present and weaken the quality of democracy.

The same conditions which undermine freedom in countries and territories with a rating of 2 may also weaken political rights in those with a rating of 3, 4, and 5. Other damaging elements can include civil war, heavy military involvement in politics, lingering royal power, unfair elections, and one-party dominance. However, states and territories in these categories may still enjoy some elements of political rights, including the freedom to organize quasi-political groups, reasonably free referenda, or other significant means of popular influence on government.

Countries and territories with political rights rated 6 have systems ruled by military juntas, one-party dictatorships, religious hierarchies, and autocrats. These regimes may allow only a minimal manifestation of political rights, such as competitive local elections or some degree of representation or autonomy for minorities. Some countries and territories rated 6 are in the early or aborted stages of democratic transition. A few states are traditional monarchies that mitigate their relative lack of political rights through the use of consultation with their subjects, toleration of political discussion, and acceptance of public petitions.

For countries and territories with a rating of 7, political rights are absent or virtually non-existent due to the extremely oppressive nature of the regime or severe oppression in combination with civil war. States and territories in this group may also be marked by extreme violence or warlord rule which dominates political power in the absence of an authoritative, functioning, central government.

Civil liberties

Countries and territories which receive a rating of 1 come closest to the ideals expressed in the civil liberties checklist, including freedom of expression, assembly, association, and religion. They are distinguished by an established and generally equitable system of rule of law and are comparatively free of extreme government indifference and corruption. Countries and territories with this rating enjoy free economic activity and tend to strive for equality of opportunity.

States and territories with a rating of 2 have deficiencies in three or four aspects of civil liberties, but are still relatively free.

Countries and territories which have received a rating of 3, 4, and 5 range from those that are in at least partial compliance with virtually all checklist standards to those with a combination of high or medium scores for some questions and low or very low scores on other questions. The level of oppression increases at each successive rating level, particularly in the areas of censorship, political terror, and the prevention of free association. There are also many cases in which groups opposed to the state engage in political terror that undermines other freedoms. Therefore, a poor rating for a country is not necessarily a comment on the intentions of the government, but may reflect real restrictions on liberty caused by non-governmental terror.

Countries and territories rated 6 are characterized by a few partial rights, such as some religious and social freedoms, some highly restricted private business activity, and relatively free private discussion. In general, people in these states and territories experience severely restricted expression and association, and there are almost always political prisoners and other manifestations of political terror.

States and territories with a rating of 7 have virtually no freedom. An overwhelming and justified fear of repression characterizes these societies.

Free, Partly Free, Not Free

The Survey assigns each country and territory the status of "Free," "Partly Free," or "Not Free" by averaging their political rights and civil liberties ratings. Those whose ratings average 1–2.5 are generally considered "Free," 3–5.5 "Partly Free," and 5.5–7 "Not Free." The dividing line between "Partly Free" and "Not Free" usually falls within the group whose ratings numbers average 5.5. For example, countries that receive a rating of 6 for political rights and 5 for civil liberties, or a 5 for political rights and a 6 for civil liberties, could be either "Partly Free" or "Not Free." The total number of raw points is the definitive factor which determines the final status. Countries and territories with combined raw scores of 0–30 points are "Not Free," 31–59 points are "Partly Free," and 60–88 points are "Free." Based on raw points, this year there are several unusual cases: Mali's and Argentina's ratings average 3.0, but they are "Free," and Chad, Côte d'Ivoire, and Swaziland are rated 5.0, but they are "Not Free."

It should be emphasized that the "Free," "Partly Free," and "Not Free" labels are highly simplified terms that each cover a broad third of the available raw points. Therefore, countries and territories within each category, especially those at either end of each category, can have quite different human rights situations. In order to see the distinctions within each category, one should examine a country's or territory's political rights and civil liberties ratings.

The differences in raw points between countries in the three broad categories represent distinctions in the real world. There are obstacles which "Partly Free" countries must overcome before they can be called "Free," just as there are impediments which prevent "Not Free" countries from being called "Partly Free." Countries at the lowest rung of the "Free" category (2 in political rights and 3 in civil liberties, or 3 in political rights and 2 in civil liberties) differ from those at the upper end of the "Partly Free" group (e.g., 3 for both political rights and civil liberties). Typically, there is more violence and/or military influence on politics at 3, 3 than at 2, 3.

The distinction between the least bad "Not Free" countries and the least free "Partly Free" may be less obvious than the gap between "Partly Free" and "Free," but at "Partly Free," there is at least one additional factor that keeps a country from being assigned to the "Not Free" category. For example, Lebanon, which was rated 6, 5, "Partly Free" in 1994, was rated 6, 5, but "Not Free," in 1995 after its legislature unilaterally extended the incumbent president's term indefinitely. Though not sufficient to drop the country's political rights rating to 7, there was enough of a drop in raw points to change its category.

Freedom House does not view democracy as a static concept, and the Survey recognizes that a democratic country does not necessarily belong in our category of "Free" states. A democracy can lose freedom and become merely "Partly Free." Sri Lanka and Colombia are examples of such "Partly Free" democracies. In other cases, countries that replaced military regimes with elected governments can have less than complete transitions to liberal democracy. Guatemala fits the description of this kind of "Partly Free" democracy. Some scholars use the term "semi-democracy" or "formal democracy," instead of "Partly Free" democracy, to refer to countries that are democratic in form but less than free in substance.

The designation "Free" does not mean that a country enjoys perfect freedom or lacks serious problems. As an institution which advocates human rights, Freedom House remains concerned about a variety of social problems and civil liberties questions in the US and other countries that the Survey places in the "Free" category. An improvement in a country's rating does not mean that human rights campaigns should cease. On the contrary, the findings of the Survey should be regarded as a means to encourage improvements in the political rights and civil liberties conditions in all countries.

Reproduced with permission from: http://www.freedomhouse.org/survey00/method/

Bibliography

Acharya, A. (1999) "Developing countries and the emerging world order," in L. Fawcett and Y. Sayigh (eds.), *The Third World Beyond the Cold War: Continuity and Change*, Oxford: Oxford University Press, pp. 78–98.

Ackerley, B. and Okin, S. M. (1999) "Feminist social criticism and the international movement for women's rights as human rights," in I. Shapiro and C. Hacker-Cordón (eds.), *Democracy's Edges*, Cambridge: Cambridge University Press, pp. 134–62 .

Africa Confidential (1995) "Ken and the soja boys," March 17, pp. 3–4.

Aglionby, J. (2001a) "Crisis after crisis threatens whole of SE Asia," *Guardian*, March 17.

Aglionby, J. (2001b) "Fisherman driven to illegal logging as pulp factory poisons river," *Guardian*, June 26.

Ajami, F. (1978) *Human Rights and World Order*, New York: Institute for World Order.

Alvarez, S. (1990) *Engendering Democracy in Brazil*, Princeton, NJ: Princeton University Press.

Arblaster, A. (1999) "Democratic society and its enemies," in P. Burnell and P. Calvert (eds.), *The Resilience of Democracy: Persistent Practice, Durable Idea*, special issue of *Democratization*, 6, 1, pp. 33–49.

Aryeetey, Bortei-Doku E. (2000) "The participation of women in the Ghanaian economy," in E. Aryeetey, J. Harrigan, and M. Nissanke (eds.), *Economic Reforms in Ghana: The Miracle and the Mirage*, Oxford/Accra/Trenton, NJ: James Currey/Woeli Publishing Services/Africa World Press, pp. 321–43.

Atkinson, P. (1999) "Representations of conflict in the Western media: the manufacture of a barbaric periphery," in T. Skelton and T. Allen (eds.), *Culture and Global Change*, London: Routledge, pp. 102–8.

Auda, G. (1993) "The Islamic movement and resource mobilization in Egypt: a political culture perspective," in L. Diamond (ed.), *Political Culture and Democracy in Developing Countries*, Boulder, CO: Lynne Rienner, pp. 379–407.

Ayubi, N. (1991) *Political Islam: Religion and Politics in the Arab World*, London: Routledge.

Bayart, J.-F. (1986) "Civil society in Africa," in P. Chabal (ed.), *Political Domination in Africa*, Cambridge: Cambridge University Press, pp. 109–25.

Bayart, J.-F. (1991) "Finishing with the idea of the Third World: the concept of the political trajectory," in J. Manor (ed.), *Rethinking Third World Politics*, Harlow: Longman, pp. 51–71.

Bayart, J.-F. (1993) *The State in Africa*, Harlow: Longman.

Bealey, F. (1999) *The Blackwell Dictionary of Political Science*, Oxford: Blackwell.

Beeley, B. (1992) "Islam as a global political force," in A. McGrew and P. Lewis (eds.), *Global Politics: Globalization and the Nation State*, Cambridge: Polity Press, pp. 293–311.

Bennis, P. (2000) "Democratizing the unborn state: Palestine, the PLO and the struggle for democracy," in H. Smith (ed.), *Democracy and International Relations: Critical Theories/Problematic Practices*, Basingstoke: Macmillan, pp. 171–91.

Berger, M. (1994) "The end of the Third World," *Third World Quarterly*, 15, 2, pp. 257–75.

Bill, J. and Springborg, R. (1994) *Politics in the Middle East*, 4th edn., New York: HarperCollins.

Black, I. (1995) "Rich talk to the poor," *Guardian*, March 4.

Black, I., Bowcott, O., and Vidal, J. (1995) "Nigeria defies world with writer's 'judicial murder'," *Guardian*, November 11.

Body Shop (n/d, but ca. mid-November 1995) "Ken Saro-Wiwa and the Ogoni fact sheet."

Borger, J. (2001) "Mapmaking martyr," *Guardian, G2*, April 12.

Braid, M. (1995) "How quality of life matches up to global sisterhood," *Independent*, August 18.

Branford, S. (2001) "Buenos Aires rallies against the bankers," *Guardian*, August 13.

Bratton, M. and Van de Walle, N. (1997) *Democratic Experiments in Africa*, Cambridge: Cambridge University Press.

Bretherton, C. (1996) "Introduction," in C. Bretherton and G. Poynton (eds.), *Global Politics: An Introduction*, Oxford: Blackwell, pp. 3–17.

Breyman, S (1993) "Knowledge as power: ecology movements and global environmental problems," in R. Lipschutz and K. Conca (eds.), *The State and Social Power in Global Environmental Politics*, New York: Columbia University Press, pp. 124–57.

Brittain, V. (1994) "Victims from birth," in Special Supplement "World on Her Shoulders," *Observer*, October 16, p. 12.

Brittain, V. (1995) "Riding the Tigress," *Guardian*, August 28.

Bromley, S. (1994) *Rethinking Middle East Politics*, Cambridge: Polity Press.

Brown, P. (2001) "World deal on climate isolates US," *Guardian*, July 24.

Brydon, L. and Chant, S. (1989) *Women in the Third World*, Aldershot: Edward Elgar.

Bunting, M. (2001) "The debate nobody wants … globalization," *Guardian*, May 21.

Burnell, P. (1998) "Arrivals and departures: a preliminary classification of democratic failures and their explanation," *Journal of Commonwealth and Comparative Politics*, 36, 3, pp. 1–29.

Burnell, P. (2000) "The significance of the December 1998 local elections in Zambia and their aftermath," *Journal of Commonwealth and Comparative Politics*, 38, 1, pp. 1–20.

Buxton, J. and Phillips, N. (eds.) (1999) *Case Studies in Latin American Political Economy*, Manchester: Manchester University Press.

Callaghy, T. (1993) "Vision and politics in the transformation of the global political economy: lessons from the Second and Third Worlds," in R. Slater, B. Schutz, and S. Dorr (eds.), *Global Transformation and the Third World*, Boulder, CO: Lynne Rienner, pp. 161–256.

Callick, R. (1991) "No blue skies yet in the South Pacific," *Pacific Economic Bulletin*, 6, 2, pp. 1–19.

Calvert, S. and Calvert, P. (2001) *Politics and Society in the Third World*, 2nd edn., Harlow: Pearson Education.

Cammack, P. (1994) "Democratization and citizenship in Latin America," in G. Parry and M. Moran (eds.), *Democracy and Democratization*, London: Routledge, pp. 174–95.

Cammack, P. (1997) "Democracy and dictatorship in Latin America, 1930–80," in D. Potter, D. Goldblatt, M. Kiloh, and P. Lewis (eds.), *Democratization*, Cambridge and Milton Keynes: Polity Press in association with the Open University, pp. 152–73.

Cammack, P., Pool, D., and Tordoff, W. (1993) *Third World Politics: A Comparative Introduction*, 2nd edn., London: Macmillan.

Carothers, T. (1997) "Democracy without illusions," *Foreign Affairs*, 76, 1, pp. 85–99.

Castañeda, J. (1994) *Utopia Unarmed: The Latin American Left after the Cold War*, New York: Vintage Books.

Chiriyankandath, J. (1993) "Human rights in India: concepts and contexts," *Contemporary South Asia*, 2, 3, pp. 245–63.

Christie. K. and Roy, D. (2001) *The Politics of Human Rights in East Asia*, London: Pluto Press.

Clapham, C. (1988) *Third World Politics: An Introduction*, London: Routledge.

Clark, I. (1997) *Globalization and Fragmentation*, Oxford: Oxford University Press.

Cohen, M. (1994) "Culture of awareness," *Far Eastern Economic Review*, November 17, p. 44.

Coles, M. (1994) "Women of Iran "treated as sub-humans'," *Observer*, December 4.

Corcoran-Nantes, Y. (1993) "Female consciousness or feminist consciousness: women's consciousness raising in community-based struggles in Brazil," in S. Radcliffe and S. Westwood (eds.), *"Viva" Women and Popular Protest in Latin America*, London: Routledge, pp. 136–55.

Coulon, C. (1983) *Les Musulmans et le pouvoir en Afrique noire*, Paris: Karthala.

Coussy, J. (2001) "International political economy," in M.-C. Smouts (ed.), *The New International Relations*, London: Hurst, pp. 140–54.

Crawford, G. (2001) *Foreign Aid and Political Reform: A Comparative Analysis of Democracy Assistance and Political Conditionality*, Basingstoke: Palgrave.

Cumming, G. (1999) "French and British aid to Africa: a comparative study," unpublished Ph.D. thesis, School of European Studies, Cardiff University.

Denny, C. (2001) "Argentina raises the stakes for IMF cash," *Guardian*, August 13.

Dessouki, A. H. (1982) *Islamic Resurgence in the Arab World*, New York: Praeger.

Diamond, L. (1999) *Developing Democracy Toward Consolidation*, Baltimore: Johns Hopkins University Press.

Dolan, M. (1993) "Global economic transformation and less developed countries," in R. Slater, B. Schutz, and S. Dorr (eds.), *Global Transformation and the Third World*, Boulder, CO: Lynne Rienner, pp. 259–82.

Dorr, S. 1993. "Democratization in the Middle East," in R. Slater, B. Schutz, and S. Dorr (eds.), *Global Transformation and the Third World*, Boulder, CO: Lynne Rienner, pp. 131–57.

Duodu, C. (1996) "Nigerian troops shoot six dead as Ogoni mourn Saro-Wiwa," *Observer*, January 7.

Durning, A. (1989) *Action at the Grassroots*, Worldwatch Papers no. 88, Washington, DC: Worldwatch Institute.

Eccleston, B. (1996) "NGOs and competing representations of deforestation as an environmental issue in Malaysia," *Journal of Commonwealth and Comparative Politics*, 34, 2, pp. 116–42.

Economist, The (1992) "Editorial," January 2, p. 3.

Economist, The (1995a) "A kept woman," July 15, p. 61.

Economist, The (1995b) "France's other blast," September 16, p 88.

Ekins, P. (1992) *A New World Order: Grassroots Movements for Global Change*, London: Routledge.

Elliot, L. (2001a) "A world still hungry for change," *Guardian*, February 26.

Elliot, L. (2001b) "Short joins push for new WTO talks," *Guardian*, March 19.

Ellis, S. (1994) "Politics and nature conservation in South Africa," *Journal of Southern African Studies*, 20, 1, pp. 53–69.

Elshtain, J. B. (1995) "Exporting feminism," *Journal of International Affairs*, 48, 2, pp. 541–58.

Emerson, R. (1975) "The fate of human rights in the Third World," *World Politics*, 27, 2, pp. 205–20.

Encarnacion, T. and Tadem, E. (1993) "Ethnicity and separatist movements in Southeast Asia," in P. Wignaraja (ed.), *New Social Movements in the South*, London: Zed Books, pp. 153–73.

Engberg, J. and Ersson, S. (2001) "Illiberal democracy in the 'Third World': an empirical enquiry," in J. Haynes (ed.), *Democracy and Political Change in the "Third World,"* London: Routledge, pp. 35–54.

Escobar, A. and Alvarez, S. (1992) "Introduction: theory and protest in Latin

America today," in A. Escobar and S. Alvarez (eds.), *The Making of Social Movements in Latin America: Identity, Strategy and Democracy*, Boulder, CO: Westview Press, pp. 1–15.

Etienne, B. and Tozy, M. (1981) "Le glissement des obligations islamiques vers le phénomène associatif à Casablanca," in Centre de Recherches et d'Etudes sur les Sociétés Méditerranéennes, *Le Maghreb musulman en 1979*, Paris, pp. 235–51.

Fals Borda, O. (1992) "Social movements and political power in Latin America," in A. Escobar and S. Alvarez (eds.), *The Making of Social Movements in Latin America: Identity, Strategy and Democracy*, Boulder, CO: Westview Press, pp. 303–16.

Fawcett, L. (1999) "Conclusion," in L. Fawcett and Y. Sayigh (eds.), *The Third World Beyond the Cold War: Continuity and Change*, Oxford: Oxford University Press, pp. 234–46.

Feijoo, M. C. and Gogna, M. (1990) "Women in the transition to democracy," in E. Jelin (ed.), *Women and Social Change in Latin America*, London, Zed Books, pp. 79–114.

Ferguson, J. A. (1986) "The Third World," in R. J. Vincent (ed.), *Foreign Policy and Human Rights*, Cambridge: Cambridge University Press, pp. 203–26.

Fisher, J. (1993) *The Road from Rio: Sustainable Development and Nongovernmental Movement in the Third World*, Westport, CT: Praeger.

Florini, A. (ed.) (2000) *The Third Force: The Rise of International Civil Society*, Tokyo and Washington, DC: Japan Center for International Exchange/Carnegie Endowment for International Peace.

Florini, A. and Simmons, P. (2000) "What the world needs now?" in A. Florini (ed.), *The Third Force: The Rise of International Civil Society*, Tokyo and Washington, DC: Japan Center for International Exchange/Carnegie Endowment for International Peace, pp. 1–17.

Forrest, J. (1988) "The quest for state 'hardness' in Africa," *Comparative Politics*, 20, 4, pp. 423–42.

Foweraker, J. and Landman, T. (1997) *Citizenship Rights and Social Movements: A Comparative and Statistical Analysis*, Oxford: Oxford University Press.

Fry, G. (1993) "At the margin: the South Pacific and changing world order," in R. Leaver and J. Richardson (eds.), *Charting the Post-Cold War Order*, Boulder, CO: Westview Press, pp 224–42.

Fukuyama, F. (1992) *The End of History and the Last Man*, London: Penguin Books.

Geisler, G. (1995) "Troubled sisterhood: women and politics in southern Africa," *African Affairs*, 94, 377, pp. 545–78.

George, S. (1993) "Uses and abuses of African debt," in A. Adedeji (ed.), *Africa within the World: Beyond Disposession and Dependence*, London: Zed Books/ ACDESS, pp. 59–72.

Ghazi, P. (1995) "Rainbow warriors defy French guns," *Observer*, July 9.

Gill, S. (1993) "Gramsci and global politics: towards a post-hegemonic research agenda," in S. Gill (ed.), *Gramsci, Historical Materialism and International Relations*, Cambridge: Cambridge University Press, pp. 1–20.

Gills, B., Rocamora, J., and Wilson, R. (eds.) (1993) *Low Intensity Democracy*, London: Pluto Press.

Grayson, J. (1989) "Korea," in S. Mews (ed.), *Religion in Politics*, Harlow: Longman, p. 153.

Green, D. (1999) "The lingering moment: an historical perspective on the global durability of democracy after 1989," *Democratization*, 6, 2, pp. 1–41.

Greenpeace USA (1990) *The International Trade in Wastes: A Greenpeace Inventory*, Washington, DC: Greenpeace.

Grugel, J. (2000) "State and business in neoliberal democracies in Latin America," in H. Smith (ed.), *Democracy and International Relations*, Basingstoke: Macmillan, pp. 108–25.

Guelke, A. (1999) *South Africa in Transition: The Misunderstood Miracle*, London: I. B. Tauris.

Gurr, T. (1994) "Peoples against states: ethnopolitical conflict and the changing world system," *Commentary* (Canada), November 30, pp. 3–4.

Hadjor, K. (1993) *Dictionary of Third World Terms*, London: Penguin Books.

Hall, S. (1985) "Religious ideologies and social movements in Jamaica," in R. Bocock and K. Thompson (eds.), *Religion and Ideology*, Manchester: Manchester University Press, pp. 269–96.

Hansen, H. B. and Twaddle, M. (1995) "Uganda: the advent of no-party democracy," in J. Wiseman (ed.), *Democracy and Political Change in Africa*, London: Routledge, pp. 137–51.

Harrison, P. (1987) *The Greening of Africa: Breaking Through in the Battle for Food and Land*, London: Penguin Books.

Harrison, P. (1993) *The Third Revolution: Population, Environment and a Sustainable World*, London: Penguin Books.

Harsch, E. (1996) "Global coalition debates Africa's future," *Africa Recovery*, 10, 1, pp. 24–31.

Haynes, J. (1991) "Human rights and democracy: the record of the Rawlings regime in Ghana," *African Affairs*, 90, 3, pp. 407–25.

Haynes, J. (1993) *Religion in Third World Politics*, Buckingham: Open University Press.

Haynes, J. (1995) "Religion, fundamentalism and identity: a global perspective," Discussion Paper no. 65, Geneva: United Nations Research Institute for Social Development.

Haynes, J. (1996) *Religion and Politics in Africa*, London: Zed Books.

Haynes, J. (1997) *Democracy and Civil Society in the Third World: Politics and New Political Movements*, Cambridge: Polity Press.

Haynes, J. (1998) *Religion in Global Politics*, Harlow: Longman.

Haynes, J. (1999) "Power, politics and environmental movements in the Third World," in C. Rootes (ed.), *Environmental Movements: Local, National, Global*, London: Frank Cass, pp. 222–42.

Haynes, J. (2001a) *Democracy in the Developing World: Africa, Asia, Latin America and the Middle East*, Cambridge: Polity Press.

Haynes, J. (2001b) "'Limited' democracy in Ghana and Uganda: what is most important to international actors: stability or political freedom?" *Journal of Contemporary African Studies*, 19, 2 , pp. 183–204.

Heine, J. (1999) "Latin America: collective responses to new realities," in L. Fawcett and Y. Sayigh (eds.), *The Third World Beyond the Cold War: Continuity and Change*, Oxford: Oxford University Press, pp.101–17.

Held, D. (1993) "Democracy from city-states to a cosmopolitan order?" in D. Held (ed.), *Prospects for Democracy*, Cambridge: Polity Press, pp. 13–52.

Held, D. (1994) *Democracy and the Global Order*, Cambridge: Polity Press.

Herring, R. (1999) "Embedded particularism: India's failed developmental state," in M. Woo-Cumings (ed.), *The Developmental State*, Ithaca, NY: Cornell University Press, pp. 306–34.

Hettne, B. (1995) *Development Theory and the Three Worlds*. Harlow: Longman.

Hewison, K. (1999) "Political space in Southeast Asia: 'Asian-style,' and other democracies," in P. Burnell and P. Calvert (eds.), *The Resilience of Democracy: Persistent Practice, Durable Idea*, special issue of *Democratization*, 6, 1, pp. 224–45.

Higson, A. (1995) "France's poisoned paradise lost," *Guardian*, December 30.

Hilton, I. (2001) "The ruins Tony Blair should visit," *Guardian*, August 8.

Hirst, P. and Thompson, G. (1999) *Globalization in Question: The International Economy and the Possibilities of Governance*, 2nd edn., Cambridge: Polity Press.

Howard, R. (1986) "Is there an African concept of human rights?" in R. J. Vincent (ed.), *Foreign Policy and Human Rights*, Cambridge: Cambridge University Press, pp. 11–32.

Human Rights Internet (1993) "Women in Bangladesh," Ottawa: Immigration and Refugee Board.

Huntington, S. (1991) *The Third Wave: Democratization in the Late Twentieth Century*, Norman: University of Oklahoma Press.

Huntington, S. (1993) "The clash of civilizations?" *Foreign Affairs*, 72, 3, pp. 22–49.

Hurrell, A. and Woods, N. (1995) "Globalization and inequality," *Millennium*, 24, 3, pp. 425–51.

Ibrahim, S. E. (1995) "Liberalization and democratization in the Arab world: an overview," in R. Brynen, B. Korany, and P. Noble (eds.), *Political Liberalization and Democratization in the Arab World, Vol. 1: Theoretical Perspectives*, Boulder, CO: Lynne Rienner, pp. 29–57.

IDEA (International Institute for Democracy and Electoral Assistance) (1998) *Voter Turnout from 1945 to 1997: A Global Report on Political Participation*, Stockholm: IDEA.

ILO (International Labor Organization) (1994) *World Labor Report 1994*, Geneva: ILO.

Inoguchi, T. (1995) "A view from Pacific Asia," in H.-H. Holm and G. Sorensen (eds.), *Whose World Order?* London: Westview Press, pp. 119–36.

Jackson, R. (1990) *Quasi-states: Sovereignty, International Relations and the Third World*, Cambridge: Cambridge University Press.

Jaquette, J. (1989) *The Women's Movement in Latin America*, Boston, MA: Unwin Hyman.

Jelin, E. (ed.) (1990) *Women and Social Change in Latin America*, London: Zed Books/UNRISD.

Jetshke, A. (1999) "Linking the unlinkable? International norms and nationalism in Indonesia and the Philippines," in T. Risse, S. Ropp, and K. Sikkink (eds.), *The Power of Human Rights: International Norms and Domestic Change*, Cambridge: Cambridge University Press, pp. 134–71.

Johnson, A. (1999) "Local forms of resistance: weapons of the weak," in T. Skelton and T. Allen (eds.), *Culture and Global Change*, London: Routledge, pp. 160–5.

Joseph, R. (1998) "Africa, 1990–97: from abertura to closure," *Journal of Democracy*, 9, 2, pp. 3–17.

Kamrava, M. (1993) *Politics and Society in the Third World*, London: Routledge.

Kaplan, R. (1994) "The coming anarchy," *Atlantic Monthly*, April, pp. 44–76.

Karatnycky, A. (1999) "The decline of illiberal democracy," *Journal of Democracy*, 10, 1, pp. 112–25.

Karl, T. L. (1990) "Dilemmas of democratization in Latin America," *Comparative Politics*, 23, 1, pp. 1–21.

Karl, T. L. (1995) "The hybrid regimes of Central America," *Journal of Democracy*, 6, 3, pp. 72–86.

Kasfir, N. (1998) "Civil society, the state and democracy in Africa," *The Journal of Commonwealth and Comparative Politics*, 36, 2, pp.123–49.

Khagram, S. (2000) "Toward democratic governance for sustainable development: transnational civil society organizing around big dams," in A.Florini (ed.), *The Third Force: The Rise of International Civil Society*, Tokyo and Washington, DC: Japan Center for International Exchange/Carnegie Endowment for International Peace, pp. 83–103.

Khan, S. (1988) *The Fifty Percent: Women in Development and Policy in Bangladesh*, Dhaka: Dhaka University Press.

Kiloh, M. (1997) "South Africa: democracy delayed," in D. Potter, D. Goldblatt, M. Kiloh, and P. Lewis (eds.), *Democratization*, Cambridge: Polity Press in association with the Open University, pp. 294–320.

King, A. Y. C. (1993) "A nonparadigmatic search for democracy in a post-Confucian culture: the case of Taiwan, R.O.C.," in L. Diamond (ed.), *Political Culture and Democracy in Developing Countries*, Boulder, CO: Lynne Rienner, pp. 139–62.

Lane, J.-E. and Ersson, S. (1994) *Comparative Politics: An Introduction and New Approach*, Cambridge: Polity Press.

Lawson, L. (1999) "External democracy promotion in Africa: another false start?" *The Journal of Commonwealth and Comparative Politics*, 37, 1, pp.1–30.

Lecomte, B. (1986) *Project Aid Limitations and Alternatives*, Paris: OECD Development Centre Studies.

Leftwich, A. (1993) "Governance, democracy and development in the Third World," *Third World Quarterly*, 14, 3, pp. 605–24.

Leftwich, A. (1997) "Conclusion," in D. Potter, D. Goldblatt, M. Kiloh, and P.

Lewis (eds.), *Democratization*, Cambridge: Polity Press in association with the Open University, pp. 517–36.

Leftwich, A. (2000) *States of Development: On the Primacy of Politics in Development*, Cambridge: Polity Press.

Leonard, H. J. (1989) *Environment and the Poor: Development Strategies for a Common Agenda*, New Brunswick, NJ: Transaction Books.

Linz, J. and Stepan, A. (1996) *Problems of Democratic Transition and Consolidation: Southern Europe, South America, and Post-Communist Europe*, Baltimore, MD: Johns Hopkins University Press.

McCarthy, R. (2001) "Pakistan's women get seats at the bottom table," *Guardian*, May 18.

McCormick, J. (1989) *Reclaiming Paradise: The Global Environmental Movement*, Bloomington, IN: Earthscan.

MacFarlane, S. N. (1999) "Taking stock: the Third World and the end of the Cold War," in L. Fawcett and Y. Sayigh (eds.), *The Third World Beyond the Cold War: Continuity and Change*, Oxford: Oxford University Press, pp. 15–33.

McGarry, J. (1998) "Political settlements in Northern Ireland and South Africa," *Political Studies*, 46, 5, pp. 853–70.

McGreal, C. (2000) "Clinton's visit shows US fears for Nigeria," *Guardian*, August 26.

McKay, A., Winters, A. L., and Kedir, A. M. (2000) *A Review of Empirical Evidence on Trade, Trade Policy and Poverty: A Report to the Department for International Development*. A Report to the Department for International Development (DFID), prepared as background document for the Second Development White Paper.

Macmillan, J. and Linklater, A. (1995) "Introduction: boundaries in question," in J. Macmillan and A. Linklater (eds.), *Boundaries in Question: New Directions in International Relations*, London: Pinter, pp. 1–16.

Magdoff, H. (1986) "Third World debt past and present," *Monthly Review*, 38, pp. 1–13.

Mainwaring, S. and Shugart, M. (1997) "Presidentialism and democracy in Latin America: rethinking the terms of the debate," in S. Mainwaring and M. Shugart (eds.), *Presidentialism and Democracy in Latin America*, Cambridge: Cambridge University Press, pp. 12–54.

Mainwaring, S. and Viola, E. (1984) "New social movements, political culture and democracy: Brazil and Argentina in the 1980s," *Telos*, 61, pp. 17–54.

Manor, J. (1991) "Introduction," in J. Manor (ed.), *Rethinking Third World Politics*, Harlow: Longman, pp. 1–11.

Marais, H. (1998) *South Africa: Limits to Change: The Political Economy of Transformation*, London and Cape Town: Zed Books and University of Cape Town Press.

Maravall, J. M. (1995) "The myth of the authoritarian advantage," in L. Diamond and M. Plattner (eds.), *Economic Reform and Democracy*, Baltimore, MD: Johns Hopkins University Press, pp. 13–27.

Marchand, M. (1995) "Latin American women speak on development," in M. Marchand and J. Parpart, *Feminism/Postmodernism/Development*, London: Routledge, pp. 56–72.

Marty, M. and Appleby, R. S. (1993) "Introduction," in M. Marty and R. S. Appleby (eds.), *Fundamentalism and the State: Remaking Polities, Economies, and Militance*, Chicago: University of Chicago Press, pp. 1–9.

Mehden, F. von der (1989a) "Thailand," in S. Mews (ed.), *Religion in Politics*. Harlow: Longman, p. 265.

Mehden, F. von der (1989b) "The Philippines," in S. Mews (ed.), *Religion in Politics*. Harlow: Longman, pp. 215–18.

Merkel, W. (1998) "The consolidation of post-autocratic democracies: a multi-level model, *Democratization*, 5, 3, pp. 33–67.

Miller, M. (1995) *The Third World in Global Environmental Politics*, Buckingham: Open University Press.

Mitchell, N. and McCormick, J. (1988) "Economic and political explanations of human rights violation," *World Politics*, 40, 4, pp. 476–98.

Mittelman, J. (1994) "The globalization challenge: surviving at the margins," *Third World Quarterly*, 15, 3, pp. 427–41.

Molyneux, M. (1985) "Mobilization without emancipation? Women's interests, the state, and revolution in Nicaragua," *Feminist Studies*, 11, 2, pp. 227–54.

Moore, M. (2001) "Liberalization? Don't reject it just yet," *Guardian*, February 26.

Morlino, L. (1998) *Democracy between Consolidation and Crisis: Parties, Groups, and Citizens in Southern Europe*, New York: Oxford University Press.

Morris, S. (2001) "Offices, schools, hospitals at end of paper trail from diminishing forests," *Guardian*, June 26.

Mosley, P., Harrington, J., and Toye, J. (1991a) *Aid and Power: The World Bank and Policy-based Lending Vol. 1: Analysis and Policy Proposals*, London: Routledge.

Mosley, P., Harrington, J., and Toye, J. (1991b) *Aid and Power: The World Bank and Policy-based Lending Vol. 2: Case Studies*, London: Routledge.

Mullin, J. (1995) "Trinidad's Islamic rebel awaits final verdict," *Guardian*, June 13.

Naanen, B. (1995) "Oil-producing minorities and the restructuring of Nigerian federalism: the case of the Ogoni people," *Journal of Commonwealth and Comparative Politics*, 33, 1, pp. 46–78.

Nonneman, G. (2001) "The Middle East between globalization, human 'agency,' and Europe," *International Affairs*, 77, 1, pp. 141–62.

O'Donnell, G. (1992) "Transitions, continuities, and paradoxes," in S. Mainwaring, G. O'Donnell, and J. Samuel Valenzuela (eds.), *Issues in Democratic Consolidation: The New South American Democracies in Comparative Perspective*, Notre Dame, IN: University of Notre Dame Press, pp. 24–52.

O'Donnell, G. (1994) "Delegative democracy," *Journal of Democracy*, 5, 1, pp. 55–69.

Ogoni Community Association UK (1995) "Ogoni campaign builds internationally," press release, November 13.

Okin, S. M. (1994) "Gender inequality and cultural differences," *Political Theory*, 22, 1, pp. 5–24.

Omvedt, G. (1994) "Peasants, dalits and women: democracy and India's new social movements," *Journal of Contemporary Asia*, 24, 1, pp. 35–48.

Organski, A. (1965) *The Stages of Political Development*, New York: Knopf.

Osaghae, E. (1995) "The Ogoni uprising: oil politics, minority agitation and the future of the Nigerian state," *African Affairs*, 94, 376, pp. 325–44.

Ottaway, M. (1999) *Africa's New Leaders: Democracy or State Reconstruction?* Washington, DC: Carnegie Endowment for International Peace.

Ottaway, M. and Carothers, T. (2000) *Funding Virtue*, Washington, DC: Carnegie Endowment for International Peace.

Owen, R. (1992) *State, Power and Politics in the Making of the Modern Middle East*, London: Routledge.

Parpart, J. (1988) "Women and the state in Africa," in D. Rothchild and N. Chazan (eds.), *The Precarious Balance: State and Society in Africa*, Boulder, CO: Westview Press, pp. 208–30.

Peluso, N. L. (1993) "Coercing conservation: the politics of state resource control," in R. Lipschutz and K. Conca (eds.), *The State and Social Power in Global Environmental Politics*, New York: Columbia University Press, pp. 46–70.

Peterson, M. (1992) "Transnational activity, international society and world politics," *Millennium*, 21, 3, pp. 371–88.

Pettifor, A. (2001) "Indonesia pays price of IMF blunder," *Guardian*, July 9.

Pinkney, R. (1993) *Democracy in the Third World*, Buckingham: Open University Press.

Pool, J. and Stamos, S. (1985) "The uneasy calm: Third World debt – the case of Mexico," *Monthly Review*, 36, pp. 7–19.

Portes, A. and Zhou, M. (1992) "Gaining the upper hand: economic mobility among immigrant and domestic minorities," *Ethnic and Racial Studies*, 15, 4, pp. 491–521.

Postel-Vinay, K. (2001) "The spatial transformation of international relations," in M.-C. Smouts (ed.), *The New International Relations*, London: Hurst, pp. 88–99.

Pridham, G. (2000) *The Dynamics of Democratization: A Comparative Approach*, London: Continuum.

Princen, T. (1994) "NGOs creating a niche in environmental diplomacy," in T. Princen and M. Finger et al., *Environmental NGOs in World Politics: Linking the Local and the Global*, London: Routledge, pp 29–47.

Przeworski, A. (1991) *Democracy and the Market: Political and Economic Reform in Eastern Europe and Latin America*, Cambridge: Cambridge University Press.

Przeworski, A., Alvarez, M., Cheibib, J. A., and Limongi, F. (1996) "What makes democracies endure?" *Journal of Democracy*, 7, 1, pp. 39–55.

Putnam, R. (1993) *Making Democracy Work: Civic Traditions in Modern Italy*, Princeton, NJ: Princeton University Press.

Putnam, R. (1999) *Bowling Alone: The Collapse and Revival of American Community*, New York: Simon and Schuster.

Putzel, J. (1997) "Why has democratization been a weaker impulse in Indonesia and Malaysia than in the Philippines?" in D. Potter, D. Goldblatt, M. Kiloh, and P. Lewis (eds.), *Democratization*, Cambridge and Milton Keynes: Polity Press in association with the Open University, pp. 240–63.

Putzel, J. (1999) "Survival of an imperfect democracy in the Philippines," in P. Burnell and P. Calvert (eds.), *The Resilience of Democracy: Persistent Practice, Durable Idea*, special issue of *Democratization*, 6, 1, pp. 198–223.

Radcliffe, S. and Westwood, S. (1993) "Gender, racism and the politics of identity in Latin America," in S. Radcliffe and S. Westwood (eds.), *"Viva" Women and Popular Protest in Latin America*, London: Routledge, pp. 1–29.

Rai, S. (1994) "Towards empowerment of South Asian women," *Third World Quarterly*, 15, 3, pp. 532–47.

Rai, S. (ed.) (2000) *International Perspectives on Gender and Democratization*, Basingstoke: Macmillan.

Randall, V. and Theobald, R. (1998) *Political Change and Underdevelopment: A Critical Introduction to Third World Politics*, 2nd edn., London: Macmillan.

Redclift, M. (1988) "Introduction: agrarian social movements in contemporary Mexico," *Bulletin of Latin America Research*, 7, 2, pp. 249–56.

Reveyrand-Coulon, O. (1993) "Les enoncés féminins de l'islam," in J.-F. Bayart (ed.), *Religion and modernité. Politique en afrique noire*, Paris: Karthala, pp. 63–100.

Rich, B. (1990) "The emperor's new clothes: the World Bank and environmental reform," *World Policy Journal*, spring, pp 305–29.

Richards, P. (1996) *Fighting for the Rain Forest: War, Youth and Resources in Sierra Leone*, London: James Currey and Heinemann.

Risse, T. (2000) "The power of norms versus the norms of power: transnational civil society and human rights," in A. Florini (ed.), *The Third Force: The Rise of Transnational Civil Society*, Tokyo and Washington, DC: Japan Center for International Exchange/Carnegie Endowment for International Peace, pp. 177–210.

Risse, T. and Ropp, S. (1999) "Conclusions," in T. Risse, S. Ropp, and K. Sikkink (eds.), *The Power of Human Rights: International Norms and Domestic Change*, Cambridge: Cambridge University Press, pp. 234–78.

Risse, T., Ropp, S., and Sikkink, K. (eds.) (1999) *The Power of Human Rights: International Norms and Domestic Change*, Cambridge: Cambridge University Press.

Risse-Kappen, T. (1995) "What have we learnt?" in T. Risse-Kappen (ed.), *Bringing Transnational Relations Back In*, Cambridge: Cambridge University Press, pp. 280–313.

Robinson, W. (1998) "Capitalist globalization and the transnationalization of the state." Presented at the Transatlantic Workshop, "Historical Materialism and Globalization," University of Warwick, April 15–17.

Rocamora, J. (1993) "The Philippines under Cory Aquino," in B. Gills, J. Rocamora, and R. Wilson (eds.), *Low Intensity Democracy*, London: Pluto Press, pp. 195–225.

Rood, D., James, C., and Sakamati, S. (1995) "Collateral damage," *Far Eastern Economic Review*, September 21, pp. 16–17.

Rosenau, J. (1993) "Environmental challenges in a turbulent world," in R. Lipschutz and K. Conca (eds.), *The State and Social Power in Global Environmental Politics*, New York: Columbia University Press, pp. 71–93.

Roy, A. Narain (1999) *The Third World in the Age of Globalization*, London/Delhi: Zed Books/Madhyam Books.

Rueschemeyer, D., Stephens, E., and Stephens, J. (1992) *Capitalist Development and Democracy*, Cambridge: Polity Press.

Sabbagh, R. (1994) "Jordanian women pay the violent price of traditional male 'honour'," *Guardian*, December 28.

Sadiki, L. (1997) "Towards Arab liberal governance: from the democracy of bread to the democracy of the vote," *Third World Quarterly*, 18, 1, pp. 127–48.

Safa, H. (1990) "Women and social movements in Latin America," *Gender and Society*, 14, 4, pp. 354–69.

Said, E. (1996) "War babies," *Observer*, January 14.

Saif, W. (1994) "Human rights and Islamic revivalism," *Islam and Christian–Muslim Relations*, 5, 1, pp. 57–65.

Saro-Wiwa, K. (1992) *Genocide in Nigeria: The Ogoni Tragedy*, London: Saros International Publishers.

Sartori, G. (1991) "Rethinking democracy: bad policy and bad politics," *International Social Science Journal*, 129, pp. 437–50.

Saurin, J. (1995) "The end of international relations?" in J. Macmillan and A. Linklater (eds.), *Boundaries in Question: New Directions in International Relations*, London: Pinter, pp. 244–61.

Scholte, J.-A. (1993) *International Relations of Social Change*, Buckingham: Open University Press.

Schulz, M., Söderbaum, F., and Öjendal, J. (2001) "Introduction: a framework for understanding regionalization," in M. Schulz, F. Söderbaum, and J. Öjendal (eds.), *Regionalization in a Globalizaing World: A Comparative Perspective on Forms, Actors and Processes*, London: Zed Books, pp. 1–21.

Sen, G. (1999) "Developing states and the end of the Cold War," in L. Fawcett and Y. Sayigh (eds.), *The Third World Beyond the Cold War: Continuity and Change,* Oxford: Oxford University Press, pp. 56–77.

Serhan, B. (1993) "The Palestinian social movement," in P. Wignaraja (ed.), *New Social Movements in the South*, London: Zed Books, pp. 164–82.

Sethi, H. (1993) "Survival and democracy: ecological struggles in India," in P Wignaraja (ed.), *New Social Movements in the South*, London: Zed Books, pp. 122–48.

Shah, G. (1988) "Grassroots mobilization in Indian politics," in A. Kohli (ed.), *India's Democracy: An Analysis of Changing State–Society Relations*, Princeton, NJ: Princeton University Press, pp. 262–304.

Shin, D. C. (1999) *Mass Politics and Culture in Democratizing Korea*, Cambridge: Cambridge University Press.

Slater, D. (1985) *New Social Movements and the State in Latin America*, CEDLA

Latin American Studies no. 25, Amsterdam: Floris.

Smith, H. (2000) "Why is there no international democratic theory?" in H. Smith (ed.), *Democracy and International Relations*, Basingstoke: Macmillan, pp. 1–30.

Smith, T. (1985) "Requiem or new agenda for Third World studies?" *World Politics*, 37, pp. 532–61.

So, A. (1990) *Social Change and Development*, London: Sage.

Sparr, P. (1994) "Feminist critiques of structural adjustment," in P. Sparr (ed.), *Mortgaging Women's Lives*, London: United Nations/Zed Books, pp. 20–35.

Stepan, A. (1988) *Rethinking Military Politics: Brazil and the Southern Cone*, Princeton, NJ: Princeton University Press.

Stiefel, M. and Wolfe, M. (1994) *A Voice for the Excluded: Popular Participation in Development: Utopia or Necessity?* London/Geneva: Zed Books/UNRISD.

Sweezy, P. and Magdoff, H. (1984) "The two faces of Third World debt: a fragile financial environment and debt enslavement," *Monthly Review*, 35, pp. 1–10.

Sylvester, C. (1995) "Whither opposition in Zimbabwe?" *Journal of Modern African Studies*, 33, 3, pp. 403–24.

Taylor, I. (n/d) "South Africa's 'democratic transition' in a globalized world: the 'change industry' and the promotion of polyarchy," unpublished manuscript, Department of Political Science, University of Stellenbosch.

Thomas, A. (1994) *Third World Atlas*, 2nd edn., Buckingham: Open University Press.

Thomas, A. (1999) "Modernization versus the environment? Shifting objectives of progress," in T. Skelton and T. Allen (eds.), *Culture and Global Change*, London: Routledge, pp. 45–57.

Thomas, C. and Reader, M. (2001) "Development and inequality," in B. White, R. Little, and M. Smith (eds.), *Issues in World Politics*, Basingstoke: Palgrave, pp. 74–92.

Thompson, M. (1993) "The limits of democratization in ASEAN," *Third World Quarterly*, 14, 3, pp. 469–84.

Timberlake, L. (1995) *Africa in Crisis*, London: Earthscan.

Tomasevski, K. (1988) *Foreign Aid and Human Rights Case Studies of Bangladesh and Kenya*, Copenhagen: Danish Centre of Human Rights.

Törnquist, O. (1999) *Politics and Development: A Critical Introduction*, London: Sage.

Törnquist, O. (2001) "Indonesia's democratization," in J. Haynes (ed.), *Democracy and Political Change in the "Third World,"* London: Routledge/ECPR Studies in European Political Science, pp. 171–97.

Tran, M. (1994) "World Bank sees Nepal project as test of credibility," *Guardian*, November 17.

UNDP (United Nations Development Program) (1994) *Human Development Report 1994*, Oxford: Oxford University Press for the UNDP.

UNDP (United Nations Development Program) (1996) *Human Development Report 1996*, Oxford: Oxford University Press for the UNDP.

UNRISD (United Nations Research Institute for Social Development) (1995) *States of Disarray*, Geneva: UNRISD.

Vidal, J. (1995a) "Localism vs globalism," *Guardian*, November 15.

Vidal, J. (1995b) "Rats of the rubbish society fight back," *Guardian*, September 9.

Villalón, L. (1995) *Islamic Society and State Power in Senegal: Disciples and Citizens in Fatick*, Cambridge: Cambridge University Press.

Villallón, L. (1998) "The African state at the end of the twentieth century: parameters of the critical juncture," in L.Villallón and P. Huxtable (eds.), *The African State at a Critical Juncture: Between Disintegration and Reconfiguration*, Boulder, CO: Lynne Rienner, pp. 3–26.

Vincent, R. J. (1986) *Human Rights and International Relations*, Cambridge: Cambridge University Press.

Vogler, J. (2001) "Environment," in B. White, R. Little, and M. Smith (eds.), *Issues in World Politics*, 2nd edn., Basingstoke: Palgrave, pp. 191–211.

Walker, M. (1995) "How the existing consensus on foreign policy goals is collapsing," *Guardian*, February 21.

Waterbury, J. (1994) "Democracy without democrats? The potential for political liberalization in the Middle East," in G. Salamé (ed.), *Democracy without Democrats? The Renewal of Politics in the Muslim World*, London: I. B.Tauris, pp. 3–26.

Watkins, K. (2001) "Thread that could span global gulf," *Guardian*, July 30.

Waylen, G. (1993) "Women's movements and democratization in Latin America," *Third World Quarterly*, 14, 3, pp. 573–87.

Weber, M. (1969) "Major features of world religions," in R. Robertson (ed.), *The Sociology of Religion*, Baltimore, MD: Penguin Books, pp. 19–41.

Webster, P. (1995) "Capital of terror," *Guardian*, September 6.

Whitehead, L. (1993) "The alternatives to 'liberal democracy': a Latin American perspective," in D. Held (ed.), *Prospects for Democracy*, Cambridge: Polity Press, pp. 312–29.

Wiebe, V. (1989) "Jamaica," in S. Mews (ed.), *Religion in Politics*, Harlow: Longman, p. 141.

Wintour, P. (2001) "Minister pins hope on fair trade," *Guardian*, July 10.

Witte, Jr, J. (1993) "Introduction," in J. Witte, Jr. (ed.), *Christianity and Democracy in Global Context*, Boulder, CO: Westview Press, pp. 1–20.

Woollacott, M. (1995) "A rage for peace and power," *Guardian*, September 9.

World Bank (1991) *World Development Report 1991*, New York: Oxford University Press.

World Bank (1995) *World Development Report 1995*, New York: Oxford University Press.

World Bank (1997) *World Development Report 1997: The State in a Changing World*, New York: Oxford University Press.

World Bank (1999) *World Development Report: Knowledge For Development 1998/ 1999*, New York: Oxford University Press.

World Bank (2000) *World Development Report: Entering the 21st Century 1999/ 2000*, New York: Oxford University Press.

World Bank (2001) *World Development Report 2000/2001*, New York: Oxford University Press

Zakaria, F. (1997) "The rise of illiberal democracy," *Foreign Affairs*, November/December, pp. 22–42.

Zinn, C. and Bowcott, O. (1995) "Storm of anti-nuclear protests mark Bastille day," *Guardian*, July 15.

Index